9 MONTHS IN,

9 MONTHS OUT

9 MONTHS IN, 9 MONTHS OUT

A SCIENTIST'S TALE OF PREGNANCY AND PARENTHOOD

VANESSA LOBUE

RUTGERS UNIVERSITY

Oxford University Press is a department of the University of Oxford. It furthers
the University's objective of excellence in research, scholarship, and education
by publishing worldwide. Oxford is a registered trade mark of Oxford University
Press in the UK and certain other countries.

Published in the United States of America by Oxford University Press
198 Madison Avenue, New York, NY 10016, United States of America.

Library of Congress Cataloging-in-Publication Data
LoBue, Vanessa, author.
Title: 9 months in, 9 months out : a scientist's tale of pregnancy and
parenthood / Vanessa LoBue.
Other titles: Nine months in, nine months out
Description: New York : Oxford University Press, 2019.
Identifiers: LCCN 2018036225 | ISBN 9780190863388 (paperback)
Subjects: LCSH: Parenthood. | Motherhood—Psychological aspects. |
Pregnancy—Psychological aspects. | BISAC: FAMILY & RELATIONSHIPS /
Parenting / Motherhood. | PSYCHOLOGY / Psychotherapy / Couples & Family. |
MEDICAL / Gynecology & Obstetrics.
Classification: LCC HQ755. 8.L63 2019 | DDC 306.874—dc23
LC record available at https://lccn.loc.gov/2018036225

9 8 7 6 5 4 3 2 1

Printed by Sheridan Books, Inc., United States of America

To Edwin, who turned this adventure in science into an unexpected love story. And to Charlie, who's inspired me to do it all over again.

CONTENTS

Part II Parenthood: The *Real* Adventure Begins

INTRODUCTION

When I was a kid, my mother told me that there comes a time in every girl's life when she wants to become a mom. I think this is what most women are taught to expect—that at some point in our lives, we will naturally want children. This idea doesn't seem too far-fetched when we're little girls, or when we're teenagers, or even when we're in our 20s, mostly because having kids seems like an abstract and distant possibility. But one day we wake up and we're not in our early 20s anymore, and the prospect of having children becomes an all too immediate reality. By this time, some of our friends have already had kids and others have plans to: They're "not trying to not get pregnant," as many of them say. Others have decided confidently and definitively that they aren't having kids at all, while the rest of us find ourselves in a position where we haven't gotten the urge to reproduce, but we are reaching the point where we have to decide soon whether or not to pull the trigger.

That's where you find me—I'm pushing 33, and I still have no natural desire to have a baby. I am not saying that I never want to have kids; I just don't have the urge to have them *right now*. I don't look at families walking by on the street and yearn to share in their magical experience. When I see a friend with a baby, I'm not compelled to hold it, I don't find myself going on and on about how cute it is, and, in fact,

I'm much more moved by pictures of cute puppies than cute babies. When I see parents struggling to drag their strollers onto the subway, or when I see an exhausted mom at the supermarket holding the hand of a screaming toddler, I think, "Thank GOD that isn't me." The truth is, when I see a baby, all I see is the immense responsibility I'm not sure I'm quite ready for and thus the inevitable decision that I have to make very soon.

Like I said before, I am nearly 33, married for less than 3 years, and I just started a job as an assistant professor of psychology at Rutgers University. Most psychology professors spend the bulk of their time teaching and doing research. I got my PhD specializing in early child development, so I teach undergraduate and graduate courses in child psychology and infancy. I run a lab where I conduct studies on infants and young children; not the kind of experiments where I wear a white lab coat and poke and prod newborn babies (although that's what my friends like to tell people)—it's the type of lab where we study children's everyday experiences by presenting them with pictures, books, videos, or toys, and by simply studying their behavior. It's a wonderful job, and I am immensely happy, but getting a job as a tenure-track professor came at a steep price.

After 4 years of college, I went straight to graduate school. A long 5 years later, I graduated with my master's degree and a PhD in developmental psychology. You'd think that having such an extensive education and advanced degree would make it easy to find a job, but it's quite the opposite. Very few industries have any need for overeducated and underexperienced 30-year-olds who have been in school since they were in diapers. Most of us go the academic route, seeking a position at a university or college, but these jobs are few and far between, and they are highly competitive. When I graduated, I hadn't published enough to get a university position, so I had to do a 2-year postdoctoral fellowship (which is pretty much just an extension of graduate school) and then a second postdoc for another year and a half just to get enough research done to become viable on the job market. Finally, in January

2011, after a grand total of 12½ years of higher education, I started my very first real job. I was 31 years old.

That might sound like a long road, but friends of mine have had it a lot worse, doing up to 7 years of graduate school followed by 4 to 5 years of postdoc work only to find that they can't get a tenure track position. Instead, they accept research scientist positions or visiting/adjunct positions (which pay notoriously low salaries and often don't include benefits) only to face an even more competitive job market a few years later. I saw just how bleak the situation is from the other side last year when I served on a search committee for a new tenure track position in my department. We had close to 200 applicants—200 amazing and intelligent individuals, all touting PhDs in psychology—competing for just one job. Academia is not an easy road, at least not at first, and I consider myself lucky to even have a job to speak of, let alone a job that I love so much. But, again, looking for a job in academia came at a steep price, and I don't mean in terms of student loans: After more than a decade of schooling, I finally have a job, a job I worked so hard for so many years to get, I'm nearly 33, just beginning my career, and I am suddenly feeling pressed with the decision of whether or not to rearrange this brand new life I've made for myself to have a baby.

Some of you might be thinking, "Oh you're still young, you have a few years to decide." People say that kind of thing to me all the time. I say it to my friends all the time, too. Maybe they're (we're) right, but as an expert in child development, I am intimately aware of the risks of having your first child when you're well into your 30s, starting with problems conceiving and ending with the frightening possibility of developmental problems for the child. The optimal age for women to have children is between 18 and 31. Once women reach 37, they might experience some difficulties conceiving (Williams & Ceci, 2012). Furthermore, as women give birth at older ages (which is becoming more and more common), the risks for complications during pregnancy, such as breech births, C-sections, and problems with labor increase as well (Luke & Brown, 2007). Beyond that, there are various developmental risks for the infant. Older mothers, for example, are at increased risk for giving birth to babies who have a low birth weight (Lee, Ferguson, Corpuz, & Gartner, 1988). Even more serious is the risk for Down syndrome, which is highly related to increased maternal age (Hook & Lindsjo, 1978).

The problems don't end there—having children as an academic brings with it a ton of issues of its own. Just being a woman in science comes with difficulties. Although psychology is a field that is becoming more and more dominated by women, female professors still make less money than male professors for doing exactly the same job. What's worse is that although women make up 76% of new psychology doctorates, they only constitute 53% of the psychology workforce (Willyard, 2011) and 33% of professors at doctoral-level institutions (Williams & Ceci, 2012). *Nature*, perhaps the most prestigious academic journal in the world, recently published an editorial that was a self-reflection on the gender bias that exists *within its own journal*. Despite the relatively high number of female editors who work for *Nature*, the number of female scholars who assess their contributions (14%), female researchers profiled by the journal (18%), and externally written comments with a female lead author (19%) are abysmally low (*Nature Editorials*, 2012).

Research echoes this trend. Recently, a group of investigators at Yale University examined the effects of gender bias in academic fields by presenting a group of college professors with an identical resume for a position as a lab manager. Half of them were told that it belonged to a female applicant, and the other half were told that it belonged to a male applicant. Even though all of the professors were asked to evaluate exactly the same resume, professors who thought the resume belonged to a man rated the candidate as more competent and offered the candidate a higher starting salary than professors who thought the resume belonged to a woman (Moss-Racusin, Dovidio, Brescoll, Graham, & Handelsman, 2012). The most surprising part about this study is that the gender of the *professor* who assessed the fictional candidate made no difference—both male and female professors were equally likely to evaluate the female candidate as less competent than the male. So, when it comes to gender bias, it looks like women are just as guilty as men.

Besides the obvious challenges of gender bias, other researchers have suggested that the major reason why women are underrepresented in academic jobs actually lies with the decision to become a mother (Williams & Ceci, 2012). As you can see from my own career trajectory, once academics finish their degrees, they are likely to first enter the workforce when they're over the age of 30 (and, on average, around 33). This means that by the time many of us get our first jobs, we are already past the optimal age for childbearing. If female academics do eventually decide to have children, they become 38% less likely to be promoted than their male counterparts (Mason, Stacy, & Goulden, 2002–3). This isn't unique for women in academia—women with their MBA's who have one or more children are significantly less likely than men to still be in the full-time workforce 10 years later (Bertrand, Goldin, & Katz, 2010).

Recent news and popular media is saturated with headlines that echo concern for this issue: "Why Women Can't Break Free from the Parent Trap" (*New Republic*, February 2, 2015), "The Motherhood Penalty vs. The Fatherhood Bonus" (*New York Times*, September 6, 2014). We're told to lean in, lean out, focus on our careers, focus on our families, stay at home, and go back to work; everyone seems to have an opinion about how to tackle the work–family balance these days. The reality is that life has changed significantly for women over the past 50 years, and we have a lot more choices than we used to: Being a stay-at-home mom is no longer required but is something many of us *choose to do*; the same is true for following an ambitious career path. Whether we choose to be academics, business executives, medical doctors, school teachers, chefs, waitresses, or stay-at-home moms, it's all about choice, and the hard truth is, our bodies haven't caught up with choices that involve a longer career path. At some point, most of us have to compromise *something*, whether it's related to our careers or to our families.

If you're like me—someone who has chosen to devote a great deal of time and effort to your career—you might not be thinking about how you're "still young" or how you have a few years left before you have to have children. Instead, there's a chance you're thinking what I'm thinking: It's time to either pull the trigger or to pull out of the baby game altogether. For some of us, that urge or pressing desire to start a family will never come, and, for *most of us*, there will never be a "good time" to have a baby. In fact, many of us face the inevitable reality that having a baby might seriously jeopardize our careers. That leaves us with a difficult decision to make, and this year I made it: I decided to start a family.

While I admit that I may not feel the immediate urge to have children, the scientist in me has been really curious about the experience of childbearing. Not to make it sound too clinical, but I've always wondered what it would be like to be pregnant—to essentially grow a human parasite inside my body for 9 months. Plus, how can I claim to be an "expert" in child development while never having experienced motherhood myself? At Rutgers, there is a large subsection of the student body that already has children, and, as you can imagine, many of these students self-select into my infant and child development classes. One student asked me in class one day what a placenta looks like. I just looked at her blankly. Finally, after what felt like a very long silence, three other students raised their hands, each of them eager to share descriptions of what *their* placentas looked like. Even worse is that, every semester, at least a few students come to my office and ask for advice about raising their kids: *Should I send him to preschool? Is it normal that she's not crawling yet? When do I stop breastfeeding?* My answer is always the same: I can tell you what research suggests would be best for your child, but research may not necessarily translate well to a mother's personal experience. I'm not saying that I decided to have a baby to see what my own placenta would look like or to enhance my career in any way—again, having a baby is like the kiss of death for women in academia. I'm just saying that I've always been curious, especially since I've devoted so many years to studying children.

Based on my chosen career path and the fact that my husband, Nick, is a middle school math teacher, people are always pointing out how "prepared" we will be when we decide to become parents. Our jobs are perfect for having children, they say, and we clearly know everything there is to know about having a baby already. I couldn't disagree more. On one hand, expertise can certainly tell you the science about what's happening to you and to your baby throughout development. In this sense, I am prepared for parenthood in many ways. On the other hand, all of the science in the world can't tell you what it *feels* like to have a baby—the pang of morning sickness, the pain of labor, the excitement of birth, and the joy that comes from seeing your baby's first smile. This book is about pregnancy and first-time parenthood, and, more specifically, what someone who is supposed to be an "expert" in infant and child development experiences during the 9 months of pregnancy and the 9 months that follow.

What makes this book different from other parenting books is that I will be telling you about pregnancy and parenthood in real time, writing about each month as it happens. There is a phenomenon that women experience when they have children that I like to call the "postnatal glow." It describes how mothers magically omit the grisly details of their experiences—the labor pain, the crying, the stress, and the lack of sleep—instead just touting the joys of motherhood. I used to think they were lying, or at least bending the truth a little, but there's actual biological evidence that moms *forget* the bad parts of pregnancy and parenthood in favor of the good. Researchers have suggested that a hormone present in mothers during labor, pregnancy, and nursing called *oxytocin* might keep women from developing negative memories about the experience (Heinrichs, Meinlschmidt, Wippich, Ehlert,

& Hellhammer, 2004), essentially stacking the deck so that we'll turn around and do it all over again.

Here, I can promise you two things. First, I will put my relatively narrow skill set to good use and give you interesting information about what's happening to the baby every step of the way and about what research says is good practice whenever possible. Second, I will juxtapose this information with how science translates to the mother's (i.e., *my*) experiences. When you don't have children, it's easy to use science to judge what good parenting should look like, but my guess is that all bets are off when you become a parent yourself. Most importantly, I will give you an account of pregnancy, birth, and the aftermath— the good, the bad, and the ugly—writing about these experiences as they are actually happening in real time, before Nature can force me to forget. And all from the perspective of someone who has more than a decade of experience studying infant and child development. After all, if anyone should be prepared for pregnancy and parenthood, it's me, right?

Right?

PART I

PREGNANCY

THE ADVENTURE BEGINS

1

CONCEPTION

THE SCIENCE OF GETTING PREGNANT

Every day, I get on the Path train and ride for 23 minutes from the World Trade Center to Newark, New Jersey, for work. Sometimes I read a book, sometimes I read news headlines on the small monitors, sometimes I look outside at the passing train yards, and today I happened to be reading the ads on the train walls. "Donate your eggs, help make a family happy," read the one directly across from me. "Looking for donations from women aged 24–32." Women aged 24 to 32. It was official: My eggs had expired.

It was April, and I just celebrated my 33rd birthday a few weeks earlier. I was already feeling old (I recently noticed gray hairs popping up in alarming numbers and a not-so-flattering roll of skin starting to form every time I bend the wrong way), but this sign said aloud what I was thinking: My body is starting to get too old for childbearing. I don't usually pay attention to media suggesting that women in their mid-30s have anything to be self-conscious about, but this sign was different. This wasn't about growing older and becoming unattractive; this was about growing older and beginning to watch your body slowly shut down.

But despite the negative implications of the sign and their effect on my self-esteem, still being childless and in my mid-30s is not at all uncommon anymore. First of all, more and more women are deciding not to have children at all these days. In fact, the number of women who choose not to have children has more than doubled since the 1970s (Blackstone & Stewart, 2016). Second, a new report from the Centers for Disease Control and Prevention suggests that, for the first time in history, there are more women having babies in their 30s than there are women having babies in their 20s (Rossen, Osterman, Hamilton, & Martin, 2017). In prior years, the most common age for women to have babies for the first time was between the ages of 25 and 29. Recently, women aged 30–34 have surpassed this younger age group, suggesting that my decision to wait to have children is consistent with current US trends (Figure 1.1). The shift is likely due to the fact that women are choosing longer career pathways and are waiting for more job security before having children.

Unfortunately, waiting longer to have children does come with some drawbacks. After age 30, pregnancy becomes increasingly risky every year you wait. As we age, it will become more difficult to conceive. If and when we are successful, there are other problems that could lie ahead. Miscarriages and complications during pregnancy, for example, increase with the age of conception (Jacobsson, Ladfors, & Milsom, 2004). To put it in perspective, for women aged 20–24—the age in which the female body is best prepared to have a baby—the risk for miscarriage is about 9%. Once a woman turns 35, the risk is greater than 20%; at 40, it is nearly 50%; and by the ripe old age of 45, 75% of pregnancies will result in miscarriage (Anderson, Wohlfahr, Christens, Olsen, & Melbye, 2000). It is likely that these problems have to do with chromosomal abnormalities or problems with the functioning of the uterus or hormones; these issues are typical of older women. But miscarriage isn't the only risk. There are other chromosomal abnormalities that can result in severe developmental disabilities for the *child*. Trisomy 21 for example—more commonly known as Down

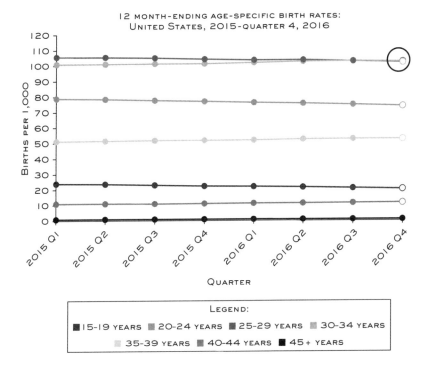

12 MONTH-ENDING AGE-SPECIFIC BIRTH RATES:
UNITED STATES, 2015-QUARTER 4, 2016

BIRTHS PER 1,000

QUARTER

LEGEND:
■ 15-19 YEARS ■ 20-24 YEARS ■ 25-29 YEARS ■ 30-34 YEARS
■ 35-39 YEARS ■ 40-44 YEARS ■ 45+ YEARS

Figure 1.1 | Average birth rates for 12 months ending with the quarter listed on the bottom of the chart. Circle on top right indicates data for the fourth quarter of 2016, demonstrating that birth rates for women between the ages of 30 and 34 are slightly higher than birth rates for women between the ages of 25 and 29 for the very first time in history.

Source: Center for Disease Control and Prevention, Vital Statistics (Rossen, Osterman, Hamilton, & Martin, 2017).

syndrome—is closely linked to maternal age during pregnancy. In women under 30, the risk of having a child with Down syndrome is less than 1 in 1,000 (Yoon et al., 1996). Once a woman is older than 40, the risk is more like 1 in 100, and once she's 45, it's about 1 in 30. Other problems include higher rates of C-section, premature birth, low birth weight, and the need for serious prenatal care (Delbaere et al., 2007).

But, it's not all bad news for older moms. Recent research suggests that there are some important benefits to waiting a while before becoming a mother. One study looking at the life-long income levels of women in Denmark found that women who have babies in their 30s make more money in the long run than women who have babies in their 20s. Although having children is costly for *all* women in terms of income, it seems to be less costly for older women who wait until they are more established in their careers before having children (Leung, Groes, & Santaeulalia-Llopis, 2016). Furthermore, the results of a recent Swedish study looking at the relationship between maternal age and child outcomes suggest that there may in fact be more positives to having a baby later in life than negatives. Children of older mothers in this study did better in school and were more likely to go to college than were children of younger mothers (Barclay & Myrskylä, 2016). In general, family income is related to a variety of positive outcomes for children, such as higher academic achievement and college success, so waiting to have children until you have a stable income might carry substantial long-term benefits for you and your future children (e.g., Morrissey, Hutchison, & Winsler, 2014).

And although it might be more difficult to get pregnant as women get older, there are several intervention strategies available to families if problems do arise. First, there are a number of genetic tests now available that can be done to screen for developmental problems before you even conceive. They usually involve getting a saliva or blood sample that is sent to a lab to determine whether parents carry a recessive gene that could cause a specific genetic disorder. To explain how this works, let's first take the simple example of eye color. I have brown eyes, and my husband has blue eyes. Brown eyes are dominant, so we'll call the genes for brown eyes uppercase B's. Blue eyes are recessive, so we'll call those lowercase b's. A child will receive one eye color gene from the mother and one from the father. In order to inherit brown eyes, all the child needs is one B gene, since it is the "dominant" trait. In order to have blue eyes, the child needs two b genes, or a recessive gene from *both* the mother and the father. So, given that my husband has blue eyes and hence two b's, if I happen to have two dominant brown-eyed genes, our kids are destined to have brown eyes no matter what. But, if I happen to have one dominant B and one recessive b, then our kids will have a 50/50 chance of having blue eyes (see Figure 1.2).

Now let's apply this example to genetic disorders. Most genetic disorders are recessive (thank goodness), so, in order for your child to develop one of these disorders, both parents need to carry at least one recessive gene. Genetic testing will tell you whether the mother has a recessive gene for a variety of disorders, and, if she does, her doctor will ask that the father get tested as well. If both parents have a recessive gene for something like fragile X syndrome or cystic fibrosis, that doesn't mean that their children will definitely develop these disorders. Instead, it means that there is about a 25% chance that their child will carry both recessive genes—a single dominant gene is all you need to avoid the disorder altogether. If this happens to you—if you have genetic testing done and find out that both you and your partner carry recessive genes for a developmental disorder—it doesn't mean that you shouldn't have children or that your child will definitely develop the disorder (remember, there's only a 25% chance that you will both pass on the recessive gene to your child if you each have one), it just means that further screening can be done during pregnancy to see what the child has inherited. At that point, you can decide on a course of action.

It's important to note a few caveats here. First, the preceding example only holds if neither you nor your partner already has one of the genetic disorders included in the screening. The chances of passing the disorder on to your child can go up to 50% if one of you has *two* recessive genes (and hence the actual disorder) and the other has one (Figure 1.3). Doctors might make stronger recommendations if you or your partner already has a genetic disorder. Second, genetic tests can be quite costly, and they are so new that many insurance companies don't cover them. So, before having genetic testing done, it is

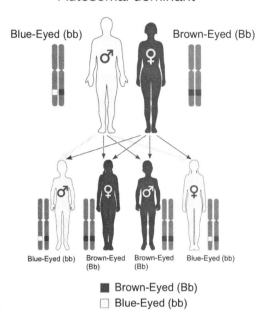

Autosomal dominant

Blue-Eyed (bb)
Brown-Eyed (Bb)

Blue-Eyed (bb)   Brown-Eyed   Brown-Eyed   Blue-Eyed (bb)
(Bb)   (Bb)

■ Brown-Eyed (Bb)
□ Blue-Eyed (bb)

Figure 1.2 | Example of how brown and blue eyes might be passed along to a child. In this example, the father has blue eyes, meaning that he has two recessive blue-eyed genes, labeled "bb" (illustrated in white); the mother has brown eyes, and one dominant brown-eyed gene and one recessive blue-eyed gene, labeled "Bb" (illustrated in blue). If they had children, two of them (50%) would likely inherit a dominant brown-eyed gene from the mother and a recessive blue-eyed gene from the father, resulting in brown eyes. The other two (50%) would likely inherit a recessive blue-eyed gene from the mother and another recessive blue-eyed gene from the father, resulting in blue eyes.

Source: Wikipedia, "Dominance (genetics)," figure adapted by Vanessa LoBue from original by Domaina.

Autosomal recessive inheritance

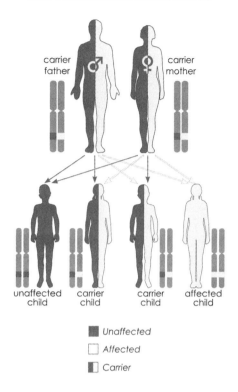

Figure 1.3 | Example of how a recessive gene for a genetic disorder might be passed along to a child. In this example, both parents have a recessive gene (illustrated in white) for a genetic disorder. If the parents have four children, one of them would likely inherit both dominant genes (illustrated in blue), and two of them would likely inherit one dominant gene from one parent and one recessive gene from the other. None of these three children would develop the genetic disorder because of the presence of one or more dominant genes. However, one in four of the children (25%) would likely inherit both recessive genes and therefore be at risk for developing the disorder.

important to think about what action you would take if you did find out that your fetus has a genetic disorder. Would you terminate the pregnancy? Would you simply use the information to prepare for intervention strategies? Or would you take no action at all? Depending on your answers to these questions, the cost of genetic testing might not be worth the extra stress it can cause you. Third, these tests can only screen for disorders that are caused by a single gene and do not screen for other developmental disabilities that are the result of an interaction between hundreds or thousands of genes, like autism or schizophrenia. *Most* of the time, developmental disabilities are the product of an interaction between many genes and environmental circumstances, so my simple example only holds for a very narrow set of genetic disorders. Prenatal vitamins, a healthy diet, and regular check-ups can help reduce the risk for other developmental problems that can't be screened for by genetic testing.

In addition to genetic screening, various interventions are available for couples that have trouble conceiving. After about 6–12 months of trying to conceive without success, doctors might recommend testing for potential fertility problems in both the mother and the father. If there are problems for the mother—perhaps she doesn't ovulate regularly—a potential treatment option is hormone therapy, where doctors inject a woman's body with hormones to facilitate ovulation. Hormone therapy can also function to make the uterus more receptive to implantation, which can be helpful for women with *endometriosis*— a condition where there is extra tissue trapped inside the uterus—as well as for men who have weak sperm. If weak sperm is the problem, artificial insemination is also an option, which involves injecting "washed" or carefully selected "super" sperm directly into the uterus to make conception easier. Artificial insemination can also be used for same-sex couples looking to conceive or for men who are carriers of genetic disorders that they don't want to pass down to their children. All of these techniques are relatively low cost and highly successful within a few months.

For couples with more serious infertility problems, such as women with damaged fallopian tubes or women with more extreme endometriosis, in vitro fertilization is an option. This procedure involves extracting sperm from the father and eggs from the mother and then mixing them in a test tube or lab dish, hopefully creating several fertilized eggs, or embryos. The embryos are then reinserted into the mother's womb in hopes that they will implant in the uterine wall and develop into a fetus. Unlike the other intervention strategies just mentioned, in vitro fertilization is very expensive and often takes multiple attempts, each one carrying steep costs. Furthermore, doctors generally insert several embryos into the mother's womb at once to maximize the chances of success. So, if in vitro is successful, it could result in twins if more than one embryo implants.

These interventions are available if a couple has trouble conceiving over a long period of time, after 6 months to a year of trying to get pregnant the old-fashioned way. On average, it generally takes 3–6 months for a woman under 35 to get pregnant. That might sound long, but, contrary to what you might learn in middle school sex-ed (and what the anxious teenage brain might have once told you), getting pregnant is not that easy—*for anyone*. A woman can only get pregnant when she is ovulating, which only happens 2–3 days out of each month. If you miss that window—if your partner is out of town or sick, if you get busy at work those few days, or if you're just not in the mood—you're out of luck until next month when you get another chance at catching that 2- to 3-day bull's-eye. Ovulation usually happens in the middle of a woman's cycle, so if you get fairly regular periods, you've got a shot at predicting when it will happen. If you're not so regular, as many women aren't, it's quite a bit harder to make predictions about when ovulation will occur.

Let's say you guessed correctly, and you've got your timing just right—it still doesn't mean you'll get pregnant. A woman's body is not exactly a safe place for sperm. It's a highly acidic environment, which makes for an unfriendly journey for tiny sperm that have to navigate their way to a single egg. One of the first obstacles the sperm will face as they travel through the vagina to get to the uterus is a pocket of heavy mucus that blocks their entry. Many of the sperm will get stuck in this pocket and never make it to the egg—only the very best sperm with good head shape and tail motion will make it through. After navigating the uterus and traveling up the fallopian tube, the sperm finally reach the egg. By this time, there are only a few of them left. Only one of these remaining travelers can penetrate the egg: Once the contents of the sperm make it inside, chemical messengers spread to the egg, causing an electrical charge that will cause the egg to shut down so that no other sperm can get in. Finally, one lucky sperm is victorious and joins the egg in the fallopian tube to form a zygote. This is what we call conception, or fertilization. Fertilization is the goal.

My husband Nick and I decided that we would start trying to conceive that summer, after the spring semester was over and after he was finished teaching. I'm a college professor and he's a middle school math teacher, so the summer is always a bit less stressful than other parts of the year. As a big planner, I wanted to try to time it so that we would have the baby next May, meaning that Nick could take advantage of his 6 weeks of paternity leave, and we could have the whole summer at home together. We tried for 7 months before I finally got pregnant (so much for planning). When I say 7 months of trying, I don't mean "not trying to not get pregnant," as many of my friends sometimes say. I used to find that phrase irritating; why not just admit that you're trying to get pregnant? But now I get it. "Not trying to not get pregnant" just means that you're not using birth control—that you've "pulled the goalie." *Trying* to get pregnant is a totally different ballgame. Trying to get pregnant means peeing on a stick every morning so that you can pinpoint the precise day that you're ovulating and then making sure that you're having sex during that window to maximize your chances of conceiving. Not trying to not get pregnant is easy—*trying* to get pregnant is hard work, and I had no idea it would take as long as it did.

Like I said, Nick and I started our journey to getting pregnant in the summer so that we would have a May baby. Turns out we didn't even get pregnant until May. I decided to go off the pill for a few months before really trying to get pregnant because you hear stories about how your body takes 6 months or a year to get back on a regular cycle after you've been on the pill. Since I had been on the pill for awhile, I figured I'd need at least a few months to get the ball rolling again. It turns out this was all a total myth. I had my period exactly 28 days after I went off the pill and consistently every 28 days thereafter. The first time I started monitoring my ovulation (a few months later), I ovulated the very first month I checked and every month after that. My doctor confirmed that it isn't quite true that your body can take 6 months or a year to readjust to not being on the pill and that we could start trying right away. In my case, she was right, and my body kicked back into gear within the first month.

In the fall, we stopped "not trying to not get pregnant" and started really trying. I bought the ovulation strips that you pee on every morning. Ovulation tests like these work by determining the level of luteinizing hormone (LH) in your urine. The amount of LH in your body conveniently increases just before you ovulate. If the ovulation test detects an elevated level of LH, it will come back positive, which means you'll likely be ovulating within the next day or two. I figured out in the very first month that I ovulated around the 19th day of my cycle, giving us a 2- to 3-day window around day 19 to try to conceive. Six months went by, and nothing happened. Every month, I hoped to skip my period, and every 28th day, Aunt Flo came for her regularly scheduled visit.

Maybe several years of worrying about getting pregnant made me think it was going to be easy, but it wasn't. It was hard, and it was frustrating. When it started taking a long time, I looked for any website that would give me statistics about how long it *should* take. Again, the standard seems to be that, on average, it takes 3 months to get pregnant if you're under 35 and that you should consult with a fertility specialist if it takes longer than 12 months. If you're over 35, you should see a specialist if you have no luck after 6 months. There's no real reason to think that 35 is a magical age in any way—the risks associated with maternal age and pregnancy increase very gradually and consistently each year—but doctors (and insurance companies) need some guideline to steer their recommendations, so 35 has become designated as the number when pregnancies go from normal to "high risk." Although I know very well that there's nothing special about 35, having a cut-off and a scary sounding label like "high risk" makes it feel like there's an exact age where things go from easy to hard, from good to bad, or from bad to worse. I'm 34, so I'm right at the edge of where doctors will tell you to wait longer or see a specialist if you go beyond 6 months; but, being a scientist, I know that there is no reason I should be having trouble conceiving. Knowing all of this did not make me any less paranoid about my age and the fast approach of that magic number.

After 6 months of no luck, I borrowed a friend's ovulation monitor. It does the same thing that the ovulation strips do, but it's more expensive, looks fancier, and gives you a cute little egg icon when you're ovulating instead of a double line. My doctor said she only recommends the monitor if you don't get any indication of ovulation from the strips. Even though the strips did seem to be working, I wasn't about to turn down my friend's offer of the fancy monitor—just in case. The monitor confirmed what I already knew, that I ovulate at around 19 days. Maybe the monitor was lucky, but finally, in that seventh month, when I was frustrated, depressed, and about to throw my arms up in the air, the biology finally worked itself out.

I didn't actually know I was pregnant at first. The 28th day of my cycle arrived, and it appeared as if my period had arrived with it. The first two days of my period are generally very light, and I got some light bleeding as usual. Disappointed about yet another failure, I told Nick that I wasn't pregnant and we begrudgingly circled the next ovulation date on my calendar. Everything seemed normal, and then, on day 3 of my period, the day it is supposed to get heavy, it just disappeared.

I thought maybe it was a fluke and waited a day. Still no bleeding. On the fifth day, I took a pregnancy test and it was negative. Given how regular I am, I didn't believe the result.

You can get a negative pregnancy test and still be pregnant. Once an egg is fertilized, a woman's body starts producing a hormone called human *chorionic gonadotropin* (hCG) to tell the body that it is pregnant. Each day, the amount of hCG increases, and pregnancy tests are designed to pick up levels of the hormone in your urine. In the first few days/weeks after conception, the level of hCG is relatively low, so you can get a negative pregnancy test and still be pregnant. I ovulate very late in my cycle (day 19 is about a week before I get my period), so when I missed my period, it was still very early after conception, which is probably why I got a negative result after my first test. I knew that if I was really pregnant, the levels of hCG in my system would be higher the next day, and I would be more likely to get a positive test. Since your body should only produce hCG if you are pregnant, it is really rare to get a positive pregnancy test if you're not actually pregnant (and probably means that something went wrong with the test). So, if you see that plus sign, even a very faint one, chances are you're pregnant. But you can get a minus sign and still be pregnant if the levels of hCG in your body aren't high enough yet to be detectable, so it's worth taking the test again in a day or two.

That's what I did—the very next day (still without my period) I took the test again, and this time I got the coveted plus sign. I was finally pregnant.

2

THE FIRST TWO MONTHS

Signs and Symptoms, From Zygote to Fetus

The first step after getting a positive pregnancy test was to call my doctor. She made me take a blood test to confirm the pregnancy and then another one a few days later to check that my levels of hCG were increasing normally. The blood test was positive, and my hormones were normal. It looks like I finally peed on my last stick.

In the next few weeks, every time I went to the bathroom I was nervous I would see blood, which is a sign that you've had an early miscarriage. *Miscarriage* is the spontaneous end of a pregnancy within 20 weeks of conception. They are quite common throughout the first trimester, which is generally why you hear that it's "bad luck" to tell people that you're pregnant before the end of the third month. Luck has nothing to do with it—miscarriages are just a lot more common in the first 3 months of pregnancy than most people think.

About 10–20% of known pregnancies end in miscarriage. A whopping 80% of those happen in the first trimester. Most of these early miscarriages—about 50–75%—are called *chemical pregnancies*, and they happen in the first 5 weeks after conception. Having a chemical pregnancy means that you were pregnant, but the egg never implanted or something went wrong and the pregnancy ended before it even began. At this point, you might not have even missed your period yet, or you might get a positive pregnancy test and then get your period a week or two later. I was terrified of that. Most early miscarriages are caused by chromosomal abnormalities, and there's not much you can do (so maybe luck does have something to do with it), but these abnormalities can become more likely as mothers get older. Doctors or loved ones might tell you to withhold your happy baby news until the end of the first trimester to save you some undue grief in case you do have a miscarriage. That doesn't mean you can't tell anyone you're pregnant until the second trimester—the general rule of thumb is that you just shouldn't tell anyone about your pregnancy that you might not want to tell that you've had a miscarriage. The old wives tale about "bad luck" is just a nice way of protecting young mothers from having to tell their family and friends that they're no longer pregnant. These days, with social media, you have to be extra careful about that. If you post pictures of your ultrasound online and then miscarry, chances are that people are going to be asking awkward and potentially painful questions several months later about the birth of your baby. Personally, I've decided to refrain from making any social media announcements until the baby is born; I'm not keen on the idea of sharing my tragedies with most people, let alone 500 of my closest friends.

When I got a positive pregnancy test, it was about 2 weeks after I ovulated, making me only about 2 weeks pregnant. I didn't really feel pregnant; nothing much felt different at all. Meanwhile, in my uterus, a lot was changing very quickly. As soon as conception took place, the newly merged sperm and egg became what is called a *zygote*. The zygote immediately began dividing as it floated down my fallopian tube to my uterus, at first slowly, and then more and more quickly. Within 12 hours of fertilization, the zygote divided into 2 cells, then those 2 cells divided into 4, then those 4 cells became 8, and so on. This dividing process usually takes about 48 hours. On the fourth day, the dividing cells formed a hollow ball called a *blastocyst*. Once the blastocyst reached my uterus, it implanted itself and burrowed beneath my uterine wall. This happened around 6–12 days after conception. It isn't uncommon to spot a little bit after implantation, which might explain why I thought I was getting my period around then (Figure 2.1).

By the time I figured out that I was pregnant, the egg was likely implanted in my uterine wall, and support structures were beginning to grow to help the zygote, which we can now call an *embryo*. The *amnion*, for example, is a membrane that forms around the embryo containing a substance called *amniotic fluid* in which the fetus will eventually float around. The *chorion* is a layer outside of the amnion that makes contact with the wall of uterus and the *placenta*— a flat organ that my students tell me looks something like a liver. The placenta will filter the exchange of materials between me and the fetus, keeping some stuff out and letting other stuff like food and oxygen in. Although fetuses make breathing motions with their lungs starting in the first trimester, they don't actually breathe until after birth. The mother breathes for them, and the fetus gets oxygen during pregnancy (and during their journey through the birth canal) through the placenta. An *umbilical cord* connects the placenta to the fetus.

In the next month, all of the fetus's most important anatomy, organs, and structures will develop. All of the newly formed cells that resulted from the multiple cell divisions I just described will move from where they first started. This is called *cell migration*. The embryo's first cells, better known as *stem cells*, will initially all be the same, without a fixed function or fate. This is why stem cells are so important—they are flexible and can become specialized to fit many different functions. Because of this utility, stem cells can be used to treat potentially serious illnesses, like leukemia and other cancers that attack the blood. In fact, these days, you can do what's called *cord blood banking* when your baby is born. Cord blood banking is the relatively new process of saving and

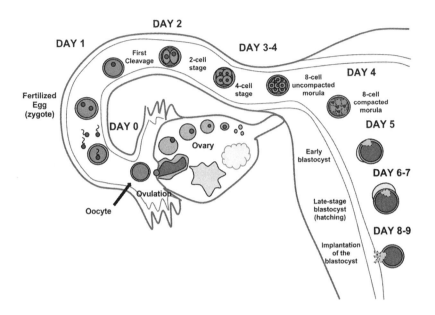

Figure 2.1 | Human fertilization. The first 10 days after fertilization. The egg is fertilized in the fallopian tube, and the newly merged sperm and egg become a *zygote*. The zygote immediately begins dividing as it floats down the fallopian tube to the uterus, at first slowly, and increasingly quickly. Within 12 hours of fertilization, the zygote divides into two cells, then those two cells divide into four, then those four cells become eight, and so on. This dividing process usually takes about 48 hours. On the fourth day, the dividing cells form a hollow ball called a *blastocyst*. Once the blastocyst reaches the uterus, it implants itself and burrows beneath the uterine wall, where it will grow into a human fetus.

Source: Wikipedia, "Human fertilization," by Ttrue12.

storing the blood in your umbilical cord—which contains stem cells—that can later be used to treat your child if he or she becomes sick with a life-threatening illness. Cord blood banking can be expensive, costing several thousand dollars for the initial extraction and then a few hundred dollars every month for storage thereafter, but it can also be life-saving in the rare instances where children do develop a life-threatening disease.

The life-saving potential of stem cells is also what makes them so controversial. In 1998, researchers first discovered how to extract stem cells from the body in order to study how we can use them to treat illnesses. The potential life-saving benefit of this new research was incredibly high, and doctors even hypothesized that one day we could use stem cells to regrow a new heart, or kidneys, or a lung. In fact, researchers recently got close and were able to regrow human heart tissue from adult stem cells (Guyette et al., 2016). The catch was, at the time, the only way to extract stem cells from the body was by destroying a human embryo. As you can imagine, this idea caused a lot of discomfort and controversy, some of which still exists today. However, in the past 20 years, we've come a long way in stem cell research and have discovered ways of extracting them safely without destroying human embryos—from the umbilical cord, bone marrow, and even from breast milk.

After a fetus's stem cells initially migrate, they differentiate and become specialized to serve different functions for different structures. This is called *cell differentiation*. As the cells differentiate in a human fetus, many of the most important organs will form quickly. The heart, for example, will begin beating around 21 days after fertilization. It will be disproportionately large compared to the overall size of the embryo as it has to work hard to keep the embryo alive. Around the same time, the neural tube, which runs down the backside of the embryo, will close, sort of like a zipper. This will make up the spinal cord. At around 5 weeks, after the neural tube zips shut, it will enlarge and soon become the brain. The spine and spinal cord will expand quickly at this point, making the embryo look like it has a tail.

By 6 weeks, the embryo will be floating in the amniotic fluid that protects it. It can move for the first time, and it can, in fact, do somersaults (albeit slowly) in the amniotic fluid. It can also hiccup, and the very first reflexes that it will have as a newborn will slowly begin to appear. Even though it can move, it's still too small for me to feel. Around 6 ½ weeks, the lobes of the brain will begin to form, and the fetus will have two primitive eyes on each side of the face, with an open cavity in the middle where the mouth and nose will be. Over the next week, sheets of cells will move over and cover the open cavity to form the mouth and nose. The indentation in the middle of your upper lip is called the *philtrum*—this is where the sheets of cells came together to fill in the open cavity that is now your nose. If these sheets of cells fail to come together fully, the result is a condition called *cleft palate*, or an opening in the upper lip.

Like I said, I didn't really feel much during any of this process, or in the first 2 months of my pregnancy at all apart from a few very common symptoms. First, I had a 3-day long headache the week after I found out I was pregnant. I've had tension headaches here and there ever since. Second, at about week 4, my breasts started to hurt like crazy. I don't mean the normal tenderness that some of us feel when we have our periods. I mean *pain*. I can't touch them (and neither can my husband as far as I'm concerned); I can't pat or bump them; my dog can't even sit on my lap because I'm afraid that she might lightly tap them. They're bigger already, and in fact it feels like I have two abnormal growths on my chest. Breast "tenderness" is common in the first trimester, and some growth is normal even this early on, but since I usually don't even fill a full A-cup, the slight increase in size was immediately noticeable.

The third symptom is that I am hungry all the time. *All the time.* To be fair, Nick claims that I was hungry all the time even before I got pregnant. But first-trimester pregnancy hunger is different. It creeps up out of nowhere and all of a sudden I can't even talk to people if I don't eat something right away. I have taken it upon myself to bring one breakfast, two lunches, and several snacks to work every day to avoid offending colleagues or students if they happen to run into me in the hallway at a particularly ravenous time. I don't know if it is because of the hormones or all the extra food, but I feel bloated despite the fact that I haven't officially gained any weight yet. When I'm not eating, I spend the rest of my day tending to the last two symptoms—frequent urination and fatigue—by taking constant trips to the bathroom or napping.

All of these symptoms—headaches, breast tenderness, increased hunger, frequent urination, and fatigue—are really common in the first trimester. And although doctors aren't exactly sure what causes all of them, they likely have to do with increased levels of hormones and blood volume flowing through the body, both of which are needed to maintain a healthy pregnancy, especially in the first trimester when all of the baby's most important organs are forming. Extra blood flow can cause headaches and makes your kidneys produce more urine. The surge of hormones can make your body work harder, needing to make extra use of every calorie (hence the increased appetite and fatigue).

One other common symptom of pregnancy in the first trimester—perhaps the most common—is nausea, which has completed escaped me so far. Three-quarters of pregnant women experience "morning sickness." I put it in quotes because it is somewhat of a misnomer, as nausea or vomiting can happen during pregnancy at any time of the day. It can begin around 4 weeks, but on average starts around 6 weeks and, for most women, lasts until the end of the first trimester; for others (like my poor mom), it can last through the entire pregnancy. Although morning sickness can be incredibly unpleasant and in some cases debilitating, it is generally thought to be a sign of a healthy pregnancy. Researchers don't know for sure what causes morning sickness, but many have long assumed that it acts to keep women from ingesting dangerous substances that can harm the developing fetus. It's not clear whether morning sickness does in fact serve a protective function, but there are several studies now showing that morning sickness is associated with better outcomes for the baby, including decreased risk of miscarriage, developmental problems, and prematurity. In other words, the sicker the mom is, the less likely she will be to have a miscarriage or problems with the pregnancy (Hinkle

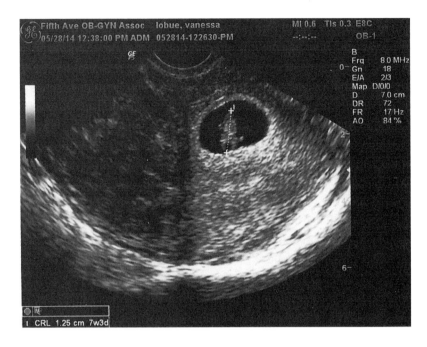

Figure 2.2 | Seven-week ultrasound. Fetus, back view, upside down.

et al., 2016; Koren, Madjunkova, & Maltepe, 2014). So, despite the fact that morning sickness can be difficult to bear, it likely means that all is well with the fetus. Only one-fourth of women escape morning sickness completely, and so far I seem to have drawn the lucky Jack. But honestly, without having the nausea, I'm constantly worrying whether the baby is really in there and whether it's healthy.

At the end of the second month, I went for my first *sonogram*. A sonogram is an internal ultrasound—it is what a doctor will do when the fetus is too small to see from outside the abdomen. My doctor showed me the image of the inside of my uterus on a large screen, and it was exactly what I expected it to look like based on photographs I show in my classes. The fetus was upside down floating in the amniotic fluid. Its heart was visibly beating and oversized, and I could see a large head, two small arm buds, what looked like a tail, and a yolk sac (which nourishes the fetus before the placenta is fully developed) floating beside it. It looked exactly like the photographs in the textbooks I assign—I could hardly believe it. To my husband, who teaches math and not infant development, it just looked like a blob. Even after the doctor pointed out the head and rear end to him on the screen, he said it looked like she was literally pointing at a picture of nothing ("Oh, you mean that blank part of the screen is the head? Got it"). That's probably what it looks like to most people. But to me, it looked picture perfect—a fully recognizable fetus, measuring only a half an inch long (Figure 2.2).

3

THE THIRD MONTH

THE DANGERS OF TERATOGENS

In the third month, I am still experiencing some of the same symptoms—headaches, painful breasts, and ravenous hunger. I was really hoping the breast pain would go away by now, but they still hurt so much that it's hard to sleep on my side or my stomach. Then again, if I'm looking on the bright side: At least they're bigger. Unfortunately, the rest of me is getting bigger too (see Chapter 2, *ravenous hunger*). I've gained a few pounds, which doesn't sound like much, but it's all in my uterus. I don't look pregnant yet, which makes it worse—I just look fatter. My jeans are getting really tight, and wearing anything fitted is completely out of the question. I'm still not feeling any nausea unless I get hungry (again, see *ravenous hunger*), but the headaches have been frequent and intense. In addition to my old symptoms, this month I had to add two new symptoms to my list—constipation and 24/7 gas. No matter what I eat or what I drink, the only thing that comes out of my bottom is gas. I'm constantly nervous that I'm going to break wind in public and clear a subway car or, worse, the hallway at work. Despite my difficulties producing a #2, I'm still having absolutely no trouble when it comes to producing #1's. In fact, my average number of bathrooms trips has doubled or even tripled. I have to get up about three times during the night to go to the bathroom and about once an hour during the day. Sometimes I'll go and then have to go again 5 minutes later. This has made long car trips hard. A few weeks ago, I visited an old friend in Virginia, which is about a 7-hour drive from my home in New York, and I had to stop five times to go to the bathroom.

Although the headaches, painful breasts, ravenous hunger, gas, constipation, and increased bathroom time might make it sound like I'm really experiencing pregnancy, honestly, I still don't *feel* pregnant at all. You could probably have any of these symptoms (or combinations of them) and never even realize that you're pregnant. Feeling relatively normal is hard to reconcile with the fact that I know that I'm pregnant and that I am now in possession of a photograph of my very real fetus. It is also hard to reconcile not feeling pregnant with the inevitable lifestyle changes I am now facing because of the pregnancy. Most notably, I have to watch what I eat, and I can't take most basic over-the-counter remedies. If you're pregnant, you can only have one cup of coffee a day, as high amounts of caffeine have been linked to miscarriage (e.g., Weng, Odouli, & Li, 2008). And, all of a sudden, there is a long list of foods that I can't eat because of the risk of ingesting bacteria, including deli meat, soft or unpasteurized cheeses, hot dogs, and sushi. Listeriosis, for example, is caused by a type of bacteria that can be found on contaminated meat. It's extremely rare, but it can have devastating effects on a fetus if a mother is infected while pregnant. And then there's the anxiety of knowing that everything I put in my body can affect my developing baby. In fact, according to *What to Expect When You're Expecting,* "each bite . . . is an opportunity to feed that growing baby of yours healthy nutrients" (p. 90). How's that for guilt?

The biggest challenge this month has been coping with the constant headaches, alongside new limitations on taking over-the-counter medications. I've had throbbing headaches about once every week since I got pregnant, and I can't really take anything to relieve the pain except for Tylenol. While doctors discourage pregnant women from taking anything with ibuprofen in it (e.g., Advil, Motrin), acetaminophen (the active ingredient in Tylenol) is one of the only painkillers that has been deemed safe during pregnancy. The US Food and Drug Administration (FDA) has a grading system for over-the-counter medications based on what research says about their risk to a developing fetus. Drugs that receive an A have been thoroughly tested in pregnant women and there is no evidence of abnormalities for the fetus when taken during any trimester. Drugs that get a B or C are a bit sketchier, and there's either no good research on the effects of these drugs on pregnant women, or the drug has shown potentially negative effects in pregnant animals. If the drug gets a D, or worse, an X, it means there's solid evidence that the drug can cause potential harm to a developing fetus and shouldn't be taken (unless there is a life-threatening situation). Prescription drugs follow the same rating system, so if you're on a prescription medication and become pregnant, check with your doctor about whether your medications are safe.

When it comes to over-the-counter meds, ibuprofen gets a B in the first two trimesters and a D in the third. Tylenol, or acetaminophen gets straight A's across the board. But just to make sure it's safe, I did an Internet search of what happens when women take Tylenol during pregnancy, and the first article that came up was a paper pointing to a relationship between taking Tylenol during pregnancy and having children with attention deficit hyperactivity disorder (ADHD; Thompson, Waldie, Wall, Murphy, Mitchell, & ABC Study Group, 2014). Of course, I freaked out. I read the original study, and the link they find between taking Tylenol and ADHD is just *correlational* and not necessarily *causal*, meaning that it isn't clear whether mothers who have headaches during pregnancy just happen to be more likely to have kids who have ADHD, or whether taking Tylenol *causes* ADHD. Logically (and as a professional researcher), I know acetaminophen has a long history of being safe during pregnancy and that it's fine to relieve my headaches with Tylenol, but this information doesn't stop me from being completely paranoid and agonizing over the decision (prolonging and probably intensifying my headache) for hours every time. I guess the mom guilt has indeed begun.

The second challenge this month has been hiding all of my new lifestyle changes from my friends. For example, I went to a wedding with all of my best friends from college in the beginning of this month. The wedding was in the Outer Banks, North Carolina, and about ten of us rented a large house on the beach for a long weekend. I don't know about you, but long weekends with college friends means drinking cold beers on the beach. What a bummer for me. As the weekend approached, I was nervous that not drinking would give away my condition. I am by no means an alcoholic, but I rarely turn down a cold beer on a hot summer day, and my friends know it well. Since I wasn't past the first trimester, and we already talked about the high risk of miscarriage (see Chapter 2), I decided to keep the news to myself and fake it. I carried around beer cans full of water, and, at the reception (which to my dismay, featured a delightful-looking open bar and sushi spread), I carried around a glass of seltzer with a lime and told everyone I was drinking gin and tonic. It went off without a hitch—no one suspected anything. Apparently, faking alcohol consumption is pretty easy around a bunch of drunk people at a wedding. But the fact that I was successful at keeping my secret doesn't make complete sobriety easy in the summertime. I love having a cold beer at the end of a long workday, and even in month three, I was already missing my favorite summer beverage.

Whether you can drink even a little bit during pregnancy is a controversial issue since there is very little research on the topic. There's plenty of research studying women who drink heavily during pregnancy, but that research is also correlational. In other words, we don't know whether differences between babies of mothers who drink and babies of mothers who don't drink are *caused* by alcohol or by some other factor altogether. This is especially problematic for research on alcohol use because women who drink heavily during pregnancy are also more likely than nondrinkers to engage in other risky activities like smoking and illegal drug use and have a poor diet and limited access to prenatal care. This makes it hard to study the unique effects of alcohol since the side effects we see in newborn babies could be attributed to any of these risk factors.

Toxins that can affect fetal development are called *teratogens*. If we wanted to carry out a good study where we could make solid conclusions about the effects of certain teratogens on a developing fetus, we'd have to randomly assign women (with no known history of drug or alcohol use) to different conditions to avoid any kind of bias. In other words, we'd have to randomly assign some pregnant mothers to drink during pregnancy and others to abstain. For obvious ethical reasons, we'd never do that (and most mothers would never agree), thus making it hard to study the direct effects of alcohol—or any teratogens—on unborn babies.

What we know for sure is that heavy drinking or incidences of binge drinking during pregnancy can lead to *fetal alcohol syndrome* (FAS). FAS results in smaller than normal babies with a smaller head circumference, lesser developed brains, and minor facial abnormalities that include widely spaced small eyes and a thin upper lip. There could also be minor ear deformities and cleft palate—which, again, occurs when the cells that make up the face fail to come together completely (see Chapter 2). The problems aren't just physical: many children with FAS suffer some cognitive deficits and behavioral problems associated with attention and learning that start early in infancy. Some infants may not meet full criteria for FAS but have some of the associated symptoms, such as alcohol-related birth defects (ARBD), or are diagnosed with alcohol-related neurodevelopmental disorder (ARND) where some of the same structural abnormalities and psychological problems related to FAS are present but to a lesser extent (Thackray & Tifft, 2001).

The question on your mind is probably how much alcohol is too much? Unfortunately, because of the ethical problems I mentioned with doing research on alcohol consumption in pregnant women, the answer isn't at all clear. A research group in Norway recently published a series of papers suggesting that mild (1–4 drinks per week) and even moderate (5–8 drinks per week) drinking during pregnancy leads to no significant adverse effects for the fetus on a variety of measures, including IQ and attention span, but that more than 9 drinks a week can be problematic (Falgreen Eriksen et al., 2012; Kesmodel, Bertrand et al., 2012; Kesmodel, Falgreen Eriksen et al., 2012; Skogerbø et al., 2012; Underbjerg et al., 2012). Even with these findings, the authors point out that there is no specific level of drinking that is deemed to be safe, so it's probably best to be cautious and not take too many risks. Some people will say that a glass of wine here and there won't hurt anything, but the truth is, we really don't know exactly what small amounts of alcohol can do to a fetus.

In addition to alcohol, smoking is another teratogen that can negatively affect a fetus. Doctors will tell you not to smoke tobacco products during pregnancy because it is bad for the baby, but most of the time they won't tell you why it's so bad. The reason is pretty intuitive—it deprives the mother of oxygen and, therefore, deprives the fetus of oxygen as well. This is bad for the fetus in two important ways. First, it can impede growth and lead to a baby who is born too small, or with a low birth weight (LBW). The average birth weight of a newborn is about 7.5 pounds, and babies who are born with a LBW are generally less than 5.5 pounds. Having a small baby may not sound like too bad of an outcome—after all, who wants to push an 8-pounder out of a hole barely the size of a lime—but being born too small (or what some doctors call *small for gestational age*) is associated with all sorts of developmental problems as infants grow up. For example, cerebral palsy (which is a blanket term for deficits in the ability to control movements) is associated with LBW and prematurity, and it often results from some sort of trauma during birth due to a lack of oxygen. The lack of oxygen leads to brain lesions that cause abnormal muscle tone and various cognitive problems.

Second, smoking and even second-hand smoke can also have a negative effect on the baby after it's born and is one of the two most powerful predictors of *sudden infant death syndrome* (SIDS). As the name suggests, SIDS is the sudden death of an infant while sleeping for no known reason in the absence of any prior symptoms of illness. No one knows what causes SIDS. What we do know is that there are two behaviors that are related to the incidence of SIDS. One is putting infants to sleep on their stomachs instead of on their backs (more on this later), and the other is smoking. The incidence of SIDS is higher in the infants of parents who smoke.

Two final teratogens that I'll mention are probably the ones that are the hardest to avoid—stress and depression. The effects of stress and maternal depression on a developing fetus is another issue that is difficult to study, especially since women who are anxious or depressed during pregnancy are also likely to be anxious or depressed during parenthood, making it difficult to study whether the anxiety and depression experienced *specifically during pregnancy* affects the fetus. Researchers in Finland found a way to do it by retrospectively interviewing people whose fathers died during World War II. They contacted these adults (who were infants or fetuses at the time of their fathers' deaths) and asked them questions about their psychological and social well-being. The researchers targeted two specific groups—one group of adults who were in their mothers' wombs when their fathers were killed, and a second group of adults whose fathers died shortly after they were born. This is a really clever way to study the effects of maternal stress and depression since both groups of children had mothers' who were likely stressed because of their husbands' deaths, but only one group of mothers experienced this stress *while they were pregnant.* The results of the study were that the adults who were in their mothers' wombs at the time of their fathers' deaths had more psychological and emotional problems than those whose fathers died after they were born, suggesting that stress while their mothers were pregnant may have had a negative impact on their development (Huttunen & Niskanen, 1978).

The death of a partner is an extreme type of stress, so maybe it's not surprising that it can affect an unborn baby. However, milder forms of stress or anxiety might also have negative effects on a developing fetus, especially chronic clinical anxiety or depression. For example, mothers who are clinically anxious while they are pregnant are more likely than nonanxious mothers to have children who have emotional problems (O'Connor, Heron, Golding, Beveridge, & Glover, 2002; Van den Bergh & Marcoen, 2004). Furthermore, babies of mothers who are clinically depressed during pregnancy can have different stress responses and even different brain activity than babies whose mothers are not depressed during pregnancy (Field et al., 2004; Jones et al., 1996). How is this possible, you might ask? Researchers have proposed that changes in a mother's mood might change the physiology of the prenatal environment (the womb) and, as a result, affect the biology of the developing fetus (Kaplan, Evans, & Monk, 2008). Thus, if you are experiencing high levels of stress or depression during pregnancy, it is important to consult a specialist. Likewise, if you're already on medication for anxiety or depression, talk to your doctor about whether your medications are safe to take during pregnancy.

To sum up, while you're pregnant it's important to listen to your doctors and stay away from teratogens like alcohol and tobacco (and, needless to say, illegal drugs), to manage life stressors, eat a healthy diet, and seek medical attention when necessary. It is perhaps *most* important to do this during the first trimester, as most of the major abnormalities that can result from all of these teratogens can occur in the very first few months of pregnancy. Why? Because this is when all of the most important organs are forming, as opposed to later in the pregnancy when the fetus is mostly growing in size.

Thalidomide is a famous example of a dangerous teratogen that is most dangerous when consumed in the first trimester. Thalidomide was an over-the-counter drug for morning sickness that was popular in the 1950s and 1960s (Frank, Macpherson, & Figg, 2004). The drug was thought to be an effective remedy for nausea, so doctors had no problem recommending it to expecting moms. Unfortunately, the drug wasn't tested rigorously on human subjects—it was only tested in animals—and women who took thalidomide in the first trimester ended up giving birth to infants who had dramatic physical abnormalities that varied depending on when the drug was taken. For example, mothers who took the drug between 34 and 38 days after conception had babies with no ears; taking it 38–46 days after conception resulted in babies with malformed arms, and taking it at 40–46 days resulted in babies with malformed legs. What was most shocking was that if women took the drug after 50 days of pregnancy, *there was no effect on their babies at all!* The reason for these dramatic differences is that all of the most important parts of the body are developing in the first trimester, often during a very small window of time. If the development of those structures is interrupted by a teratogen, even for just a few days, the effects can be devastating (Figure 3.1).

Spina bifida is another example. Spina bifida is a developmental disability that involves an open or protruding spinal cord. It is a serious disorder that can result in neurological deficits, orthopedic abnormalities, and even paralysis. In the previous chapter, I mentioned that the fetus's neural tube zips shut in the first month after conception (see Chapter 2). The neural tube eventually makes up the fetus's spine—clearly an important part of human anatomy. If something interrupts this process and the neural tube fails to close completely, serious problems with the pregnancy can occur, most commonly resulting in some form of spina bifida. This usually happens because of a lack of folic acid (or B vitamin), and your doctor will probably tell you to start taking folic acid supplements daily (prenatal vitamins usually include 100% of your recommended daily intake of folic acid) before even trying to get pregnant to prevent this kind of thing from happening. It can happen so early

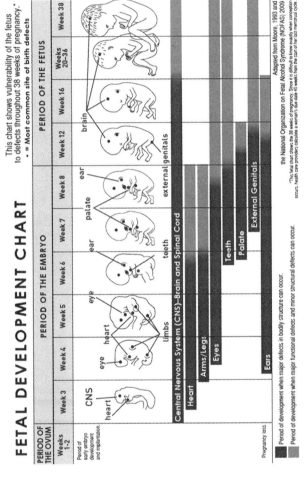

Figure 3.1 | Chart demonstrating when major defects in pregnancy can occur. In purple are when major deficits in the bodily structure of the fetus (e.g., eyes, head, feet) can occur, as in the case of the deficits caused by thalidomide and spina bifida. In pink are when major functional deficits (e.g., deficits in cognition) and minor structural deficits can occur. As you can see, the most major structural deficits to the body are likely to occur early in pregnancy.

Source: Centers for Disease Control and Prevention.

in the pregnancy that the mother may not even know that she's pregnant yet.

These are clearly very extreme cases. When doctors say that we shouldn't eat raw meat, soft cheeses, or drink alcohol even socially, it's either because these things can make *us* sick (which isn't good for the fetus) or because the effects of these potential teratogens are still *unknown*. Given the extremity of the developmental problems that can happen at this important point in my pregnancy, I've again chosen to take the cautious route and do what my doctors have advised. Better to be safe than sorry or constantly worrying.

The end of the first trimester is marked by the 12-week ultrasound. This ultrasound would include an important test—a test for Down syndrome. These days you can have a blood test and get ultrasound measurements to test for Down syndrome with 97% accuracy at the end of the first trimester. Down syndrome is not generally caused by any sort of teratogen; it is a chromosomal abnormality that is closely linked to the mother's age. In women under 30, the risk of having a child with Down syndrome is less than 1 in 1,000 (Yoon et al., 1996). Once a woman is over 40, the risk is more like 1 in 100; and once she's 45, it's about 1 in 30. At age 34, my risk is approximately 1 in 450—not huge, but also not nothing. The genetic test involves taking blood and measuring the width of the skin in the back of the fetus's neck via ultrasound. The doctor will also look for the presence of a nasal bone—75% of individuals with Down syndrome don't have one. Then the doctor enters your age, data from your blood test, presence/absence of the nasal bone, and the width measured from the ultrasound into a formula to calculate your baby's risk (Figure 3.2).

Based on the ultrasound, my fetus looked to be developing typically so far. What used to look like buds on either side of the fetus's body have developed into fully formed arms and legs, with (hopefully) 10 fingers and 10 toes. The fingers don't grow out of the buds; instead, the cells between each finger and each toe die off to create the contours of the hands and feet. This is called *programmed cell*

Maternal Age Incidence of Down syndrome	Maternal Age Incidence of Down syndrome	Maternal Age Incidence of Down syndrome
20 1 in 2000	30 1 in 900	40 1 in 100
21 1 in 1700	31 1 in 800	41 1 in 80
22 1 in 1500	32 1 in 720	42 1 in 70
23 1 in 1400	33 1 in 600	43 1 in 50
24 1 in 1300	34 1 in 450	44 1 in 40
25 1 in 1200	35 1 in 350	45 1 in 30
26 1 in 1100	36 1 in 300	46 1 in 25
27 1 in 1050	37 1 in 250	47 1 in 20
28 1 in 1000	38 1 in 200	48 1 in 15

Figure 3.2 | Risk of Down syndrome by maternal age.
Source: National Down Syndrome Society (NDSS, 2016).

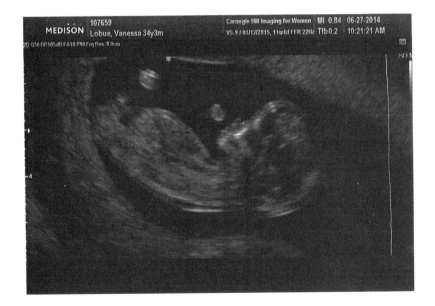

Figure 3.3 | Twelve-week ultrasound.
Source: Vanessa LoBue.

death—it's written into our biology. At this point, my fetus has its own blood type, fingernails, and a unique set of fingerprints. There is no more yolk sack to feed the fetus while the placenta grows, which means that my body is now passing food to the fetus directly. My fetus's neck width is about 1.7 mm (anything above 3 mm is a marker for Downs), and it has a fully formed nasal bone, so my risk went from 1 in 450 based on just my age to 1 in 6,281 after the test. There will be a second test at 16 weeks where my doctor will be able to quantify the risk even more precisely (Figure 3.3).

4

THE FOURTH MONTH

Developing Sex and Gender

As I moved into the fourth month and out of the first trimester, my symptoms changed quite a bit. The breast pain receded, so now they're still big, but they don't hurt anymore. I'm still peeing a lot, but not as much as before, and the constipation is completely gone. Even the ravenous hunger has subsided, which is good because my weight gain is now at about 8 pounds. My attitude about the weight gain changes daily. Sometimes I feel fat and depressed. Yes, I know I'm pregnant, and yes, I know I'm supposed to be gaining weight, and yes, pregnancy is beautiful and blah, blah, blah, but telling myself these things doesn't help when I get dressed in the morning and none of my clothes fit or when I look at myself in the mirror and I see my protruding belly. There are other days when I feel OK, and I think it's really an amazing thing that I'm growing so fast because that means that the fetus is growing fast, but those days are few and far between. I'm still in that in-between stage where I don't exactly look pregnant yet—I mostly look like I eat a lot of Hot Pockets.

Despite the fact that some of the more unpleasant symptoms of the first trimester have subsided, the second trimester has also brought with it two brand-new symptoms—both of which are strange and un-expected but apparently very common. The first and most noticeable is vertigo. If I'm lying down and I get up quickly, or if I am sitting and stand up too fast, I feel incredibly dizzy for a few seconds—I've never experienced anything like it. At this point in the pregnancy, the fetus is growing and putting more and more pressure on the body's blood vessels. This can be especially noticeable when you're lying down and the weight of the fetus is pressing on important blood vessels in the lower back, which is probably why I feel it so strongly after I've been lying down. Another weird and unexpected symptom is nosebleeds. I've never had a nosebleed before in my life, and this month I've had three. Apparently it's also completely normal and another result of the increased volume of blood flowing through my body.

In addition to the disappearance of several of my more unpleasant symptoms, the most exciting part of the fourth month of pregnancy is that I will find out the sex of the baby. I can see why a lot people want to be surprised, but delay of gratification isn't really my thing, so I elected to find out. The reason you typically don't find out the sex of your baby until about 16 weeks is because it's the first time doctors can actually see the fetus's genitals on the ultrasound. But despite having to wait 16 whole weeks for this important piece of information, the fetus has a sex right from conception. In fact, if you don't want to wait until the 16-week ultrasound, there are genetics tests you can take to determine the sex of the fetus much earlier in the pregnancy (see Chapter 2).

Sex is determined by the chromosomes that are in the nucleus of every cell in our bodies. Each cell has 46 chromosomes, and the sperm of the father and the egg of the mother each only have half—23 each. At conception, the chromosomes of the sperm and the egg come together to form 22 pairs; the 23rd and final pair is the sex chromosome. For the most part, XX chromosomes will guide the development of female sex organs and XY chromosomes will guide the development of male sex organs. Since women have two X chromosomes, the egg always has an X chromosome to contribute to the pair. Males have an X and a Y chromosome, so the sperm can either contribute another X or a Y, meaning that the sperm always determines the sex of the fetus.

The presence of two X's is what makes a female fetus develop female sex organs, and the presence of a Y is what makes a male fetus develop male sex organs. But that isn't always the case. At some point during prenatal development, fetuses that have a Y chromosome begin to produce a hormone called *androgen* that causes the fetus to develop testes, which in turn produce testosterone. However, without androgen to get the ball rolling, the embryo will remain female, regardless of the sex chromosomes that it might have. If for some reason the prenatal environment keeps a fetus that has a Y chromosome from producing enough androgen for the testes to fully develop, the fetus can appear as if it is a girl when it's born, which is what happens to babies with *androgen insensitivity syndrome* (AIS). The opposite developmental problem can also occur when the prenatal environment causes fetuses with two X chromosomes to overproduce androgen; as a result, their genitals appear to be male even though they're genetically females. This condition is called *congenital adrenal hyperplasia* (CAH).

This brings us to an important difference between the terms "sex" and "gender." Sex is what is determined by the sex chromosomes or what is written into our biology—this is called the fetus's *genotype*. But the sex chromosomes themselves aren't the only factor that determines gender. Gender is a construct, or what actually gets expressed—how the child looks, acts, and what it feels like. This is the fetus's *phenotype*, or another word for how the fetus's biology (genotype) interacts with the environment. This means that what happens in the fetus's environment does indeed play a role in determining its gender. This shouldn't be all that surprising since gender and sex aren't always consistent, as we can see from the examples of AIS or CAH. Individuals who are *transgender* also identify with a gender that is not consistent with their biological sex. For others, gender can be non-binary, existing on a spectrum of masculinity and femininity, kind of like sexuality.

In fact, some species of animals don't have sex chromosomes at all, and sex is determined *entirely* by conditions in the environment. For example, some female coral reef fish will literally become male if the dominant male in their school has an unfortunate encounter with a larger (hungrier) fish. Similarly, the sex of turtles, crocodiles, alligators, and some lizards is determined by the temperature of the surrounding environment while their eggs are being incubated. Moreover, there are species of rodents that only have X chromosomes, no Y's; researchers still don't know how exactly they become male versus female, but recent research suggests that their stem cells are sufficiently flexible to develop into either ovaries or testes (Honda et al., 2017) (for more on stem cells, see Chapter 2).

The point of all of this is that while *sex* in human fetuses is based on the content of our chromosomes, *gender* is quite flexible. And, in fact, young children think more flexibly about gender than many adults do. For example, children under the age of 5 don't really understand that gender is something that's relatively permanent. A child might ask his mom whether she was a girl or boy when she was a kid, or say that she wants to grow up to be a daddy. Don't believe me? Just ask a 3-year-old. World-renowned psychologist Sandra Bem did. In one of her most famous studies conducted at Cornell University, she showed preschool-aged children several photographs of a little boy and a little girl. In one photo, the child was naked so that his or her "private parts" were clearly visible. In a second photo, the same child was dressed in gender-stereotyped clothing—a dress and pig-tails for the girl and a collared shirt for the boy. Finally, in the third photo, the same child was dressed in clothing of the *opposite* gender—this time, a dress for the boy and a collared shirt for the girl.

Bem first asked children whether the child in the first naked photograph was a boy or a girl, and then she asked them whether the same child dressed in gender-stereotyped clothing in the second photo was a boy or a girl. Most of the children she tested answered these questions correctly. But then she told them that the child in the third photo was playing a silly dress-up game and asked them whether the child was *still* a boy or a girl, even when dressed as a member of the opposite sex. Most 3- to 5-year-olds thought that the boy who decided to dress up like a girl was now a girl and that the girl who decided to dress up like a boy was now really a boy. It wasn't until children learned about the relevance of sex organs in predicting gender—usually after the age of 5—that they reliably said that a girl who dresses up like a boy is still a girl, and a boy who dresses up like a girl is still a boy (Bem, 1989).

After the age of 5, children begin to understand that changes in their clothes or hairstyle don't necessarily constitute a change in gender and believe that gender is a stable trait. During this time, children are often pretty stringent about maintaining gender stereotypes. This is around the time you'll see a lot of girls wearing pink princess dresses to school every day and boys refusing to wear pink altogether. These behaviors actually make sense if you're 5 years old and don't fully understand that small changes in your appearance won't necessarily change your gender; to young children, wearing a dress or, conversely, wearing boys' pants might make a big difference in how others identify you (Martin & Ruble, 2004). Recent research suggests that this rigidity is pretty consistent across cultures and ethnicities, with kids getting more and more rigid about adhering to gender stereotypes between the ages of 3 and 5. By 5 or 6, this rigidity loosens up a bit, and boys and girls accept that they can adopt behaviors more stereotypical of the opposite sex and still maintain their gender identity (Halim, Ruble, Tamis-LeMonda, & Shrout, 2013).

Recently, social issues revolving around transgender rights have highlighted the fact that biology isn't the only determining factor in the development of gender identity. In fact, many children are now identifying as transgender before they reach adulthood or even adolescence. Skeptics have expressed disbelief at the idea that children have the cognitive capacity to identify as transgender at an early age and argue instead that these children are confused about gender or that they're just pretending, like they'd pretend to be a cat or a dinosaur.

Given Bem's research, it's not necessarily an unreasonable assumption as gender is not the easiest thing to reason about at an early age. Unfortunately, since this issue is relatively new and scientific research is a slow-moving process, there isn't much that the science of child development has contributed to this area so far. But there are now a handful of studies suggesting that, by the age of 5 or 6, children are not confused about their gender identities and do know enough to accurately identify themselves as transgender.

Kristina Olson and her colleagues from the University of Washington, for example, wanted to know whether transgender children are really just confused about their gender identities or, instead, whether they consistently demonstrate thoughts, preferences, and behaviors that match with their self-identified gender or the opposite sex. To answer this question, they gave groups of 5- to 12-year-old transgender and non-transgender (or *cisgender*) children a series of tests. The researchers reasoned that if transgender children were just confused about gender or they were just pretending to be a member of the opposite sex, they should either answer questions consistently with the cisgender children of the same sex, or they should flip-flop their answers, providing some answers consistent with their self-identified gender and some answers consistent with their sex.

Across a variety of tests, the transgender children looked identical to the other children with the same gender they identified with (the gender opposite their sex). In other words, transgender girls (who's sex is male) consistently showed a preference for interacting with other girls and playing with girls' toys; in fact, they behaved just like the cisgender girls in every way. In fact, the transgender children were practically indistinguishable from the cisgender children, meaning that you could not tell the difference between a transgender girl and a cisgender girl. The remarkable consistency across a variety of measures suggests that, by the age of 5 or 6, transgender children are not necessarily confused about their gender and truly identify with a gender that is opposite their sex (Olson, Key, & Eaton, 2015).

Despite this promising new research, skeptics still claim that the growing population of transgender children is likely due to confusion about gender norms based on societal changes. However, experts in this area think it is much more likely that such increases are due to the fact that transgender children are being raised in supportive environments for the first time. In fact, more recent research on transgender children's mental health suggests that if these kids grow up in a loving environment with parents who support their child's gender identity, transgender children are no more likely to grow up feeling depressed or anxious when compared to their non-transgender peers (Olson, Durwood, DeMeules, & McLaughlin, 2016).

In terms of my own fetus's sex, I haven't really been "feeling" like I'm having a boy or a girl, and I don't have a preference for giving birth to a baby of one sex over the other. But I did recently decide that, even though I'm going to find out my baby's sex, I'm not going to tell anyone else (besides Nick, of course) until the baby is born. I know this may seem over the top or even cruel to family and friends who are probably dying to know (I'm looking at you, Mom), but I have a few real reasons for keeping it a secret. First and foremost, I don't want to end up with a wave of blue or pink overwhelming my house. Picture yourself walking into any child's room; you could almost certainly guess the sex of the baby just from the color of his or her clothes, blankets, and toys. Girls' rooms are virtually covered in pink, and boys' rooms tend to be plastered in blue. This phenomenon isn't limited to newborns. If you look at the kids' section of a department store catalogue you'll see countless little girls dressed in pink clothes, playing with pink toys, carrying pink lunchboxes, and typing on pink computers.

I'm not just speaking from personal experience. A group of researchers at SUNY Stonybrook studied this phenomenon by observing parents and their infants at suburban shopping malls, simply recording what the infants wore. Not surprisingly, they reported that 75% of infant girls were wearing pink, and 79% of infant boys were wearing blue (Shakin, Shakin, & Sternglanz, 1985). Similarly, girls and boys are generally given different toys based purely on their gender, and, when asked what to get a hypothetical child for a holiday or birthday, adults generally cite nurturing toys for girls, such as dolls, dollhouses, and housewares, and they name active or competitive toys for boys, like trucks, battle games, and sports equipment (Ruble, Martin, & Berenbaum, 2006).

You might be saying to yourself, who cares? A little bit of blue and pink never hurt anyone, and what little girl doesn't like playing with a doll once in awhile? It turns out that the toys children play with can bring out gender-stereotyped behaviors. For example, when you give preschool-aged children both girl and boy toys, both boys and girls play more actively with the boy toys. In other words, we always assume that boys are naturally more active than girls (and some of them they might be), but boy toys actually *bring out more active play*, and *both* boys and the girls actually enjoy jumping on the trampolines and throwing balls once in awhile (Maccoby, 1988).

So, the bigger reason I'm keeping it a secret is that gender-stereotyped behavior is something that can be affected by the environment—how we treat our kids, the toys we give them, and our expectations for how they should behave. I know that some gender-stereotyped behavior is inevitable, but I'd really like my future child to choose what he or she would like to play with and, on a broader level, how he or she wants to behave, without setting up too many biases or expectations early on in development. It's hard to avoid this altogether—parents have expectations about their children based on gender before they're even born, whether they realize it or not. In one study on the topic conducted at Auburn University, expecting parents were asked to choose from a set of adjectives—firm or soft, large or small, coordinated or awkward, strong or weak—to describe their unborn babies. Just based on knowing the fetus's sex (and pretty much nothing else given that their babies hadn't even been born yet), parents typically chose gender-stereotyped adjectives like strong, noisy, big, and hardy to describe their unborn boys and adjectives like soft, small, and quiet to describe their unborn girls (Sweeney & Bradbard, 1988). So, even before babies are born, parents have expectations about what they are going to be like based purely on their gender.

It is true that boys and girls are different, and they're different from the very first year of life, but these differences are pretty small. Boys are more aggressive, more active (even in the womb!), and less fearful than girls. Girls are more emotional, more verbal (they speak and read sooner), and generally more compliant than boys (Ruble et al., 2006). Boys are physically stronger than girls—they are naturally taller, more muscular, and have a broader chest. Girls are physically weaker than boys, but have more long-term endurance and generally live longer (the average life expectancy in the US is about 76 years for men and 81 years for women). Evidence for this long-term endurance starts in the womb: male fetuses are more likely to be miscarried than female fetuses; there are 140 males for every 100 females at conception, but 106 males for every 100 females at birth (Siegler, DeLoache, & Eisenberg, 2011). Similarly, male babies are more susceptible to disease than female babies after they are born, and they are more likely to die in infancy. Males are also more prone to genetic disorders than females, such as Huntington's disease, color-blindness, hyperactivity, and more. This is generally because the X chromosome is much bigger than the Y and carries more genes. So, if there is a recessive gene on the X chromosome for a genetic disorder, females who have a second X chromosome are more likely to have a dominant gene on it to override the recessive one than are males with a smaller Y (see Chapter 2) (Figure 4.1).

That's about it for gender differences in the first year of life. Most of the other differences you generally associate with gender don't emerge until later in development and are likely the product (at least to some extent) of a child's environment. Some of these differences are driven by the child's own desire to identify with his or her gender. As I mentioned earlier, when children start noticing and talking about gender, they often seek out gender-related information and adhere to very strict gender stereotypes. This begins around the ages of 2 ½ or 3. For example, my own research has shown that boys and girls start to show a preference for gender-stereotyped colors like pink and blue around this time: when given the choice between pairs of toys, all of which were identical except for color, children under the age of 2 chose somewhat randomly. However, around age 2½ half, girls started choosing pink toys more and more often with age, while boys began avoiding all things pink like the plague (LoBue & DeLoache, 2011).

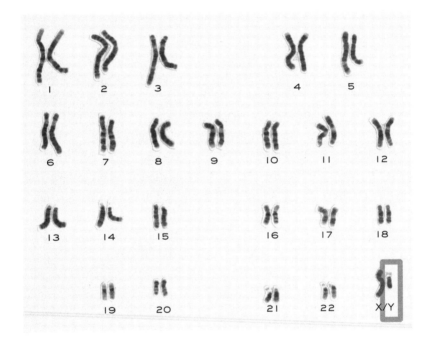

Figure 4.1 | Humans have 23 pairs of chromosomes; the twenty-third pair are the sex chromosomes. Pictured here are X and Y chromosomes; in the red box, you can see that the X chromosome is significantly larger than the Y.
Source: Wikipedia, "Y chromosome," by National Human Genome Research Institute.

Similarly, the reason you see so many preschool-aged girls dressed like princesses and boys dressed like superheroes is that they are looking for ways to identify with their gender and can sometimes go overboard to stay true to the stereotypes they learn (Figure 4.2).

But children don't create gender stereotypes on their own; they learn these stereotypes from the people around them—from us—and often our own expectations about how girls and boys *should* behave play a major role in promoting children's stereotyped behaviors. For example, although gender differences in reading (favoring girls) and spatial abilities (favoring boys) can be found in many countries from around the world, the magnitude of these differences varies based on the amount of gender inequality found within that culture. In countries with more gender inequality, the advantage for boys in spatial ability and math is much greater, presumably because boys are given more advantages in these areas by their parents and teachers (Miller & Halpern, 2014). This suggests that the way boys and girls are treated might have a large impact on gender differences.

Similarly, although there is some research suggesting that boys perform slightly better than girls at spatial tasks from a very young age, large differences in spatial ability and math don't emerge until adolescence (Miller & Halpern, 2014). Before that, in the first to third grades, girls do just as well as boys in math, and they perform *better* than boys in other subjects like reading. In fact, in a large study examining more than a thousand children from grades 1–6, researchers found very little evidence of any gender differences in a variety of basic math skills (Hutchison, Lyons, & Ansari, 2018). However, despite the fact that boys aren't better than girls at math in these early years, parents *expect* boys to outperform girls in math as early as first grade (Entwisle & Baker, 1983) or even in kindergarten (Miller & Halpern, 2014). Expectations really matter to kids, and there are countless studies showing that the expectations of authority figures can affect children's behavior and even their IQ (e.g., Rosenthal & Jacobson, 1968).

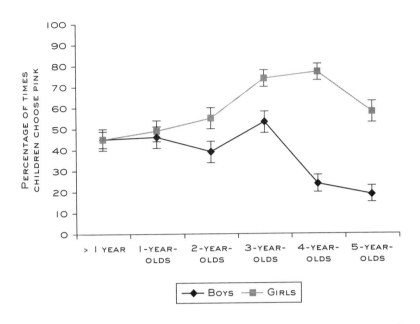

Figure 4.2 | In a study from my own lab, we presented boys and girls between the ages of 7 months and 5 years with a set of 10 toys that were identical except for color and let them choose which one they wanted to play with. It wasn't until about 2½ or 3 that girls started showing a preference for pink and boys started showing a clear avoidance of it. This is about the same time that children start recognizing and talking about their own gender.
Source: LoBue, V., & DeLoache, J. S. (2011). Pretty in pink: The early development of gender-stereotyped color preferences. *British Journal of Developmental Psychology, 29*, 656–667. Reprinted with permission of John Wiley & Sons, Inc.

In a recent study looking at the relationship between parents' expectations of their 6-year-old children's math abilities, parents' gender stereotypes, and children's expectations about their own math abilities, a group of Italian researchers found that mothers' gender-stereotyped beliefs about math predicted their daughters' perceptions of their own math ability. In other words, the more mothers believed that math was something that boys are better at, the worse their daughters felt about their own math abilities in school (Tomasetto, Mirisola, Galdi, & Cadinu, 2015). The point here is that our expectations about gender stereotypes—whether we are aware of them or not—affect our children's behavior. This can be especially problematic for girls since the most common assumption is that girls aren't going to do as well in math and science when compared to boys. In fact, recent research suggests that, by the age of 6 or 7, girls are less likely to associate intelligence with their own gender (even though on average they perform better than boys in school) and become increasingly less interested in games tailored to "really, really smart" kids over time (Bian, Leslie, & Cimpian, 2017).

But gender bias doesn't always go in boys' favor. In fact, recent research has shown that mothers talk more to their baby girls than to their baby boys (Johnson, Caskey, Rand, Tucker, & Vohr, 2014). Parents also use more emotion words when they talk to girls than when they talk to boys (Adams, Kuebli, Boyle, & Vivush, 1995). And this isn't just true of English-speaking parents—a recent study found that the same is true of Spanish-speaking parents as well (Aznar & Tenenbaum, 2013). It isn't just true of mothers either: Fathers use more emotion words with their daughters than with their sons, and they even sing to their baby girls more than they sing to their baby boys (Mascaro, Rentscher, Hackett, Mehl, & Rilling, 2017). I know this may not sound like a big deal, but the ability to understand one's own emotions has been linked to a variety of other skills, such as academic performance in school and important social skills like the ability to make and maintain friendships. So the fact that parents use fewer emotion words with boys than with girls at such an early age (and fewer words in general) sets boys up for some disadvantages as well.

I'm sure I have my own expectations for my unborn child already, whether I realize it or not. We all have them, and, as hard as we try, I don't think there is any way to shield our kids from gender stereotypes that we all carry with us to some extent. It's not unlikely that I will give birth to a girl who will eventually like pink and play with dolls or a boy who will eventually like blue and play with cars, but I can do my best right now to avoid getting bombarded with gender-stereotyped toys and clothes. Well, at least until after the baby is born.

I was pretty nervous when I showed up for my 16-week ultrasound. Today, I would have a full screening of the fetus's anatomy to look for any abnormalities, I would find out the sex, and I would have Part 2 of the Down syndrome screening—it's a big day. I relaxed a little bit once I saw the heart beating. My blood test showed that the chance my fetus has Down syndrome is even lower now than it was last time, estimated at 1 in more than 250,000. I got to see all of my fetus's bones,

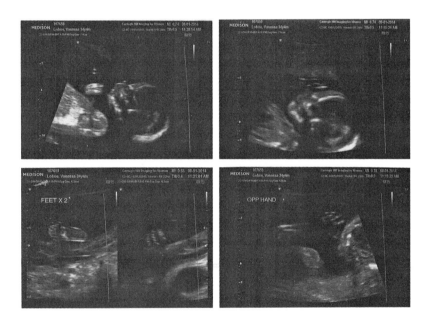

Figure 4.3 | Sixteen-week ultrasound. Left to right, top to bottom: 1. Profile. 2. Profile with open mouth. 3. Feet. 4. Back view with hand to the face.

Source: Vanessa LoBue.

fingers, toes, face, and even the four chambers of its hearts and the two hemispheres of its brain. At one point, the fetus was touching its ear—it is amazing how clearly I could see it on the screen.

After what felt like forever, the doctor made it to the genitals to check the fetus's sex. I didn't see the twig, but I definitely saw the berries. It's a boy. As soon as she said it, it felt like I knew all along (Figure 4.3).

5

THE FIFTH MONTH

THE SCIENCE OF SLEEP

After my 16-week ultrasound, I felt significantly less anxious and was now confident enough to tell my friends and family that I'm pregnant. I'd told a few friends and my immediate family already, but I kept most people in the dark; they are all starting to wonder why I'm not leaving the house much and why I'm constantly turning down happy hours. I probably could have told them after 12 weeks—the official end of the first trimester and when the risk of miscarriage significantly drops—but I decided to be extra cautious because I still didn't really *feel* pregnant. Since I didn't get morning sickness at all in the first trimester, I never really had daily proof that the baby was still there (see Chapter 2). Even at 16 weeks, I held my breath during every ultrasound until I could see with my own eyes that my baby was actually there on the screen. Without seeing it, I had no real evidence that it was alive and healthy.

All of that changed in the fifth month. First of all, I actually *look* pregnant for the first time now. I can't wear most of my clothes, and my giant belly sticks out like a sore thumb. Because I literally have nothing I can wear, this week I ventured out to buy my first pair of pregnancy jeans—the ones with the ugly elastic. I have to admit, although they look hideous on the hanger, *I absolutely love them.* How have I never discovered jeans with elastic before? When you put them on, it's like wearing yoga pants that look like regular jeans. If you wear a long enough top, you can't see the ugly elastic band and it's not obvious at all that they're for pregnant women. I never want to stop wearing them. Sure, I miss my cute little skinny jeans that look great with every pair of shoes you can imagine, but at this point, after gaining about 15 pounds, I'm thrilled to be wearing a comfortable pair of pants that I can actually leave the house in. They are so comfy that I'm not sure I'm going to trade them in for regular clothes when this debacle is over in January . . . I might just keep wearing them all winter long. I know that being so big might sound like a bad thing, but for the first time I don't feel all that overweight anymore—I finally just feel pregnant. I stopped wearing my baggiest clothes that hide my belly, and I have now borrowed maternity clothes from friends that show it off. At this point, why not just own it?

Another big change that has affected the way I feel about the pregnancy is that, at exactly 20 weeks to the day, I felt the baby move for the very first time. Like I said a few chapters ago, the baby has actually been moving since early in the first trimester (which is abundantly clear when you see it on the ultrasound). But between 18 and 25 weeks, the fetus is usually big enough that the mother can feel it move. This phenomenon is called *quickening*—it feels kind of like gas or indigestion at first. In the past few weeks, there were plenty of times when I felt some weird gas-like feelings in places where I shouldn't feel gas, which could have been the baby moving. But at 20 weeks there was no mistaking it—I felt a weird bubbly sensation that actually made my skin move. I was lying down to go to sleep when I first felt it. I immediately woke Nick up to feel it, too. He could sort of feel it (maybe 10% of the time that I can feel it), but he was excited anyway. After that first night, I've been able to feel him move every night since. It feels a little weird and uncomfortable to be honest, but I still like it. My mood is more positive than ever now that I have a daily reminder that he's in there, alive and kicking (literally).

A week after I started to feel the baby move, I went for my 20- to 22-week ultrasound. At this point, the fetus's taste buds are fully developed, and he can taste sweet, sour, salt, and bitterness from my food. Fine hairs on his head and eyebrows are beginning to form. Last time I went to the doctor, I was showing signs of *placenta previa*—a condition where your placenta is partially covering your cervix, which will obviously make it difficult for the baby to come out when it's time to give birth. My doctor said that in 95% of cases the placenta will naturally start growing up the belly, moving away from the cervix, but it is something that they are going to watch out for in the next ultrasound and every one that follows. If the placenta continues to grow over my cervix, I will definitely need a C-section, which is something I am mildly nervous about. For some reason, giving birth vaginally doesn't scare me at all, but being cut open, having my organs pushed aside, removing the baby, and then being put back together again is something that I really don't want to do, despite knowing full well that it's safe and doctors do it every day.

The ultrasound went well, and the placenta had already moved away from my cervix completely, so that's one thing I no longer have to worry about. The technician told me that she was going to do another full anatomy scan and that I would again get to see all of the baby's parts, including the four chambers of the heart and the two hemispheres of his brain. Seeing my baby on the screen again was great; he had grown so much since last month, now weighing 1 pound, 1 ounce. He wasn't all that active. This wasn't necessarily anything to be concerned about, it was just an issue for the technician who needed him to turn over to get a full view of his face and heart. We tried to get him to move by tapping my belly, then stretching my limbs, and even coughing. When that didn't work, the tech had me drink a full can of sugary cranberry juice to get him going. One can turned into two, and stretching turned into jumping jacks (yes, they really did make a pregnant woman do jumping jacks at a doctor's office). Finally, after 30 minutes of walking around and lots of sugar, he started moving. Apparently he had been asleep and all of the activity and sugar from the juice woke him up. In fact, we could actually see him *yawning* on the screen! It was the single most adorable thing I've ever seen in my life. He did it so many times, we were able to get a picture of it (Figure 5.1).

So it appears that after only 5 months of fetal development, my future child was already spending most of his time sleeping. Although it might sound like I have a lazy kid in my future, sleeping is something that fetuses start doing early in the pregnancy—in the second trimester—and, once they start, they do it a lot, especially during the

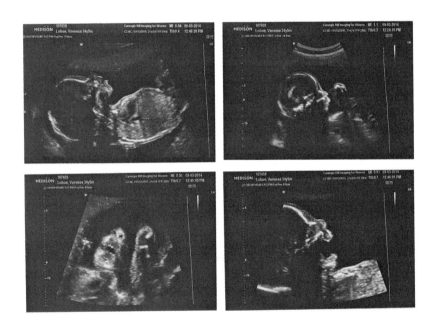

Figure 5.1 | Twenty-one-week ultrasound. Left to right, top to bottom: 1. Profile with open mouth. 2. Profile. 3. Mouth and nose. 4. Yawn.

Source: Vanessa LoBue.

day when the swaying motion of their mothers' walking lulls them into a sleepy state. Unfortunately for moms, that means fetuses are often most awake at night, when mothers are laying flat on their back and not moving, which is why I typically feel him move when I'm getting ready to go to sleep. Because of this pattern, when babies are born they will have day and night mixed up, wanting to be awake most often through the night and wanting to sleep through most of the day.

This pattern is starting to develop even in the fifth month of pregnancy, and my fetus is likely spending most of his days asleep. So it's not all that surprising that we found him taking an afternoon nap during the ultrasound. Fetuses sleep most of the time in fact, and they will sleep more and more as the pregnancy progresses, up to 90–95% of the time by the third trimester. Like newborns and adults, fetuses engage in rapid eye movement (REM) sleep cycles (named after the fact that this sleep stage causes the eyes to move back and forth), and it is the deepest cycle of sleep. Perhaps because REM sleep produces a large amount of brain activity, scientists have speculated that it is during this phase of sleep that dreaming occurs. In fact, during REM sleep, various areas of the brain involved in learning are active, and, as a result, REM is thought to be important for maintaining a healthy memory and for brain rejuvenation.

REM sleep is particularly important for newborns and fetuses who not only spend most of their time sleeping, but also spend a large percent of their total sleep time in this REM cycle. The total amount of time they sleep and the percentage of sleep time they spend engaged in REM will gradually decrease over the entire lifespan. On average, newborns will spend up to 16 hours a day sleeping, 50% of which is made up of REM sleep, whereas an adult in his or her 20s or 30s will spend between 6 and 8 hours a day sleeping, only 22% of which is made up of REM. By the time that adult is in his or her 60s or 70s, only 6–7 hours a day will be spent sleeping, only 13% of which will be REM (Pandi-Perumal et al., 2002) (Figure 5.2).

Why do babies need so much sleep, and why do they need so much REM sleep in particular? One hypothesis posed by researchers is *autostimulation theory*. It sounds dirty, but it isn't . . . it is actually quite practical, involving the amount of sensory stimulation that a fetus gets on a daily basis. Let's think for a minute about the potential for a fetus to have sensory experiences from inside the womb. As I mentioned earlier, in the fifth month, the fetus has fully formed taste buds and can taste the different kinds of food that the mother passes through the umbilical cord. In fact, the fetus can even develop specific taste preferences based on his or her experiences in the womb (more on this later). The point is, the fetus can taste. Let's move on to smell. Taste and smell are very closely linked, and there is evidence that the fetus can smell its own amniotic fluid, developing a preference for this familiar scent after it's born. The fetus can also hear. It can hear its mother's voice, it can hear the internal sounds that her body makes, and, to some extent, it can hear loud (although somewhat muffled) noises from the world outside. Touch is there as well; the baby is constantly moving; it can feel its own body and it can feel itself rubbing against the uterine wall. It might even grab on to the umbilical cord from time to time.

This just leaves sight, and, as I'm sure you can guess, it's pretty dark inside the womb. The fetus will react if you point a flashlight right into the mother's abdomen, but this not a common occurrence during most pregnancies, so the fetus isn't getting many opportunities to see before it's born. This is where autostimulation theory comes in. Visual stimulation is central for both visual and brain development. The theory is that, while the baby is sleeping, and specifically, when it is engaging in REM sleep, the high amount of activity in the brain produced by REM sleep provides much-needed stimulation to the baby's developing visual system. In other words, the brain is providing fetuses with the visual stimulation that they aren't getting otherwise (Boismier, 1977).

A classic study with newborn babies supports this theory. James Boismier and his colleagues at the University of Nebraska showed a

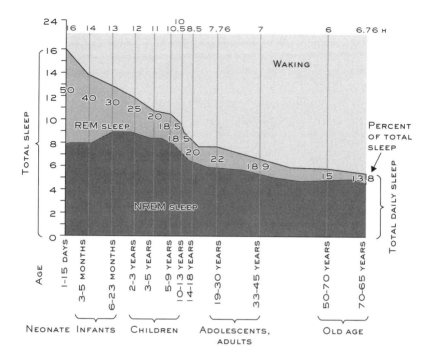

Figure 5.2 | Percentage of time humans spend sleeping and what proportion of that sleep time is spent engaged in rapid eye movement (REM), from birth to old age. The graph shows two important things. First, the total amount of time we sleep decreases with age, starting with up to 16 hours a day in newborns and ending with 5–6 hours a day in old age. Second, the proportion of total sleep time engaged in REM also decreases with age, with newborns spending about 50% of their total sleep time engaged in REM when compared to 65- to 70-year-olds who only spend about 13.8% of their total sleep time engaged in REM.

Source: Reprinted from Pandi-Perumal, S. R., Seils, L. K., Kayumov, L., Ralph, M. R., Lowe, A., Moller, H., & Swaab, D. F. (2002). Senescence, sleep, and circadian rhythms. *Ageing Research Reviews*, *1*(3), 570, with permission of Elsevier.

group of newborn infants one of two images while they were awake lying in their cribs. One of the images was a complex checkerboard, aimed at giving the newborns a large amount of visual stimulation. The other was a boring gray square, providing the newborns with very little visual stimulation. Next, the researchers simply measured how much the newborns slept after they were presented with the squares and how long they spent engaged in REM sleep. They found that newborns who looked at the complex checkerboard were more alert and they engaged in less REM sleep than the newborns who looked at the boring gray square. This supports autostimulation theory, suggesting that REM sleep serves to make up for the lack of visual stimulation newborns and fetuses aren't getting while they're awake; when they get visual stimulation elsewhere (like from an interesting checkerboard image), they don't need as much REM sleep (Boismier, 1977) (Figure 5.3).

After babies are born, they will continue to sleep a lot. Unfortunately, their sleep patterns (or lack thereof) will be highly disruptive to *your* sleep. As I said before, at first they will have day and night mixed up and keep you up all night. Once they get day and night straightened out, they will still sleep a lot, but not in long stretches, waking up every few hours to eat or nurse. By 3 months, they might sleep for up to 6 hours straight, giving you a much needed break. But, in general, it isn't until about 6 months that they "sleep through the night," which means from about 8 PM to 5 AM without waking up. And even then, they sometimes need a little bit of help to get there.

The topic of infant sleep has become a rather hot button issue in recent years. Parents, physicians, and researchers all argue about where babies should sleep, when they should sleep, what position they should sleep in, who they should sleep with, and just about every other thing concerning infant sleep that you can think of. One of the biggest arguments is about *where* babies should sleep. In the United States, most doctors will recommend that babies share a room with their mothers for some period of time as this type of co-sleeping has some

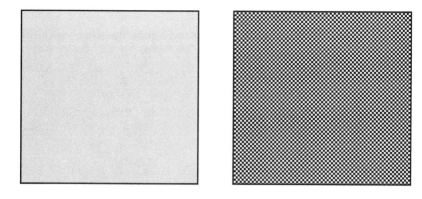

Figure 5.3 | Sample stimuli from Boismier's (1977) study. Some babies were given a boring gray square to look at while they were awake (*left*), while others were given a more complicated checkerboard (*right*). Babies who spent time looking at the checkerboard while they were awake spent less time in rapid eye movement (REM) sleep than those who looked at the gray square and were more alert.
Source: Samples created by Vanessa LoBue.

important benefits. For example, it can make nursing in the middle of the night easier, and, most importantly, when newborns sleep in the same room as their mothers the incidence of sudden infant death syndrome (SIDS) decreases dramatically. In fact, to encourage co-sleeping, in 2017, the state of New Jersey began offering new parents a sturdy box for their babies to sleep in for free. The box has a firm mattress, a waterproof cover and fitted sheet, and is intended to reduce infant mortality, presumably because it will encourage co-sleeping.

However, in many other countries, while co-sleeping is also the norm, most mothers co-sleep with their newborns *in the same bed* for years before separating. This type of co-sleeping—called *bed sharing*—is something that doctors in the United States (and the American Academy of Pediatrics) will tell you absolutely *not* to do, warning you of the dangerous risk of rolling over and suffocating your baby in the middle of the night. Although co-sleeping has been linked to maternal stress (e.g., Teti, Shimizu, Crosby, & Kim, 2016), most studies looking at fatal accidents that have occurred during bed-sharing found that infant death in these circumstances usually involved some other risk factor, such as placing infants to sleep under pillows or duvets, co-sleeping in unsafe places like a couch, maternal exhaustion, or alcohol and drug use (e.g., McKenna & McDade, 2005). Furthermore, according to two studies that examined cases of infant death during bed-sharing that did not include any of these "high-risk" behaviors, there was still an increased risk of infant death during sleep for bed sharers over non-bed sharers, but there were very few cases overall. In other words, in the absence of risk factors like drinking and drug use, there is still a greater chance of infant death for infants who sleep in the same bed as their mothers than infants who sleep in a crib, but the overall chance of death is incredibly low. And for babies older than 3 months, these studies report *no increased risk* for bed sharers at all (Blair, Sidebotham, Pease, & Fleming, 2014; Carpenter et al., 2013). This suggests that there is a risk associated with sharing a bed with your infant, but the risk isn't the same for all babies. Babies younger than 3 months seem to carry the most risk, along with babies who are premature or have parents who frequently drink or engage in drug use. In the end, co-sleeping is still a contentious issue, and although current US recommendations are to share a room but not to share a bed, the factors that go into deciding where babies should sleep are quite complicated, and traditions vary between families and cultures (McKenna & McDade, 2005).

Another infant sleep issue that gets a lot of attention has to do with whether you should *sleep train* your baby in the first year of life. The debate is about whether sleep training methods that let babies cry (or "cry it out," CIO) are cruel and have negative consequences for the baby's development. Critics of CIO methods have called parents who decide to sleep train selfish or even abusive. The controversy has left many tired parents feeling stressed about whether or not they should try sleep training and guilty about wanting to get some much needed rest. The big questions are: Is sleep training really harmful? And is it okay to let your baby cry?

The logic behind sleep training is rather simple: at an early age, babies rely on their parents to soothe them to sleep, either by rocking or nursing or by some other method. Eventually—around 4–6 months of age—infants become capable of soothing themselves to sleep, but they don't have the opportunity to learn self-soothing strategies if mom and dad keep doing it for them. That's where sleep training come in. Most sleep training methods involve putting babies to bed when they are drowsy but not fully asleep. Then, parents are told to gradually pull back on soothing methods like rocking and nursing so that babies have the chance to learn to fall asleep on their own and, importantly, go back to sleep on their own if they wake up during the night. These recommendations make sense as parents' presence at the time that the baby first falls asleep is the factor most related to babies *not* sleeping through the night (Touchette et al., 2005), and babies who can fall asleep on their own are the ones most likely to fall back to sleep on their own in the middle of the night (Anders, Halpern, & Hua, 1992).

The controversial part is that removing parent-centered soothing methods results in some initial crying. But most sleep training methods do not recommend just putting babies in their beds and letting them cry for hours and hours without any type of comfort. Most recommend only letting them cry for a predetermined (and relatively short) period of time and slowly pulling back on soothing methods so that babies can learn to soothe themselves over the course of a few days. Furthermore, sleep training advocates don't recommend trying sleep training before babies are capable of self-soothing (around 4–6 months of age), and they don't recommend sticking with it if sleep training doesn't show results within the first few days of trying it.

The little research that exists on the effectiveness of sleep training suggests that it is indeed effective within a very short period of time (e.g., Mindell, Kuhn, Meltzer, & Sadeh, 2006). In fact, most sleep-training methods are designed for effectiveness within just a few days. In a recent study of more than 600 parents who sleep-trained their infants, the vast majority reported success within a week or two, and while the average amount of crying in the first night of sleep training was about 43 minutes, it was down to an average of 8.5 minutes after a week (Honaker, Schwichtenberg, Kreps, & Mindell, 2018).

So the consensus is that sleep training does work, but is it harmful? Sleep training critics argue that letting a baby cry, even for a relatively short period of time, causes the baby undue stress and leads to elevated heart rate, a spike in blood pressure, and might even be detrimental to brain development. On top of all that, many suggest that by letting babies cry, they learn not to trust that their parents can be relied on as a constant source of comfort or support and, as a result, develop an insecure attachment. To a new parent, this sounds pretty scary, which is why a lot of people end up forgoing sleep training altogether. But, despite widespread claims of these potentially harmful consequences, there is no evidence to back it up. The only evidence that crying can cause harm to babies comes from studies on the effects of long-term abuse and neglect on children. In other words, the studies that show long-term negative consequences of crying focus on babies who have endured years and years of physical abuse or neglect by their families (e.g., Shonkoff et al., 2012).

There is very little research on the effect of very brief periods of crying in an otherwise loving family. The studies that do exist show no negative consequences of brief periods of crying for infants' development or on their relationship with their parents in any way (e.g., Price, Wake, Ukoumunne, & Hiscock, 2012; Van Ijzendoorn & Hubbard, 2010). In fact, in one recent study that examined children who were sleep trained as babies versus children who weren't 5 years later, researchers reported that there were no long-term consequences or benefits of sleep training in infancy: 6-year-olds who were sleep trained as babies looked just like 6-year-olds who weren't, and there were no differences between these children in terms of sleep problems, emotional problems, or attachment issues (Price et al., 2012). This suggests that whether you decide to sleep train your babies or not, they'll be fine and eventually sleep through the night.

Despite the fact that there is no evidence that sleep training causes any harm, there's lots of evidence that sleep *deprivation* can be harmful to both adults and children. For example, sleep deprivation has been associated with inattentiveness, depression, and even marital difficulties in adults (Medina, Lederhos, & Lillis, 2009; Meltzer & Mindell, 2007). Furthermore, waking up several times in the middle of the night (e.g., for nursing or soothing) has been associated with similar problems, even if you're getting a full 7–8 hours of sleep total (Kahn, Fridenson, Lerer, Bar-Haim, & Sadeh, 2014). Even moderate sleep deprivation has effects on adults that look similar to being drunk and, just like alcohol use, puts you at a higher risk of getting into a car accident (Williamson & Feyer, 2000). Sleep deprivation affects babies, too, in similar and predictable ways, making them cranky and possibly interfering with attention and learning (Scher, 2005).

Despite the fact that my fetus is apparently having no trouble sleeping, it looks like my sleep deprivation problems have already begun. Sleeping is getting increasingly difficult and uncomfortable as my belly is becoming larger and rounder. Sleeping on my stomach is completely out of the question, and sleeping on my back puts the entire weight of the pregnancy on my spine, so sleeping on my side is starting to be the only option. Even on my side, I feel really off balance. It helps to put a pillow between my legs (as recommended by some friends and *What to Expect When You're Expecting,* Murkoff & Mazel, 2008), but I always end up tossing and turning. I've been coping with this by taking a small nap during the day, which helps but by no means solves the problem. I can imagine that as I get bigger, the problem of being uncomfortable while sleeping will get worse, so I'm mentally preparing myself now for lots of sleepless nights ahead. In fact, maybe the increased difficulty sleeping as pregnancy progresses is nature's way of preparing you for what lies ahead—I don't exactly imagine that the sleep situation is going to get *better* once the baby is born, so might as well practice now, right?

6

THE SIXTH MONTH

Reflexes and Newborn Screening

I welcomed the sixth month with more growth and changes in my symptoms. I'm still hungry quite often, but this month, all of a sudden, I can't eat much in one sitting. It's as if the fetus is using up most of my belly space, leaving only a tiny spot for food, so I get full really fast, and, if I overeat even just a little bit I feel achy and bloated. The headaches are receding but all of a sudden heartburn has become a problem, and my doctor gave me the OK to pop a few Tums whenever it flares up. At this point, it is obvious to everyone that I am pregnant (weight gain is up to 18 pounds) and random strangers have been asking about my due date. One pair of maternity pants has turned into many, and I'm almost exclusively wearing maternity tops.

I learned this month that once you look pregnant—like, really, really pregnant—people are nicer to you. The custodian in my building, whom I see daily but with whom I only exchange casual hellos, knit me two beautiful baby bibs, just because. People open doors for me, give me their seats on the subway, offer to buy me lunch (or offer to give me a free bag of potato chips with my lunch, which has happened twice now), throw me showers, and make sure that I essentially don't need to do anything by myself. This week, I asked my parents and brother to help me paint the baby's room because Nick was busy with work. They happily agreed. Sure, that's nice of them, but what's *really* nice is that after going to Home Depot to get paint and finding out that I shouldn't actually paint the room myself because of the fumes (which a nice check-out clerk was quick to point out), my parents' response was a cheerful, "No problem at all, we can handle the job ourselves."

In earlier months, I found this kind of thing annoying—I don't generally like to be taken care of, and there is very little I feel that I can't do by myself. But the tide is now turning. I am starting to get winded by easy tasks like going up and down the stairs; standing for long periods of time is taxing on my feet and back, and wearing heels is completely out of the question. Bending over to put on shoes isn't all that easy anymore, which is slightly disconcerting since I have 3 months of belly growth left. So, this month, I've accepted some help for the first time as I can see that some of my normal daily activities (which have not changed at all up to this point) might get more difficult in the near future.

The fetus is kicking a lot more forcefully in month 6, and you can see my skin move dramatically with some especially strong movements. It feels a little uncomfortable, but I still love the constant reminder that he's in there. Nick can feel the fetus a lot more easily now, too: Last night, he rolled over in his sleep, and, after wrapping his arm around my belly, was surprised to feel that the fetus was doing "late night gymnastics routines" in my uterus. Another new development is frequent hiccups. Not mine—*the fetus's.* Often I feel a repetitive movement in the lower part of my belly that resembles the rhythm of hiccupping. The low location of the sensation tells me that the fetus's head might now be positioned downward, which is common by the sixth month to help prepare for birth.

At this point in the pregnancy, besides hiccupping, the fetus also has all of the reflexes that he will have at birth—if I'm lucky, I might even catch him sucking his thumb at the next ultrasound. This is because the brain is developing quickly, and there is even evidence that it is already becoming *lateralized* at this point in the pregnancy, meaning that one side of the brain might already be showing signs of dominance. That means that if my fetus is indeed sucking his thumb, there's a good chance it will be his right thumb over his left, as 90% of us are right-handed. This has to do with the fact that the right side of the body (including the right hand) is controlled by the left side of the brain, and the left side of the body (including the left hand) is controlled by the right side of the brain. For most (but not all) of us, the left side of the brain, which is responsible for language, is dominant, and thus our motor abilities tend to be dominant on the right side as well (Scharoun & Bryden, 2014). Researchers have observed that, starting in the second trimester, a similar percentage of fetuses (~87%) can be seen sucking their right thumb over their left (Hepper, Shahidullah, & White, 1991).

Reflexes like sucking are simple, automatic, involuntary biological responses to changes in the world, and all animals have them. Usually reflexes help animals—including humans—quickly respond to a change in the environment and can often serve a protective function because they are automatic and don't require specific thought or effort. Dogs, for example, reflexively pull their legs back if you touch their toes. Cats have what's called a "righting reflex" where they will automatically reorient themselves when falling so that they always land on their feet. Humans have reflexes, too. Imagine that you accidentally put your hand on a hot stovetop. What is likely to happen is that you'll move your hand away from the surface before you even realize how hot it is. That kind of reflex protects you from getting hurt.

One of the first things the doctors will do when my baby is born will be to check his reflexes. Humans have a set number of reflexes that are present in the second trimester and are universal across all healthy newborns; they are generally taken as evidence of normal brain growth. For example, when you stroke the side of a newborn baby's cheek, the baby will often turn its head toward your hand. This is called the *rooting reflex*. Similarly, if you touch the middle of a newborn's tongue, you will evoke sucking, or the *sucking reflex*. When a baby is born, it won't know how to drink milk or where to find it. The sucking and rooting reflexes thus have clear value—they help the newborn find the mother's nipple when it touches the side of his face (*rooting*) and suck when the nipple is placed in his mouth (*sucking*).

Reflexes can help the newborn do other things besides feeding. The *grasping reflex*, for example, is evoked when you stroke a newborn's palm with your finger; in fact, a newborn's grasp can be so strong that he can hold his entire weight for a second or two if you were to lift him up in the air (but please don't). You can see a newborn's *stepping reflex* by holding him upright so that the bottoms of his feet touch a flat surface. When this happens, the newborn will move his legs and feet up and down and back and forth as if to mimic walking. Some parents will notice right away that their newborns have an intense *Moro* or *startle reflex*. When moved very quickly, a newborn will throw his arms out to either side and then quickly bring them back in, as if trying to grab hold of something to keep from falling. Many parents swaddle their infants in wraps to keep the *startle* reflex at bay because it can result in crying. Although the *grasping, stepping,* and *startle* reflexes don't have the obvious immediate value that the *sucking* and *rooting* reflexes have, they could conceivably help the newborn hold on to or signal a parent when he's falling or help him practice the walking motion that will become so important at the end of the first year.

Other reflexes have no apparent value at all, but they appear prenatally and are present at birth nonetheless. The *Babinski* reflex, for example, can be elicited by gently stroking the bottom of a newborn's foot. When stroked, the newborn will fan his toes one by one for no apparent reason. Similarly, the *tonic neck reflex* (perhaps the weirdest of all newborn reflexes) happens when a newborn naturally turns his head to one side. This head turn is usually accompanied by an extended arm and leg on the same side of the body as the neck turn, with the opposite arm and leg bent upward. This reflex is so common that you can observe it in many resting babies (Figure 6.1).

Why do babies have these reflexes? It isn't completely known. As I mentioned before, some of them have clear adaptive value for helping humans cope with a potentially important challenge, especially the ones that help the newborn with feeding. Others—reflexes like Babinski and tonic neck—are still a mystery. Perhaps what makes reflexes even stranger is that they disappear sometime within the first few months after birth just as mysteriously as they first appeared. The traditional explanation for why they disappear is similar to the explanation for why they're there in the first place—their presence at birth is a marker of brain health, and their disappearance shortly afterward is a marker of brain growth. And it is indeed the case that the absence of some or all of these reflexes at birth can be a sign that something might

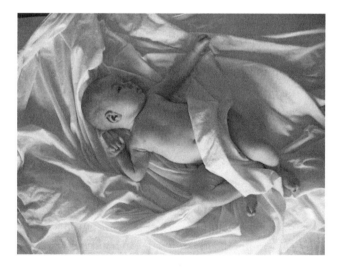

Figure 6.1 | Tonic-neck reflex.
Source: Margo Hofman Jurgens.

be wrong neurologically with the baby. However, more contemporary research into the *disappearance* of certain reflexes suggests that there are a lot of reasons why a reflex might disappear, many of which have nothing to do with brain development.

One explanation is that once babies learns a few simple daily routines, they can also learn to control their bodies and respond accordingly. For example, once newborns become accustomed to a feeding routine, they can override their *rooting* and *sucking* reflexes by intentionally seeking out a nipple and turning their head to follow the sight of their mother's breast or a bottle full of milk. Similarly, once infants learn what types of objects afford sucking, they can intentionally suck objects like pacifiers and choose not to suck other objects like stuffed animals that don't produce a soothing sensation on their gums. In other words, once babies gain control over their bodies and can move them intentionally, they don't need their reflexes anymore—intentional or learned behaviors override reflexive ones.

There are other reasons reflexes might seem to disappear. In the 1980s, Esther Thelen at Indiana University was interested in studying the disappearance of the stepping reflex in particular. After observing countless infants in her lab, she noticed some strange things that didn't fit with our old concept of why newborn reflexes disappear. First, she noticed that the motion that makes up a newborn's stepping reflex is remarkably similar to the kicking motion infants show when they are lying on their backs. In fact, she found that the muscles infants use in both stepping and kicking are nearly identical. So why then, she asked, does the stepping reflex disappear around 2 or 3 months of age, but infants continue to kick when placed on their backs throughout infancy? Second, she also noticed that the stepping reflex disappeared sooner in some babies than in others. If the disappearance of stepping is an index of brain maturity, you'd expect that it would disappear in babies who somehow matured the fastest, right? Wrong. Instead, the reflex seemed to disappear the soonest in the largest, *chubbiest* babies who passed through the lab—not necessarily the most "mature" ones.

Based on these simple observations, Esther guessed that the real reason the stepping reflex disappeared a few months after birth had nothing to do with the brain and had everything to do with *gravity*. She hypothesized that as babies' legs got heavier, their weak muscles were no longer strong enough for them to lift their legs up and down when fighting against the force of gravity. This would explain why chubbier babies (with heavier legs) lose the stepping reflex sooner and why all babies continue to kick when lying on their backs and gravity isn't as much of a problem. She systematically tested this hypothesis by first making thin babies (who still had their stepping reflex) *heavier* by fastening weights to their legs to see if the stepping reflex would disappear. It did. Next, she made heavy babies (who's stepping reflex had already disappeared) *lighter* by submerging their legs in water to see if the stepping reflex would reappear again. It did. Finally, she took babies who's stepping reflex had disappeared and made it absolutely necessary for them to step—she held them over a tiny baby treadmill. Once again, the mysterious disappearing stepping reflex returned (Thelen, 1996).

We still don't know why babies have all the reflexes that they do at birth, and we still don't know why some of them disappear, but what Thelen's clever research shows us is that the reason reflexes come and go might have nothing to do with brain growth and, instead, have everything to do with infants gaining (in the case of *sucking* and *rooting*) and/or losing (in the case of *stepping*) control of their rapidly changing bodies.

Again, all of these reflexes should already be intact in my fetus, and my doctor will check for their presence when he's born in a few months. The absence of one or more of these reflexes could mean that something might be wrong. In fact, my doctor will do a whole battery of tests when he's born to make sure everything has developed properly. The most well-known newborn test is called the APGAR; it's designed to see if the newborn needs immediate medical attention after birth. APGAR is an acronym that stands for Appearance, Pulse, Grimace, Activity, and Respiration, each of which is given a score from 0 to 2 and is then totaled. A score 7 or above means that the newborn is functioning normally; a score of 4–6 is fairly low, and usually a score of 3 or less means the newborn could need immediate medical attention. The test includes examining the baby's skin color (not too pale or blue), pulse rate (greater than 100 beats per minute), responses to the reflexes I mentioned earlier, activity in the arms and legs, and normal breathing.

Next, a blood sample is usually taken from the baby's heel to look for problems the newborn might have internally, such as issues metabolizing food or potential heart defects. One common test is for *bilirubin*, or a substance that the body makes when it breaks down red blood cells. The mother's body does this for the fetus during pregnancy, but, after birth, the baby's body has to do it on its own for the very first time. High levels of bilirubin in the body cause *jaundice*, or a yellowish tint to the skin. Mild levels of jaundice are common in some newborns, and bilirubin screening tells doctors whether a newborn's body is getting rid of bilirubin effectively.

Another common newborn test is for PKU, or *Phenylketonuria*. PKU is a genetic disorder caused by a recessive gene on a particular chromosome. PKU is a deficit in the body's ability to break down an amino acid called phenylalanine. Doesn't sound so bad at first, but phenylalanine can be found in a lot of the common foods we eat, such as cow's milk, bread, eggs, and fish. If a newborn has PKU and goes on to continually eat foods or drink milk that contain phenylalanine, it will build up in the newborn's body and can permanently damage the baby's brain by the time he's a year old.

A child can only get PKU if both parents carry at least one recessive gene for it. If both parents carry a recessive gene for PKU, any newborn offspring from those parents will have a 25% chance of getting it (see Chapter 2). The good news is that newborn screening usually catches PKU right from birth. Doctors will place babies with PKU on a phenylalanine-free, high-protein diet, and the child will grow up just fine, with a normally developing brain (Figure 6.2). As long as there is no (or very little) phenylalanine in the baby's system while the brain is developing, there is nothing to worry about. The point here is that newborn screenings are really important and can give you vital information about how the baby is functioning and whether you need to take any precautions in the first few weeks, months, or years of your newborn's life.

Speaking of blood testing, in the sixth month of pregnancy, doctors typically test both the mother and the fetus for blood sugar issues like diabetes and anemia. The test involves drinking a nasty orange liquid (to call it juice would be too generous) that tastes something like flat orange soda in under 5 minutes and then having your blood drawn precisely an hour later. If you mess up the timing, you have to take the test again because it's very sensitive to sugar content in your bloodstream. Being the overachiever that I am, I timed everything to the second so that I would not have to take the test a second time—chugging that orange stuff once was enough for me.

The blood test came back normal, but the doctor decided that next month and all of the months following she wants me to continue to have regular ultrasounds. For the first time since the beginning of my pregnancy, I shouldn't require an ultrasound at my monthly

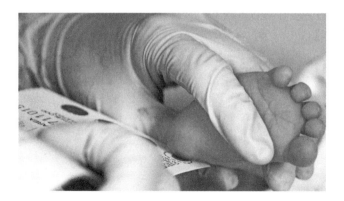

Figure 6.2 | Phenylketonuria (PKU) testing.
Source: Wikipedia, "Phenylketonuria," by USAF Photographic Archives.

(25-week) doctor's visit as it's common at this point in the pregnancy for doctors to forego the ultrasound and just listen to the baby's heart rate or measure the circumference of the mother's belly if all previous ultrasounds came back normal. Unfortunately, my doctor spotted a fibroid on my ultrasound early in the pregnancy that she wants to keep an eye on. A *fibroid* is a benign growth on the side of the uterus. It's common in many women, and this particular fibroid has probably been living in my uterus for decades now undetected. It may not necessarily pose a problem, but pregnant women who have fibroids could experience some complications. First, my belly might measure bigger than other women's since the fibroid is taking up extra space in my uterus (which probably explains why I feel so big). Second, it could get in the way of delivery if it gets any bigger, or it could prevent the baby from growing by taking up too much real estate. My doctor said that the best thing to do is to take a look at the fibroid every month via

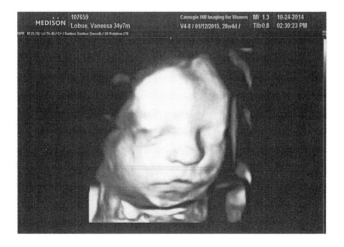

Figure 6.3 | Twenty-eight-week ultrasound, three-dimensional image of the fetus's face.
Source: Vanessa LoBue.

ultrasound to make sure it isn't growing too much or getting in the way of the fetus's growth.

Perhaps I should be concerned—Nick certainly is—but honestly, my only thought when she told me that I'd be getting a full ultrasound every month was that I'm going to get to see my baby again really soon. In fact, just to be safe, my doctor had me do an extra ultrasound to check the status of the fibroid at 28 weeks. Everything looked completely fine: The fibroid is showing no signs of growth, it doesn't look like it will get in the way of a natural birth, and it certainly doesn't appear to be impeding the baby's growth—he's a whopping 3 pounds, 3 ounces now (Figure 6.3). The best part is that I get to see his face again in 4 short weeks. That's enough to keep this expecting mother very happy, despite the sad fact that I can hardly see my own toes.

7

THE SEVENTH MONTH

Fetal Learning

I have just begun the seventh month of pregnancy and am officially in my third trimester. By the time you reach the third trimester, some women might be excited that the trials and tribulations of pregnancy are almost over, but the near finale to my adventure in human reproduction is already feeling bittersweet. I started this process dragging my feet, resigning myself to it because of my age. I never thought that I'd grow to love the experience as much as I have, and, in month 7, I'm not quite ready to be finished just yet. Luckily, I still have 3 more months left before I have to share my baby with the rest of the world.

It is crystal clear at this point that my weight is going to be the biggest impediment to daily activities from now on. Because of his growing size, the fetus is pushing up against my diaphragm and lungs; I get short of breath very easily, sometimes just by sitting. When my friends ask how I'm feeling, my response is generally "huge." Unfortunately, as one of my close friends put it, the seventh month is the point where you feel so big that you couldn't possibly get any bigger only to find out that you will, and you do. The frequency of peeing that

I experienced in the first trimester is nothing compared to what I'm dealing with now, with 22 pounds of uterus sitting on my bladder all day. I have to pee about once an hour, and sometimes, after I'm done, I have to sit right back down again for an immediate second go. The doctor said I could gain 10 more pounds or more, but I have no idea where it will go—it already feels like I have a bowling ball strapped to my belly. Lucky for me, looking so pregnant gets me out of any sort of heavy lifting or physical activity, so at least I've got that going for me.

Despite feeling that my abilities are getting increasingly limited, the fetus's abilities are becoming increasingly more advanced. In fact, starting around the seventh month, there is evidence that the fetus can *learn*. Yes, you heard me right—my 2–3 pound fetus is starting to learn and remember the things that are most familiar to him, including familiar sounds, tastes, and smells. Learning doesn't begin the day a baby is born—development is continuous, which means that birth isn't a magical start button for when babies start learning from their environments. In fact, there isn't much difference between a fetus that is still in the womb after 42 weeks and a baby that has been born already.

I mentioned in an earlier chapter that a fetus has full use of all of its five senses by the third trimester—it can see, feel, hear, taste, and smell. Most impressively, by the seventh month, it starts to *learn* from these senses and develop *preferences* for the experiences that are most familiar. The most noteworthy of these preferences comes from what the fetus can taste and smell from inside the uterus. Ever wonder why children (and many, many adults) have a sweet tooth? It turns out that even fetuses have a preference for sweet flavors and will "drink" or ingest larger amounts of amniotic fluid when it is injected with a sweet solution than when it tastes bitter, sour, or salty. This preference for sweet will continue after they are born, and if you put a sweet solution on their tongues, you are likely to see babies lick their lips and open their mouths; for bitter ones, you'll probably see a baby grimace (Figure 7.1) (Ventura & Worobey, 2013).

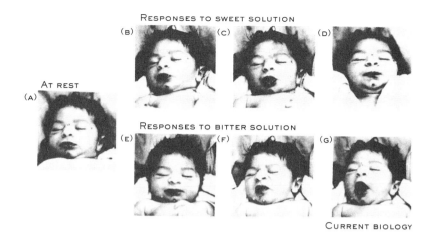

RESPONSES TO SWEET SOLUTION

(B) (C) (D)

AT REST
(A)

RESPONSES TO BITTER SOLUTION

(E) (F) (G)

CURRENT BIOLOGY

Figure 7.1 | Newborns' responses to sweet (*top row*) and bitter (*bottom row*) tastes. They generally lick their lips in response to sweet flavors and grimace in response to bitter ones.

Source: Reprinted from Ventura, A. K., & Worobey, J. (2013). Early influences on the development of food preferences. *Current Biology, 23*(9), 403, with permission of Elsevier.

The classic explanation for why even fetuses prefer sweet flavors is that such a preference is an evolutionary adaptation; in other words, we evolved a preference for the taste of foods that are high in calories (which tend to be sweet) and therefore likely to keep us alive longer (e.g., Ventura & Worobey, 2013). An alternative (and not mutually exclusive) explanation is that we develop a preference for sweet flavors because it's what's most familiar to us, and amniotic fluid itself generally has a sweet smell.

Several researchers have tested the second possibility—that we learn taste preferences based on what's familiar to us from our experience inside the womb—in both humans and a variety of animals. Much of the research on fetal learning of tastes and smells started with rat fetuses. Elliot Blass from Johns Hopkins University (1990), for example, wanted to know whether rats could remember smells from the uterus once they were born, and he took advantage of the fact that each rat dam's (i.e., rat mother's) amniotic fluid has a particular smell and taste. What he did was simple: After a litter of rat pups was born, a team of researchers varied the type of amniotic fluid that was present on their mother's nipples. The researchers wiped some of the nipples with the mother's own amniotic fluid and others with another rat's amniotic fluid. The question was which nipples would the rat pups choose to nurse from. Not surprisingly, they chose the ones wiped with their own mother's amniotic fluid—the smell was familiar to them and helped them latch on.

In follow-up studies, the researchers fed the mother with specific flavors (e.g., lemon) before the pups were born and then painted some of the mother's nipples with those familiar flavors or different ones when it came time for feeding. The results were the same: The rat pups chose to nurse from the nipples that had the familiar smell and taste. In fact, rat pups are born pretty helpless—they can't see or hear at first—so they rely on familiar tastes and smells in order to find their own mother's nipples for feeding. Without that learned familiarity to guide them, rat pups wouldn't know where to latch on, and hence they wouldn't survive for very long (Figure 7.2).

A group of French researchers did a similar taste preference experiment with human babies and their moms and found that human babies also show a preference for familiar tastes and smells. These researchers fed a group of expecting mothers with candy, cookies, and syrup that contained anise flavoring during the third trimester, and they compared these moms to a second group of expecting moms who were not given anything with anise flavoring. For those of you who are unfamiliar with anise, it smells and tastes like black licorice (yuck!), so it is a potent and unmistakable flavor. After the two groups of mothers gave birth, the researchers presented their newborns with a gauze pad on each side of their faces, one soaked with anise and the other soaked with some other scent, and they noted which to direction the newborns turned their heads. They also held cotton swabs soaked

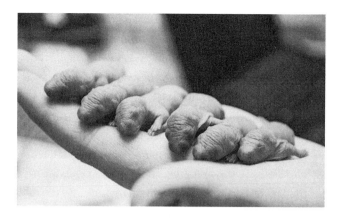

Figure 7.2 | Newborn rats are born deaf and blind; they use the familiar smell of their mothers' amniotic fluid to know where to find her nipples in order to nurse.
Source: Wikimedia Commons, by Amanda Fjordell.

with anise under the newborn infants' noses and studied their facial expressions in response to the unique smell. Newborns of mothers who ate anise cookies and candy during pregnancy reacted much more positively to the anise smell when compared to newborns of mothers who didn't eat anise—they turned their heads *toward* the anise smell, and they made positive facial expressions when the coated swab was held under their noses. The other infants (not surprisingly) were more likely to turn *away* from the anise and make negative facial expressions in response to the potent smell (Schaal, Marlier, & Soussignan, 2000). Like Blass's (1990) research with rats, this work shows that the infants remembered the familiar taste and smell of anise from their mothers' wombs and *preferred* that smell to other smells when they were born. It suggests that infants can develop taste and smell preferences based on what their mothers eat while pregnant.

Newborns can also develop preferences for familiar smells and tastes that they are exposed to via breast milk. Similar to the study conducted by the French group, Julie Mennella and her colleagues at the

Monell Chemical Senses Center in Philadelphia studied three groups of women. They asked one group to drink carrot juice in the third trimester of pregnancy, a second group to drink carrot juice during the first few months of breastfeeding, and a third group not to drink carrot juice at all (they were given water instead) during pregnancy or while nursing. The researchers then studied infants' reactions to carrot juice and carrot-flavored cereal after their mothers started introducing them to solid food. Infants who were exposed to carrot juice either prenatally or via breast milk showed fewer negative facial expressions in response to the carrot flavor and smell when compared to the group of infants who's mothers drank only water. They were also willing to eat more carrot-flavored cereal than the infants of mothers who only drank water, thus reinforcing the idea that taste preferences can develop based on what the mother eats when she's pregnant and even later when she's breastfeeding (Mennella, Jagnow, & Beauchamp, 2001). Makes you want to rethink beef jerky and potato chips, doesn't it?

In addition to learning preferences for familiar tastes and smells, fetuses can also develop preferences for familiar *sounds*. For example, in the last trimester, a fetus can recognize its own mother's voice and discriminate it from another woman's (Kisilevsky et al., 2003). How do we know? Researchers can tell by measuring the fetus's heart rate responses to different sounds. More specifically, they press a speaker to a mother's abdomen and play different sounds to the fetus and measure how its heart rate changes. These particular researchers found that a fetus's heart rate goes up when it hears its own mother's voice and goes down when it hears a stranger's voice, suggesting that it can tell the difference between the two.

Fetuses also learn to prefer the sound of their own native *language* in the third trimester. For example, when a group of researchers presented newborns that were only 2 days old with two recordings—one of a woman speaking in English and another of a woman speaking in Spanish—newborns of English-speaking mothers preferred the recordings of the English-speaking woman and newborns of Spanish-speaking mothers preferred the recordings of the Spanish-speaking woman (Moon, Cooper, & Fifer, 1993).

In fact, several animals show similar patterns and prefer the sound of their own species' calls when they are born. There are species of ducklings, for example, that prefer the sound of the adult duck's (i.e., their mother's) call to the calls of other species of birds right from birth. Although it is possible that this preference is written into the brain, world-famous psychologist Gilbert Gottlieb at the North Carolina Division of Mental Health in Raleigh found instead that ducklings' preference for the sounds produced by their own species had to do with specific auditory experiences they receive before hatching. More specifically, ducklings can hear themselves, their nest-mates, and their mother's calls from inside their eggs before they're hatched. If un-hatched ducklings are prevented from hearing these sounds by having their vocal cords altered and/or by being incubated alone, they no longer show a preference for their own mother's call after they hatch (Gottlieb, 1980). Thus, like human babies, animals can develop a preference for sounds that are most familiar to them prenatally.

Perhaps what is most surprising is that there is evidence that fetuses can develop preferences for the sound of familiar *stories* that they are exposed to prenatally as well. Anthony DeCasper and Melanie Spence at the University of North Carolina at Greensboro studied women in the beginning of their last trimester of pregnancy. Half of the women were told to read their fetuses (i.e., their stomachs) a rhythmic story like the *Cat in the Hat* twice a day for the last 2½ months of pregnancy. The other half of the women didn't read a story to their fetuses during this time frame. Shortly after the infants were born, the researchers tested whether there was any evidence that the infants recognized the familiar story. To do this, they used what is called a *conditioned sucking procedure*. It entailed giving the newborn a pacifier that was connected to two speakers; one of the speakers played the familiar *The Cat in the Hat* story read by an unfamiliar woman, and the second speaker played a new story that the infants did not hear prenatally. The pacifier and speakers were set up so that if the infants sucked very quickly, producing short, quick sucks, one of the speakers was activated. If the infants sucked slowly, producing long sucking motions, the other speaker was activated. Even newborns learn very quickly in this procedure that they are controlling the scenario and that the speakers played different sounds based on how the newborns chose to suck. The newborns whose mothers read *The Cat in the Hat* to them during pregnancy modified their sucking in order to hear the familiar story. The other infants didn't show a preference for either one (DeCasper & Spence, 1986).

You might find this amazing (I certainly did when I first read it), but it's important to note that the fetuses didn't necessarily learn the content of the story or even the specific language in the story. They probably just learned the *rhythm* of the story, as Dr. Seuss books have a very distinct rhythm. The point of telling you about this study isn't so that you'll read to your stomachs; it is only to illustrate that fetuses begin to familiarize themselves with their surroundings before they are born, and learning begins very early in development. In fact, it's beginning right *now*, at the start of the third trimester.

One more point about all of this that I want to make is that just because your fetus *can* learn in the third trimester, it doesn't mean you should try to *teach* it anything. Yes, your fetus can hear you, it can taste what you eat, and it will remember some of these familiar things when it is born, but all of this happens naturally, and trying to expose your fetus to very specific types of information this early in development isn't going to make your baby *smarter*. I feel an obligation to bring this up because lots of companies have now made millions of dollars selling products to parents based on this premise. The famous *Mozart Effect*, for example, has perpetuated the myth that playing classical music for your fetus or for newborn will increase his or her IQ. There is absolutely no evidence that this is the case.

The original Mozart Effect study was done by Frances Rauscher, Gordon Shaw, and Katherine Ky (1993) at the University of California,

Irvine. The researchers found that college students performed better on portions of an IQ test if they listened to Mozart before taking it. Their findings were published in the prestigious academic journal, *Nature*, and sparked a barrage of media attention. The media eventually dubbed this finding the "Mozart Effect," and somehow applied it to babies even though the actual research was only done on adults. Rauscher and her colleagues never intended for their findings to be applied to infants, but nonetheless the media ran with it. The notion that playing classical music can increase your baby's IQ is still quite popular, and, in fact, several states including Georgia and Tennessee have state funded programs that provide all new moms with a Mozart CD after they give birth. Products like Baby Einstein and Baby Mozart soon followed, going with the same unsupported claim that playing infants certain music or videos would somehow enhance their intelligence.

Marketing for "genius" products won't end once your baby is born; in fact, it's just the beginning. If you walk down the aisles of a toy store, most of them are lined with products that flash bright lights, play music, and even talk to you as you walk by. Many of them will tout their usefulness in teaching your baby new words or even early math skills. The flashing lights and loud sounds are enough to make your head spin. The truth is, there is no evidence that these products effectively teach infants anything. In fact, there is evidence that these toys might in fact do the opposite. For example, one study looked at how parents talk to their babies while playing with different kinds of toys. They found that the amount and quality of the language parents use while playing with electronic toys is *lower* than the language they use while playing with more traditional toys or books (Sosa, 2016). This is an important finding as children whose parents talk to them more have an advantage in school when compared to children of parents who spend less time talking to them out loud (Hart & Risley, 1995). Since some "genius" and electronic toys do all the talking for you, parents don't have to say a word, which isn't the best thing for learning.

The take-home message here isn't that "genius" toys are necessarily *bad* for your kids; it just means that talking and playing with parents is always *better* if learning is the goal. Sometimes you're not looking to teach your kids anything, and you just want to keep them entertained while you're making a cup of coffee or taking a shower. In that case, electronic toys can be very helpful and engaging. And don't get me wrong, I'm not saying that playing Mozart for your babies or exposing them to Baby Einstein videos can necessarily hurt your children either—in fact, I've heard that lots of infants really *like* them—and when is listening to a little classical music a bad thing anyway? I'm just cautioning that there is no evidence that these products will elevate your child's IQ or make him into any sort of genius, so it's important to be realistic about what these products can and can't provide you with before purchasing them (more on this in Chapter 17).

Another take-home message that can be gleaned from this work is that fetuses are developing preferences for what's familiar to them before they are born and that they carry these preferences with them after birth. This is important because familiarity is *comforting* to babies—just like it is to children and adults. And, as a result, you can use information about what's familiar to comfort your newborn during stressful times after he or she born. For example, one common practice that many parents use to soothe newborns or to promote sleep is *swaddling*, or wrapping your baby tightly in blankets so that he or she can't move. This is exactly what a fetus experiences in the third trimester (increasingly so every day) when the uterus fits tighter and tighter around their growing bodies. Parents also commonly use baby noise-makers that contain the sound of waves, whales making faint noises, and even the sound of a beating heart, all of which mimic the sounds fetuses hear internally from their mothers' bodies. Other parents commonly find that rocking their babies helps them to stop crying or quickly fall asleep; rocking also mimics the motion fetuses feel during the day in the uterus while mom is walking around. What all of these techniques have in common is that they create situations that are familiar to the newborn from when it was inside the womb. In fact, pediatrician Robert Hamilton became a YouTube sensation after he modeled how to quickly stop newborns from crying by simply holding them at a 45-degree angle and rocking them slowly, mimicking the head-down position and swaying motion that infants experience in the third trimester.

Similarly, it's important to remember that early food preferences might possibly be traced back to the third trimester when the fetus is developing a familiarity with certain flavors for the first time. This suggests that you can introduce a fetus to a variety of flavors during this period to possibly promote preferences for certain cultural foods or flavors that are sometimes difficult for young children to palate. Furthermore, you also might want to watch out for foods that you don't necessarily want to promote in your kids, like junk food. Indeed, recent research suggests that rats who eat a lot of "junk food" while they are pregnant tend to have babies that have an enhanced preference for foods high in fat and sugar and that are subsequently more likely to be obese. Furthermore, a very recent study from Australia showed that eating large amounts of "junk food" during pregnancy actually altered the reward system in baby rats, desensitizing them to high-fat foods, similar to the way alcoholics and drug addicts become desensitized to the object of their addiction and eventually need more and more of that substance to induce the desired high (Gugusheff, Ong, & Muhlhausler, 2013). Of course, this research was done in rats, not in humans, but, given the other parallels between animals and humans we've talked about in this chapter, these studies raise red flags about what you want to be eating during pregnancy and how your food choices might affect the food preferences of your child. Research suggests that the types of foods parents have at home and make available to their children tend to be the types of foods that children prefer to eat (Ventura & Worobey, 2013), so perhaps it's not a huge jump in logic to think that patterns like these might begin before a baby is born.

One final take-home message here is that, in the third trimester, the fetus is starting to function more and more like a newborn baby and is absorbing information from his or her still very limited fetal environments. Again, that doesn't mean you should start worrying about teaching your unborn baby the alphabet or math problems just yet; instead, it means that, by the time he's born, he'll already have experience familiarizing himself with the world around him, which to me, is pretty impressive stuff for a 7-month-old fetus.

8

THE EIGHTH MONTH

Infant Temperament

As I start my 33rd week of pregnancy, I'm finally beginning to see why women get sick of this by the end. I've now gained 23 pounds, which is only 1 more pound than last month, but it feels significantly bigger because it's all baby. I'm tired all the time, and I'm experiencing the lower back pain pregnant women complain about in books and in movies. The baby is now 4 pounds 7 ounces, and his movements are forceful and distinct. I still like feeling him in there, but his growing size and constant movement make it hard for me to be comfortable in any position, sitting, standing, or lying down. I went for my monthly ultrasound and doctor's appointment at 32 weeks, and they gave me a 3-D image of his face—he's really starting to look like a baby, and he even has my lips! (See Figure 8.1.) He's starting to act like a baby, too: Last week, I was running (for a pregnant person, that means walking at a moderate pace) around the dining room table playing with my dog, and, after about 30 seconds, I realized that the rapid movement gave the baby the worst case of the hiccups he's had so far. I guess I should have known that shaking up a little baby would result in 30 minutes of

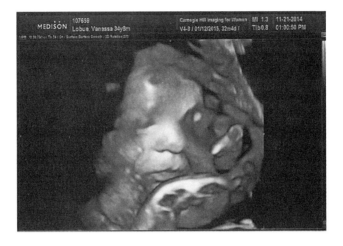

Figure 8.1 | Thirty-two-week ultrasound, three-dimensional image of the fetus's face.

Source: Vanessa LoBue.

belly-thumping gurgles, but I keep forgetting how close he is to being ready for life in the outside world.

My symptoms haven't changed much since last month—I'm still tired, still getting bigger, and still experiencing shortness of breath from as little activity as sitting up straight. The number of bathroom trips I'm forced to make has increased dramatically, to the point where it has gotten to be almost unbearable, especially on days when I have to go to work. I can barely make the 35-minute drive to the office without having to stop to go to the bathroom. The baby is now putting a lot of pressure on my bladder, so it feels like I have to pee constantly, even if nothing comes out when I finally make it to the toilet. Sleeping is still difficult as well (especially with 3–4 bathroom trips per night), but prenatal yoga has helped with managing back pain and relaxing me enough to sleep better. I borrowed a prenatal yoga DVD from a friend and have been doing it sporadically since the beginning of my second trimester. I felt pretty ambivalent about it at first, but now in the eighth month it's making a real difference—I highly recommend it, at least for the later months of pregnancy.

One weird thing is that strangers are more likely to randomly strike up a conversation with me as I've gotten bigger, asking questions about my due date or even telling me that I have a "beautiful round belly." An older woman (who I have never seen before in my life) stopped me in the grocery store yesterday as I was stocking up on ingredients to make pies for Thanksgiving dinner, incredibly concerned about the prospect of me cooking. "You're not making Thanksgiving dinner by yourself this year are you? You shouldn't be doing that in your condition." Nope, not dinner—lately, I only care about dessert—but thanks for your concern.

What is most notable is that when you're visibly pregnant, other new mothers jump at the chance to talk to you. "When are you due? Where are you delivering? Are you having an epidural? Have you found a pediatrician yet? How long will you stay home with the baby before going back to work?" Even acquaintances with kids who never paid much attention to me before are suddenly interested in what I have to say. It's like I'm in this secret club now that I never knew existed before I got pregnant. On one hand, it's kind of nice as I (clearly) like talking about my experience with pregnancy so far; but on the other, it's also a little weird, because I'm not really sure why I'm all of a sudden more interesting just because I'm having a baby. Being included in this new club has made me a little uneasy; I'm not really sure yet whether I want to be a member. It's making me think that what I once thought was an imaginary divide between couples that have kids and couples that don't isn't so imaginary after all. I guess I'll find out for sure in a couple of months.

Besides lots of peeing, friendly faces, and lack of sleep, the eighth month also came with the dreaded baby shower. Like I mentioned earlier, Nick and I didn't want to tell anyone the sex of the baby until he's born in order to avoid getting gendered gifts. This decision was displeasing to a subset of people I happen to share DNA with (sorry

Mom), so, to appease them, I offered to have a "gender reveal" baby shower, where part of the fun would be finally letting everyone know about the bundle of testosterone that has been inhabiting my uterus for the past 8 months. The unveiling would involve a cake filled with either a blue or pink center that, once cut, reveals the sex of the baby. I figured that if friends and family members are going to give us gifts, they'd do it at the shower, so we'd be able to avoid gendered gifts as much as possible and still let everyone know the sex of the baby before my due date.

For many people, along with a baby shower comes the daunting task of thinking about what you might need for the baby. If this is your first child, as it is for me, this feels a little like trying to learn to drive while blindfolded. To make matters worse, I had never even been inside of a baby store before. To see what I was getting myself into, I decided to go to the local Buy Buy Baby just to take a look around. I lasted about 5 minutes before I turned around and walked out. The store is gigantic (think Bed, Bath, and Beyond except full of baby stuff) and the number of choices for every baby item you can think of—big or small, from strollers to pacifiers—is completely and utterly overwhelming. It turns out that knowing about the science of infant development is about as useful as a trapdoor in a lifeboat when it comes to knowing about the daily needs of a newborn. There was no way I was going to be able to tackle this without doing some research first. But, since research is my day job, it was fairly easy to come up with a viable plan.

I had lots of friends who already had children, many of whom had them very recently, so I decided to email them and ask which items they absolutely could not live without and, conversely, which items they never used. My plan was to only ask for items that three or more of my friends said were "must haves" and to stay away from items that were on more than two of my friends' "never used" lists. I found out quickly that friends who had kids that were well past infancy (i.e., 2 years old and older) already had trouble remembering what sorts of things they needed when their kids were really young (like I said earlier, nature makes you forget), which narrowed down my sample size to about four friends who currently had infants (i.e., babies under the age of 2). My method generally worked, and I found that there was a lot of overlap between their lists and even in the different kinds of baby products that they all preferred. This made choosing basics like a stroller and car seat much easier than I thought. But there were a lot of differences as well, mostly based on each infant's individual personality, which made it sound like it's hard to guess exactly what you're going to need until you meet your very own newborn, as each one is different right from the very beginning.

This might sound surprising, but babies have their own unique personalities right from birth. This is often called *temperament,* or an infant's own individual style of responding to the environment. An infant's temperament is present very early in development and has been studied in infants as young as 3 or 4 months of age. What's most impressive about temperament is that distinct temperament profiles can be identified in the first year of life and remain somewhat stable into the preschool years and beyond. That isn't to say that infants can't change their temperament over time; it's just not common to move from one extreme to the other.

Alexander Thomas, Stella Chess, and Herbert Birch were the first researchers to study temperament in the 1960s. They interviewed hundreds of parents asking them specific questions of about their babies' behavior, and they used their answers to come up with nine different dimensions of infant temperament, each relating to how infants respond to some sort of change in the environment, including how adaptable they are to new situations, how they behave when presented with a stranger, and their general mood.

Based on these nine dimensions, Thomas, Chess, and Birch identified three distinct infant temperament types. Most babies (~40%) had what they called an *easy* temperament. These infants easily adapted to changes in the environment, were quick to fall into regular feeding and eating routines, and welcomed new people and situations. Other babies (~10%) had *difficult* temperaments; these infants had some trouble adapting to new experiences and routines and had a fairly negative reaction to change. Babies who were *slow to warm up* (~15%) were somewhere in the middle—they behaved like difficult babies at first, but, after taking some time to get used to new people and places, eventually embraced them. Many children (~35%) didn't fit neatly into any of these categories and fell somewhere in between two of them (Thomas, Chess, & Birch, 1970).

Jerome Kagan from Harvard University also wanted to know whether he could identify temperamental traits in the first few months of life and whether these traits persist into early, middle, and later childhood. Kagan didn't have nine traits—instead, he used one or two really simple behaviors in 4-month-olds to predict their emotional responsiveness to new objects and situations several years later. He found that infants who were "reactive" and became physically and emotionally distressed when shown a simple mobile were likely to be shy and withdraw in social situations 5 years later, a temperamental style he called *behaviorally inhibited*. Like Thomas, Chess, and Birch's "difficult" babies, reactive 4-month-olds who were likely to become behaviorally inhibited toddlers were really sensitive to changes in the environment. In contrast, the infants who barely reacted to the mobile at all—the ones who were quiet and laid back—were the ones most likely to become talkative and highly social 5 years later, a temperamental style he called *uninhibited* (Kagan, 1997). These babies are generally "easy" and respond to new people and situations quite positively. Amazingly, Kagan has now been tracking the same 4-month-olds for almost 20 years, into adolescence and adulthood, and has found that the individuals who were distressed by the mobile as infants are still the most likely to be shy as adults, while those who were the most quiet and laid back as infants are still the most socially competent and outgoing.

For the most part, temperament appears so early in infancy and is stable enough across development that most researchers believe it is biologically based. Nathan Fox from the University of Maryland studies how temperament might be represented in the brain. Classic research from his lab, in collaboration with Richard Davidson from the University of Wisconsin, has shown that babies as young as 9 months of age show different brain activation to various objects. Using a technique called electroencephalogram (EEG, a test that can detect electrical activity in your brain; Figure 8.2), they find that the left side of the prefrontal cortex—the part of the brain that is thought to be responsible for thinking and planning—is more active when we are shown something positive that we might want to approach, while the right side is more active when we are shown something negative that we might want to avoid. Furthermore, even newborns show this pattern. For example, when a group of newborns are given a sweet liquid to taste, they show more activation on the left frontal side of the brain than the right (Fox & Davidson, 1986). Similarly, when 10-month-olds are shown videos of a person posing a happy smiling face versus a sad frowning face, the infants show more left frontal brain activity when viewing the happy face (Davidson & Fox, 1982).

Most importantly, there seem to be differences in left versus right frontal activation early on for infants and children of different temperaments. For example, 10-month-old infants who are more likely to cry when separated from their mothers or when approached by a stranger—and are thus more likely to have a reactive temperament—show more right frontal activity *in general* when compared to babies who don't cry (Davidson & Fox, 1989; Fox & Davidson, 1987). Similar findings have been shown with 4-year-old children who are shy versus outgoing; children who are more withdrawn in social interactions with other kids show more right frontal activation in the brain when compared to kids who are more outgoing. More outgoing children, in contrast, tend to show more left frontal activation (Fox et al., 1995). The implication here is that, in general, children who have a more difficult or behaviorally inhibited temperament show more activity in the part of the brain that is associated with negative emotion or withdrawal from social situations: As Fox and colleagues would say, it's like they

Figure 8.2 | Baby with electroencephalogram (EEG) cap. EEG works by detecting electrical activity in different regions of the brain.

Source: Cat Thrasher Photography.

are born with a bias to have a "glass half-empty" perspective on the world, whereas uninhibited children who show more left frontal activation have more of a "glass half-full" bias (Fox & Helfinstein, 2013).

Although EEG is useful in studying those areas of the brain that might show differences in activity based on different temperaments, more recent advancements in brain technology have allowed researchers to dig a little deeper and look at the specific parts of the brain that might function differently for individuals with different temperaments. For example, in addition to global differences in activation of the front part of the brain, researchers have also found differences based on temperament in a specific region of the brain called the *amygdala*—an area where emotions like fear are processed (Roy et al., 2014)—and the *striatum*—an area that is involved in social interactions and the anticipation of social rewards (Guyer et al., 2014). Children who have a behaviorally inhibited temperament also react physically to new objects and situations more quickly than do children of other temperaments and, for example, startle more easily to a flash of light or loud noise (Barker, Reeb-Sutherland, & Fox, 2014).

Besides biological differences, different temperamental traits might also develop in part because of biases in where babies look. It should be obvious by now that babies are born with very little information about the outside world. In the first few months of life, they learn what to do by interacting with the world using their five senses, the most important of which is arguably vision. In this way, what babies look at might be a window into what they are given the opportunity to learn about (Oakes, 2015). For example, if infants see faces that are all smiling all the time, the feedback they get about the world is likely to be quite positive. In contrast, if they see mostly neutral or sad faces—for example, if they have a depressed mom—they might develop a very different view of the world (more on this later). But it's important to note that babies aren't just passively viewing the world as it comes to them, at least not after the first couple of months. They can eventually control where they look, and differences in where they *choose* to focus their attention could also alter their view of the world.

This is where temperament comes in. As I mentioned before, you can think of a difficult or behaviorally inhibited temperament as a bias to have a "glass half empty" view of the world. My own research in collaboration with two of my favorite colleagues—Kristin Buss and Koraly Pérez-Edgar from Penn State University—suggests that individuals with an inhibited temperament might also *pay more attention* to negative things in the environment compared to noninhibited individuals.

For example, Koraly and I conducted a study several years ago where we presented 5-year-old children who were either incredibly shy (or behaviorally inhibited) or very social (or uninhibited) with nine photographs on a large touchscreen monitor, arranged in three-by-three matrices. For each matrix, there was one target and eight distractors, and we instructed the children to find and touch the target on the screen as quickly as possible. The key part of the experiment was that the targets had different emotional meanings, with some targets carrying a scary or threatening meaning and the other carrying a positive or neutral meaning. In one condition, we asked them to find snakes (which are threatening) among frogs (which are not) or frogs among snakes. In another, we asked them to find angry faces (which are threatening) among happy faces (which are not) or happy faces among angry faces.

Overall, all of the children were faster at finding the targets and touching them on the screen when they were threatening (snakes and angry faces) as opposed to happy or neutral (frogs and happy faces). In fact, it turns out that we are all pretty good at finding things that are threatening (LoBue, 2009, 2010; LoBue & DeLoache, 2008). Most importantly, the shy children were even better at finding social signals of threat—angry faces—when compared to their non-shy counterparts (Figure 8.3). So, even though all of the children detected angry faces more quickly than happy faces and snakes more quickly than frogs, children who were shy were particularly fast when it came to angry faces. This suggests that children who are shy or have a behaviorally inhibited temperament pay more attention to negative social information than do kids of easier or uninhibited temperaments (LoBue & Pérez-Edgar, 2014). Importantly, very recent work from our labs suggests that this heightened bias for negative facial expressions in individuals with inhibited temperaments appears in the first 2 years of life, suggesting that these babies might pay special attention to negative social information in the environment, possibly molding a more negative view of the social world (LoBue, Buss, Taber-Thomas, & Pérez-Edgar, 2017; Pérez-Edgar et al., 2017).

Figure 8.3 | Touchscreen study from my lab. Five-year-old children were presented with nine photos—one target and eight distracters—and were asked to find the target as quickly as possible on the screen by touching it. In LoBue and Pérez-Edgar (2014), we found that children who were temperamentally shy detected angry faces more quickly than their non-shy counterparts.
Source: LoBue, V. & DeLoache, J. D. (2008). Detecting the snake in the grass: Attention to fear-relevant stimuli by adults and young children. *Psychological Science, 19(3)*, 284–289. (Association for Psychological Science). Reprinted by permission of SAGE Publications.

So far, it sounds like babies who are born with the predisposition or the requisite biology for an inhibited temperament are just screwed and there's nothing you can do about. But that isn't true. Yes, children who have more inhibited temperaments are going to be a bit more challenged in social situations than children lucky enough to be born with a bias to more positively engage with the social world, but that doesn't mean all is lost for inhibited kids. First, it's important to point out that very few children have this temperamental trait—on average, only between 10% and 15% of children in the United States are behaviorally inhibited. Furthermore, behavioral inhibition is not a disorder, and while a behaviorally inhibited temperament is the best predictor we have for the later development of anxiety disorders, having a behaviorally inhibited child doesn't mean that you will have an adolescent with social anxiety later in life; only a subset of these children (around 40%) end up developing social anxiety problems. So, although interventions are available to prevent anxiety disorders from developing in the first place, some researchers have questioned whether these interventions are necessary, as they can be costly and might even stigmatize children who are otherwise just quiet in the extreme (Fox, Barker, White, Suway, & Pine, 2013). Indeed, there is nothing wrong with being a little bit shy and reserved, and if that's the personality that our children happen to have, why would we want to step in and try to change it before we know whether there's even a real problem to address?

Furthermore, parenting does play a role in how behaviorally inhibited children fare when they are placed in social situations like daycare or preschool. To illustrate to you how this might work, let's take a quick look at temperament in monkeys. Like humans, rhesus monkeys are born with different temperaments that somewhat resemble the inhibited versus uninhibited human temperaments that Jerome Kagan studies. Research from Stephen Suomi's Laboratory of Comparative Ethology at the National Institute of Child Health and Human Development suggests that parenting does matter—even in monkeys.

To see if parenting style might help shift different temperaments, Suomi and colleagues selected a group of baby monkeys that had a temperamental profile similar to the inhibited or difficult human infants I described earlier. These "reactive" baby monkeys are highly nervous in new situations and generally cling to their mothers, even when they are perfectly safe. Suomi selected a group of these monkeys and placed with them with "foster mothers" of a very different temperament. These mothers were exceedingly relaxed and nurturing, unlike the overprotective mothers that typically birth reactive babies. After letting these reactive babies grow up with relaxed and nurturing foster mothers, Suomi and his colleagues found that these once reactive babies grew up to be quite daring—exploring their environments without fear, much like babies born with more relaxed temperaments (Suomi, 1997).

Research with human children echo this finding, suggesting that parenting style can help to alleviate some of the potential challenges that inhibited children might face because of their temperament. Research has shown, for example, that while a difficult or reactive temperament at 9 months of age is related to less social engagement when these babies are older, this relationship goes away for babies with mothers who are sensitive and responsive to the child's needs. In other words, having a reactive temperament does put a baby at risk for being shy or withdrawing from social situations as a toddler or preschooler, but having a parent who is loving and supportive creates a buffer for these effects. And, despite having temperamental challenges, these inhibited babies don't necessarily grow up to be particularly shy (Penela, Henderson, Hane, Ghera, & Fox, 2012).

This research suggests that parenting does matter, and different parenting styles are optimal for different temperaments. Furthermore, if you end up with a difficult child, you shouldn't lose sleep over what you might have done wrong because chances are that certain personality traits were already set in place before your baby was even born. But although it's easy to be the parent of an easy child, parenting a child who is biased towards shyness or who is a bit slow to warm up in social situations may require a bit more sensitivity to the child's individual needs. Forcing inhibited children into new situations too quickly might intensify their fear, so letting them grow accustomed to new situations at their own pace can be important. Furthermore, it's important to note that while temperament has a biological basis, no two children are alike, and you may very well give birth to two children with totally different temperaments. There are also cultural differences in the way different temperamental characteristics might be viewed by others (e.g., Ahadi, Rothbart, & Ye, 1993). So, adjusting your parenting style to fit your child's individual needs is important; and keep in mind that what works for one child may not work as well for the next.

It's hard to tell what my baby's personality is going to be like before meeting him, so for the upcoming baby shower I just had to wing it. It was actually a really fun day, and I got to see how truly happy our friends and family are about our pending new addition. There were cheers and shrieks of excitement from my aunts and cousins as we cut the cake to reveal a blue-filled center, and we opened gifts to find adorable baby clothes in the gender-neutral colors of green and yellow that I was hoping for. We played silly games, where Nick and I had to guess the flavor of various baby foods (which has officially inspired us to make our own), and where our closest friends were tasked with quickly fastening tiny diapers to baby dolls while blindfolded. The impending shower also motivated us to get the nursery together, so, after this month, I am feeling for the very first time like pregnancy will be coming to an end soon and that we are rapidly approaching our new lives as first-time parents.

9

THE NINTH MONTH

LABOR AND DELIVERY

Today I went to the doctor for my 36-week visit and for my last ultrasound. Apparently, I am in the home stretch—doctors consider 37 weeks to be at term—and I can technically go into labor at any time and it wouldn't be considered premature. From this point on, I will have to go to the doctor every week until the baby is born, and the visits will become increasingly unpleasant as she will have to estimate the size of my cervix with an uncomfortable internal exam instead of simply gauging the width of my belly with a measuring tape. I had my first one of those today, and, yes, it was uncomfortable but not terrible. The doctor just used her fingers to feel around my cervix and to estimate the baby's position. My cervix is not yet dilated, and the baby is still high up in my uterus, so my doctor's guess is that I have a few more weeks left before labor kicks in.

My main symptom this month is that I'm completely and utterly uncomfortable pretty much all the time. I feel huge and have lost the ability to estimate how much space my body takes up. In fact, I was in a clothing store the other day and accidentally knocked over a mannequin with my belly. I've gained 26 pounds, and the baby is 6 pounds 7 ounces, 49th percentile (at least *his* size is perfect). His head is down near my cervix, and the doctor said it is unlikely that he will reposition himself at this point, so there should be no problem (that she can foresee) with having a vaginal birth (Figure 9.1). He moves around all the time, causing the skin on my belly to move in weird and uncomfortable ways. It often looks like I'm a character in a horror movie (think *Alien*) as elbows and other miscellaneous baby parts spontaneously protrude from my stomach. Besides lots and lots of kicking, the baby also gets the hiccups at least once or twice a day now, and he's big enough that the hiccups make my whole stomach rumble with each gurgle. I am still going to the bathroom constantly, and the pressure on my bladder only gets heavier with each passing day.

Since I could technically go into labor at any time now, we've finally started thinking about labor and birth and what our plan should be. Some people take a birthing class, and I've heard mixed reviews

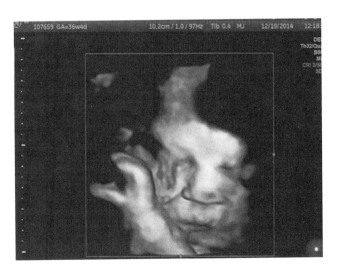

Figure 9.1 | Thirty-six-week ultrasound, three-dimensional image of the fetus's face and hand.

Source: Vanessa LoBue.

from friends about whether or not it is useful. Many of them say that they learned a lot from taking a class and are happy that they did. Others report that taking a class was somewhat useful, but the best part of it was meeting other expecting parents. Others have said that they didn't learn much in the class but felt better that they had at least listened to what the instructors had to say, feeling more prepared afterward for labor and delivery. It's important to relieve anxiety about labor and delivery in any way you can, as the more anxiety women have about labor, the more labor pain they report experiencing and the longer labor can last (e.g., Beebe, Lee, Carrieri-Kohlman, & Humphreys, 2007). In fact, relatively recent research from Norway suggests that fear of childbirth might actually prolong labor. When you're afraid or anxious, your body releases stress hormones; the researchers suggest that these stress hormones might weaken the strength of each contraction, effectively prolonging the process (Adams, Eberhard-Gran, & Eskild, 2012). So it makes sense to do whatever you can to feel relaxed and prepared as you approach the big day.

Being prepared is something that I value in most aspects of life, so I can relate to this sentiment. But instead of taking a class, I decided to read a book on labor and delivery called *Laboring Well*, written by a labor nurse named Elizabeth Allen (2012). It was exactly what I was looking for and provided me with all of the facts I felt like I needed to be prepared to make decisions about labor and delivery. I'd highly recommend something like that if you're just looking for plain facts about the process (e.g., how long contractions last, how an epidural is administered, when you'd need to have a C-section, etc.), but if you're looking for help on breathing techniques to use during labor, positions that help reduce pain, or you simply want to be a part of a community of expecting mothers, it sounds like a class might be more beneficial.

How we choose to experience labor and to ultimately deliver our babies is a very personal and sensitive topic for many women. We all share the common goal of wanting the experience to be as healthy and stress-free as possible, but, other than that, theories and methods of birthing and delivery vary widely across cultures and between generations. The classic view of birth used to be that it is a very traumatic experience for babies. In the early 1920s, Otto Rank, an Austrian psychoanalyst, wrote a book called *The Trauma of Birth* (1929) where he described birth as a horrific experience that takes a lifetime to recover from. Frederick Leboyer, a French obstetrician, perpetuated a similar idea in his book *Birth Without Violence* (1975). He advocated a new birthing method that is still popular today called a "water birth" (or a "LeBoyer birth") that involves giving birth in a warm pool of water. The idea behind water births is that a newborn's natural environment is the uterus where it is surrounded by amniotic fluid. Being born into a warm pool of water—an environment very similar to what the baby experiences in the womb—welcomes it into the world peacefully, without any sort of trauma.

The truth is that there is absolutely no evidence supporting the idea that birth is a traumatic or uncomfortable process for the baby in any way (although laboring in water might have comforting benefits for the mother). Contrary to what you might think, the newborn doesn't feel pain during birth; it mostly just feels pressure. The following demonstration (stolen from my brilliant mentor, Dr. Judy DeLoache from the University of Virginia) can illustrate what a baby might experience during birth—one that I ask all of my undergraduate students to perform in my developmental psychology class every year. Here's what to do: Put your dominant hand on your opposite wrist and squeeze it as hard as you possibly can. Squeeze *hard*. What you might find is that no matter how hard you squeeze, it doesn't hurt that much. This is what the baby experiences during birth—significant pressure, but not necessarily pain. The mother, on the other hand, has a different experience altogether. This time, instead of squeezing your wrist, pull the skin away from the bone. What you're probably thinking is: *Ouch!* While pushing on your skin doesn't really hurt so much, pulling does. In fact, it hurts a lot. Pulling is what the mother feels as the baby travels through the birth canal.

Despite the pain that the mother will endure during the early stages of labor (particularly the first stage), doctors and psychologists are beginning to find evidence that the birthing process itself might even be an adaptive one for both the baby and for the mother. For example, when compared to C-sections, vaginal births result in shorter hospital stays, lower risk for infection, shorter recovery time for the mother, and lower risk of breathing problems for the baby. Furthermore, recent research suggests that infants get bacteria through the birth canal that can be helpful in fighting diseases (Dominguez-Bello et al., 2010). In fact, infants born via C-section are more likely to develop asthma (e.g., Neu & Rushing, 2011), various allergies (Renz-Polster et al., 2005), and even childhood obesity by the time they reach preschool age (Huh et al., 2012) when compared to babies born vaginally. The hypothesis surrounding these findings is that babies who are delivered vaginally ingest a variety of bacteria from the birth canal that are important in establishing both a healthy digestive system and a healthy immune system (Neu & Rushing, 2011).

Birth itself happens in three stages. In the first stage, the cervix opens up, which is called *dilation*, and becomes thinner, which is called *effacement*. The cervix has to open up to about 10 cm before the fetus can pass through, so you'll hear doctors refer to the number of centimeters the cervix is dilated, with 10 as the ultimate goal. This is the longest stage of labor—it can last for more than 24 hours. The contractions will initially be short and far apart and gradually become longer and closer together. Once the mother's cervix is close to 10 cm, the fetus's head should begin to enter the mother's vagina. The doctors will refer to this as *transition*, where labor moves from stage one to stage two. Stage two is where the mother pushes the baby out and is usually the one you see in movies and on television. It is much shorter than the first stage and generally lasts for a little less than an hour, but can go for up to two. The pushing stage can be tiring for the mother and potentially stressful for the baby, so if the baby hasn't descended through the birth canal after 2 hours of pushing, doctors will often recommend doing a C-section. After the baby is finally born, the mother has one more stage left (stage three) in which she will push out the placenta and everything else that remains in the uterus (Figure 9.2).

There are lots of ways to go through the process of birthing. Decades ago, most women were anesthetized during labor so that they didn't feel a thing, but they also couldn't move or feel their legs. Often doctors would have to use forceps to take the baby out because mothers couldn't feel themselves push, which can cause complications for the baby. Nowadays, an epidural is used to *lessen* pain, but not so much that the mother can't move or feel herself push. This change has resulted in the less frequent use of forceps and the need for interventions if something goes wrong, which is better for the newborns. Another new development is the practice of inducing labor by administering a hormone (Pitocin) that generally gets and keeps the process of labor moving. Doctors might recommend inducing labor if there is a reason to think there might be a complication or even if mothers go too far (more than 2 weeks) past their due dates. This is again to avoid complications, like the baby getting too big for a vaginal birth.

Some parents choose to go drug-free during labor and delivery because of concern about the potential negative consequences of pain-reducing drugs on the baby. Research suggests that there are no major long-term consequences for babies whose mothers choose to have pain-reducing procedures like an epidural during labor; if there were, I doubt these practices would be so common. However, there may be some short-term consequences to keep in mind. For example, there is research suggesting that although there doesn't necessarily seem to be any negative consequences of an epidural for the baby, use of an epidural is associated with longer labor for the mother (Hasegawa et al., 2013). In fact, one study estimated that labor could last more than 2 hours longer with than without the epidural (Cheng, Shaffer, Nicholson, & Caughey, 2014). Besides the obvious benefits of pain relief, a potential plus of an epidural is that it can often make labor a lot less stressful, and, again, stress can also prolong the pain. So there's a bit of a tradeoff here: Although

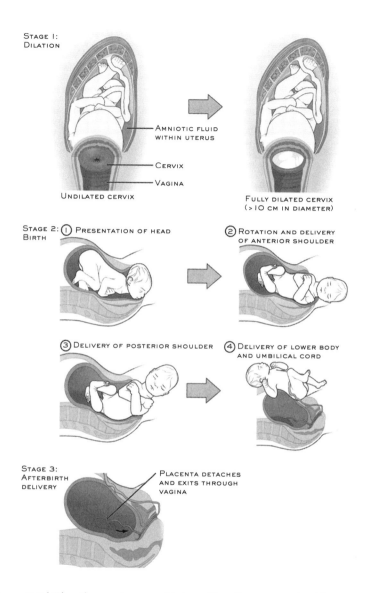

Figure 9.2 | The three stages of labor. The first stage is dilation (the longest stage), followed by birth or delivery of the baby, and finally delivery of the afterbirth.

Source: Wikipedia, "Childbirth," Adapted by Vanessa LoBue from original by OpenStax College.

an epidural might prolong labor, stress can have a similar effect, so the reduction in stress produced by having an epidural might potentially make up for any worries you have about the epidural prolonging labor.

Sometimes mothers will sidestep the pain of labor and delivery altogether and schedule a cesarean, or C-section. Both doctors and mothers have elected to use C-sections more and more over the past several decades. For example, the rate of C-section in the United States was 4.5% in 1965 (Taffel, Placek, & Liss, 1996) and was a staggering 33% in 2010–2011 (Hamilton, Martin, & Ventura, 2011). There are lots of reasons for this increase, and expecting mothers vary widely in how they feel about birth via C-section, but, for the most part, C-sections are a safe way of getting the baby out if there happens to be a complication, like if the baby is facing the wrong way (feet down, called a *breech birth*), if the baby is in the wrong position, or if labor isn't progressing and the baby is in distress.

Women didn't always give birth in hospitals with the option of a planned C-section. In the early part of the twentieth century, half of all births in the United States took place at home (Zielinski, Ackerson, & Low, 2015). Although home births have decreased dramatically since the turn of the century (less than 1% of women in the United States delivered at home in 2012), home births are still an option, and they're on the rise: In 2013, home births in the United States were at their highest rate since the late 1980s (Martin, Hamilton, Osterman, Curtin, & Matthews, 2015). Furthermore, there are large cross-cultural differences in how often mothers choose to have their babies at home, even in industrialized countries like the Netherlands, where up to 20% of women choose home births (Zielinski et al., 2015).

Along with the rise in C-sections, there's also been a rise in home births in the United States over the past decade and, relatedly, a rise in the use of midwives and doulas without or in combination with physicians. A midwife is an expert in pregnancy and childbirth and is trained to deliver babies at home. In the United States, some midwives have nursing degrees, and all of them are generally trained to recognize problems with labor that require intervention from a hospital. In other words, you can choose to have a midwife deliver your child in place of a medical doctor, particularly if you decide you want a home birth. A doula, in contrast, is a birth companion or instructor. Doulas don't deliver babies themselves, but they can accompany a midwife, or they can come with you to the hospital when you deliver with a physician to provide guidance and support. There are fewer interventions associated with home births and a lower incidence of C-sections (Newhouse et al., 2011; Zielinski et al., 2015), which is likely why more and more mothers who would like to avoid unnecessary interventions are choosing this option. Death of the newborn is slightly higher for home births than hospital births, but the difference is small and the overall rates of newborn death in the United States are pretty low in both cases (Snowden et al., 2015).

A current problem in the United States is that home births using midwives is generally discouraged by physicians, whereas in many other countries midwives are quite common, and local hospitals work hand in hand with midwives to deliver most babies. In Germany, for example, births *most often* take place in hospitals by midwives. German midwives oversee most births working directly with hospitals or birthing centers while doctors generally play a background role, ready to step in only if intervention is needed. The US system is quite different, and midwives do not necessarily work directly with hospitals or physicians. That means that midwives in the United States may or may not have an established relationship with a local hospital, and, if something goes wrong with your labor and it becomes absolutely necessary for you to go to the hospital, whoever takes care of you there won't know anything about the history of your pregnancy. This doesn't generally happen in the European system, where midwives deliver your baby in the hospital and have an established partnership with a doctor.

Another concern is that there are various ways of becoming a certified midwife in the United States, which means that different midwives might have different kinds of certifications and/or experience. By contrast, in many European countries where giving birth with a midwife is the norm, the certification process is standardized so that you can trust that all midwives have the same credentials and necessary experience (Allen, 2012). That doesn't mean you shouldn't opt to have your baby at home with a midwife instead of a physician, but it does mean that steps should be taken to look into your midwife's certification and whether he or she has a partnership with a hospital in case anything goes wrong.

Ultimately, what you choose has to do with how you envision giving birth and what kind of support system you'd like to surround yourself with on that important day. There are a lot of ways to give birth, and the traditions from country to country vary almost as widely as the babies themselves, ranging from restricted diets for new mothers for a predetermined number of weeks, to traditions in handling the placenta (e.g., eating it or burying it in your backyard). Since there are so many ways that women can decide to go through labor and birth, it's important to have an idea of how you might want to do it before those contractions start.

Nick and I made a very loose birth plan this month based on our own personal preferences and priorities. Birth plan worksheets are available on countless baby websites, and they can help you through the process; they offer a wide range of choices for how you want to give birth, from small decisions like whether you want to light candles or listen to music in the birthing room, to big decisions like whether you want to be induced or have a planned C-section. However, a word of caution: Although having a plan is important to some people, there are a lot of factors that are beyond your control. On average, the first stage of labor lasts between 8 and 12 hours, with 1–2 hours of pushing after that. And, although it usually doesn't take longer than 18 hours, it's certainly possible for it to go even longer without your cervix ever progressing all the way to 10 cm. If labor isn't progressing after 20 hours, doctors might offer Pitocin to move the labor along, or a C-section might be necessary. In fact, a third of all C-sections are the result of labor failing to progress. The main worry here is stress to the baby, possibly because of a lack of oxygen from the placenta.

Similarly, while the ideal position for the baby at the time of birth is head down, facing toward the back of your body, there are babies who are "sunny side up" or facing your abdomen, and even babies who are feet down, or breech. A baby can be born "sunny side up," but it is more difficult to get him or her through the pelvis and it could increase the pain of birth for the mother, so doctors will often try to turn the baby around in these cases. Having a baby that is breech is more serious and generally requires a C-section, but only 3–4% of babies are breech at the time of birth. There are other complications that could happen as well: The umbilical cord could be wrapped around the baby's neck; you could have placenta previa (as I did for a while), where the placenta grows over the cervix and prevents a natural birth; you may have trouble with the pain and ask for an epidural even though you initially wanted a natural birth; in contrast, you may have planned for an epidural, but for some reason it ends up not working, wearing off too soon, or only working on half of your body; you could need an *episiotomy* (a surgical cut at the opening of the vagina) to make more room for the baby in the birth canal, or you might experience tearing that requires stitches; or you might experience some combination of these things, all unexpected and most completely out of your hands. That doesn't mean you shouldn't make a birth plan—it can be helpful if you have specific ideas of what you want for your child's birth. But always remember that not everything on your birth plan will necessarily work out exactly as you planned, and ending up with a healthy baby is always the ultimate goal.

We have decided that we would like to have a vaginal birth with an epidural. We are comfortable with having a C-section or with using any other method necessary to birth a healthy baby if there are complications, but we would like to have a vaginal birth if at all possible. We would like to give birth in a hospital with my doctor—whom I have known for more than 5 years and trust immensely—as opposed to at home with a midwife and/or doula. We will circumcise our son shortly after birth, and we plan to breastfeed. Other than that, we do not have preferences for how to labor, how the hospital room should be set up, or for anything else.

Some women have much more detailed birth plans—ours is rather skimpy—but regardless of how skimpy or detailed your plan is, or whether you have one at all, it should outline what you think is most important during labor and delivery. We have really only come up with one major priority—to have a vaginal birth if possible. We have chosen to have an epidural because it seems important to stay as relaxed as possible during labor, and an epidural will likely make that easier for me. We have chosen to give birth at a hospital with my doctor instead of at home with a midwife because I trust my doctor and have full confidence in her recommendations. After the birth, we'd like to circumcise my son because it has health benefits, such as reducing the prevalence of certain bacteria on the body (Liu et al., 2013), and we'd like to breastfeed because it has other health benefits like protecting the baby against infection (e.g., Howie, Forsyth, Ogston, Clark, & Florey, 1990). Again, everyone is different, so what I am choosing should in no way impact what *you* choose to do as there is no right or wrong way to bring a baby into this world, as long as it's healthy and safe.

Again, it's good to have a plan if you feel like you want one, and it's good to feel prepared to some extent, but I really don't think there are any right or wrong decisions if you end up with a healthy baby. Even if nothing in our birth plan works out—if the baby is breech and we need to have an emergency C-section, or if for some reason I am unable to breastfeed, or if my doctor is out of town during my labor and someone else has to delivery our baby—it will be OK. Anything can happen during labor, delivery, and beyond, and, in my case, having too many expectations might lead to disappointment. After all, I don't want to start motherhood feeling like a failure because something out of my control happened to keep me from having the kind of birth I wanted. The goal of labor and delivery is to end up with a healthy baby. If at the end of the process I get a healthy baby boy, that's what's most important. Everything else is just gravy.

10

THE STORY OF
MY SON'S BIRTH

Right at the beginning of the ninth month, I started getting mild menstrual cramps on a daily basis. I had a feeling that these were *Braxton Hicks contractions*—or pre-labor contractions—but I wasn't sure. At my 36-week visit, my doctor asked me if I was having any contractions, and, after feeling my belly, she said, "You're actually having one right now!" My stomach was rock hard and my belly button that usually sticks out was now completely flat. I didn't really feel much—just some tightening of the stomach muscles and another mild menstrual-like cramp—but she made me feel around my belly so that I could get used to the way contractions would feel on my skin. She said I could have these Braxton Hicks contractions for weeks and weeks before going into labor and that some women even have them throughout most of their pregnancies. She did an internal exam, and my cervix wasn't dilated or effaced yet, so her prediction was that I would go to term. I went back a week later (on New Year's Eve)—at 37 weeks—and this time I was 1 centimeter dilated and the internal exam hurt a lot more than it had at the last visit. My doctor said I could stay pregnant for weeks at 1 cm, so there was still nothing to get excited about. I went home thinking that we still had at least 2 weeks left before anything would happen.

By the time I got home from the appointment, I had a huge pounding headache. I hadn't gotten headaches like this since the first and early second trimesters, when a surge of new hormones was streaming through my body. By 11:30 PM that night—30 minutes until the ball dropped in Times Square—my headache hadn't backed off despite taking several Tylenols. That's when I felt something weird happen in my uterus. I can't really describe it as anything other than a "pop." Immediately after, I felt a trickle of liquid coming out of me. Honestly, I just assumed that I peed myself. No, I've never peed myself before (at least not since I was a toddler), so I really had no prior basis for this assumption, but I was 37 weeks pregnant and feeling like I had little enough control over my body that peeing myself wasn't outside the realm of possibilities. The odd thing was that the trickle didn't stop; it wasn't a gush, but it was enough that I had to put on a maxi pad to keep from wetting myself again. Half an hour later, literally as the ball dropped in Times Square at midnight to signal the start of 2015, I felt a really strong cramp. It lasted for about 30 seconds. About 10 minutes later, I felt another one, just as strong as the first. I knew at that point that the trickle of liquid could have been my water breaking and that I might be in labor.

What my mom and most of my friends told me about labor is that the contractions start out feeling like mild menstrual cramps and gradually get stronger over several hours. In fact, most of my friends weren't even sure they were in labor at first and were only certain after hours of contractions that got progressively stronger and more consistent. My experience couldn't have been more different. My contractions didn't start out slow or mild; they were fast and furious from the very first one. I read (in *Laboring Well*) that you'd know you were in labor when the contractions "mean business." This seemed like a vague (and mildly silly) statement at the time, but it turned out to be completely true: From my very first contraction, I knew that they were qualitatively different from the Braxton Hicks contractions I had been experiencing for a few weeks; these new ones meant business.

After only a few, I calmly told Nick that I was in labor. We started timing the contractions using a cell phone app. From the beginning (around midnight), each one lasted for about 30–45 seconds and were 8–10 minutes apart. We decided to try to relax and watch some TV, as my doctor said to call her when they were 5 minutes apart, 1 minute long, and coming consistently for about an hour (the 5–1–1 rule). By 2 AM, we called. My doctor said that we should think about coming to the hospital soon, but could take our time since we likely had several hours of laboring ahead of us. My husband quickly packed a bag and wanted to head to the hospital immediately—Mount Sinai was a 20-minute drive directly into Manhattan and it was New Year's Eve (technically New Year's day by that time).

We ended up getting there at about 3 or 3:30 in the morning. I was immediately put in a wheelchair and taken to a temporary room where an intern could check my cervix. I was 4 cm dilated by then, and my contractions were a minute long and 3 minutes apart. They were excruciating. The intern who examined me asked casually if I was interested in an epidural. I immediately said "yes" (followed by "please, please"). She looked at me hesitantly and said, "I'm not going to sugarcoat this for you, but it's a bit early for an epidural." I could tell by the look on her face that she had never been pregnant before and had never experienced anything close to the pain of a 1-minute-long contraction (that was the first of two times I wanted to slap someone that night).

Although 4 cm may be "a bit early" for an epidural, I was dilated enough that I was admitted and moved to a labor and delivery room. By 4 AM, the anesthesiologist came in to place my epidural. I was really nervous about this part—having a needle inserted into my spine is about the scariest thing I can think of—but I was in so much pain from the contractions that I didn't care. The pain was just like everyone says—the worst pain you will ever experience—and *intense* to say the least. No amount of breathing or squeezing Nick's hand or fidgeting was going to ease this pain. The local anesthetic for the epidural was even more painful than a contraction, and, to make matters worse, I had to sit still while they placed the needle in my back during contractions that were less than 3 minutes apart. This was probably the most difficult part of the entire labor.

Despite the unpleasantness of having the epidural placed, after it was in, everything was *fantastic*. The male intern who accompanied the anesthesiologist even commented, "I can tell it's working, you look a lot more human now." (This was the second time I wanted to slap someone that night; he was lucky I was on drugs.) I could no longer feel the contractions, and I could finally relax and rest a bit while we waited for my cervix to dilate. By this time, it was about 4:30 in the morning. Nick and I tried to sleep a bit and decided to wait to call our families until about 6:30 or 7 AM since it was New Year's morning and everyone we knew would likely be sleeping in. I was on the phone with my mom around 6:30 telling her to take her time coming to the hospital when my doctor arrived to check my cervix. She was shocked to find that I was already 10 cm dilated and fully effaced. She said we could push whenever I was ready. I called my parents back and told them to come now.

I wasn't ready to push just yet, since the epidural was still in full force and I couldn't really feel much below the waist. We decided to wait half an hour and let the epidural wear off enough so that I could feel the contractions again. When they started to feel like mild cramps, we decided to start pushing. Pushing didn't hurt exactly (with the epidural that is), but it was *hard work*. It entailed holding my legs up as close to my face as possible and pushing as hard as I could for three 10-second periods while holding my breath. Doesn't sound like a lot of work, I know, but it's a huge workout when you're 37 weeks pregnant. My contractions were coming every 30 seconds now, so we tried to push during every other one so that I could rest for a minute or two and catch my breath.

The vibe of the room while I was pushing wasn't at all like you see in movies. It was quiet, the lights were dimmed, and only my nurse and Nick were in the room for most of the pushing, each holding up one of my semi-limp legs. I pushed for an hour and a half, all the while relying on the nurse and Nick to give me progress reports since I couldn't see what was going on down below. Finally they called my doctor in, suggesting that we were close to being done. As the sun rose over Central Park on New Year's morning, my doctor held my son's head up between my legs and placed him on my chest. Edwin Henry Reeb was only 6 pounds, 9 ounces, but he looked gigantic. I imagine that anything even resembling a 6-pound object looks huge when it just came out of your vagina. I didn't even notice the cord getting cut or delivering the placenta or getting stitched up—it all happened very quickly while Edwin was crying on my chest. It was 8:59 AM on New Years morning, 2 weeks before my due date, after 9 hours of labor.

All in all, despite the fact that I didn't expect Edwin to come 2 weeks early on New Year's Day, I didn't expect the labor to move so quickly, and I certainly didn't expect to walk away from this experience *still* not knowing what a placenta looks like, I got incredibly lucky. My labor was relatively short for a first timer, the epidural kept everything relaxing for the second half of labor, my cervix fully dilated and effaced easily and without any labor-augmenting medications, I had a vaginal delivery with very little tearing (I needed one stitch), and my own doctor was there with me. I can't imagine it going any more smoothly. There were some bumps along the way of course—after the epidural, my blood pressure dropped so I had to be on oxygen the whole time; Edwin was "sunny side up," meaning that it looked like he was going to come out face up, which isn't ideal, but he turned himself around during delivery; and the umbilical cord was wrapped around his neck when he came out, which could be very dangerous. All of these issues turned about to be fine, and my doctor didn't even let on that I should be alarmed about any of them. "It's not worth worrying until there's something to worry about," she said. I couldn't agree more.

Sometimes, the unexpected surprises that come with labor are not so positive. The day I was being discharged from the hospital, the nurses rolled a woman into the empty bed space next to mine in the hospital room. The woman was about my age, she was in tears and holding a vomit bucket. She told me that she went through 30 hours of labor, tried to get an epidural but an intern placed it incorrectly so it wasn't effective, and after all of that, her cervix only dilated to 7 cm so she had to get an emergency C-section in the end. She was exhausted, in pain, and clearly distressed that the nurses wouldn't let her see her newborn baby; she had a fever, and they insisted on her getting some rest first. Labor and delivery did not go according to her plan, and she looked (understandably) devastated. But, despite the trauma of the birth, it turned out that her baby boy was perfectly healthy and weighed in at over 9 pounds. I didn't get to meet her son, but I'm sure that after I was discharged, when the nurses finally let her hold him in

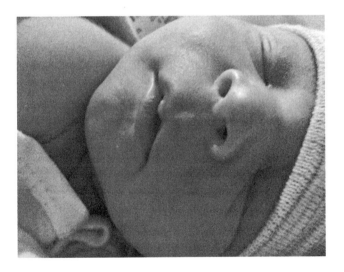

Figure 10.1 | Edwin Henry Reeb, born at 8:59 am on January 1, 2015.
Source: Vanessa LoBue.

her arms, the unexpected trauma of birth would soon become a distant memory.

The moral of the story is that labor is never what you expect, even when it does go smoothly. It could come 2 weeks early, 2 weeks late, last for too long, end in a C-section, or it could all go much better than you expected. This holds not just for labor and delivery, but pregnancy in general: I started out quite skeptical about whether or not I even wanted to have a baby, and everything about pregnancy ended up coming much more naturally than I thought it would. Somewhere along the way, I got excited about being a new mother, I fell in love with being pregnant, and began to feel a connection with my fetus even before he was born.

About 36 hours after his birth, I looked at Edwin and knew that my life was never going to be the same, in the best and worst ways possible. The pain of labor was a blur, and I was already reflecting romantically on the night before. All of the science in the world could not have prepared me for that, and I assume the same will be true for what lies ahead (Figure 10.1).

PART II

PARENTHOOD

THE *REAL* ADVENTURE BEGINS

11

THE FIRST MONTH

Postpartum Depression, Crying, and Nursing

"Are you ready?" People kept asking us in the last few weeks of pregnancy (which, who are we kidding, is actually almost 10 months long, not 9 months). I had no idea how to answer that question. Is there really such a thing as being ready for parenthood? Before getting pregnant, everyone just assumed that I would be highly prepared for being a mother. I'm a college professor who's an expert in infancy, right? Who is more prepared than me? I can now tell you now with the utmost certainty that nothing could have prepared me for how difficult the first month of parenthood would be.

Like I said in the last chapter, I fell in love with Edwin Henry Reeb about 36 hours after he was born. At this point, I was still in the hospital and euphoric over the entire experience. Plus, we had ecstatic friends and family members coming to visit constantly, toting food and gifts as an excuse to drool over our beautiful newborn baby. It was a happy and exciting few days. I was also getting quite a bit of help from the hospital staff in terms of learning how to change diapers, swaddle the baby, and nurse. They let me keep Edwin in my room most of the time but were happy to cart him off to the nursery if I wanted some time to take a shower, eat my breakfast, or get a little bit of much needed rest. I didn't know how good I had it. As soon as Nick and I walked out of those revolving hospital doors 2 days later, it hit me that we no longer had an army of expert helpers at the press of a button. All of a sudden, I was terrified. Are they really just letting us walk out of the building with a newborn baby? Shouldn't this be illegal?

Fear followed me around for the next few weeks, which proved to be the most difficult of my life. I'm not sure what people did before Google or smartphones, but I found myself constantly typing "Is it normal for my newborn to . . . " and "When will my newborn . . . ?" into my browser. I was in a constant state of panic that I was going to drop the baby or bend him the wrong way, and every little change in his behavior immediately made me think that I was doing something wrong. But the anxiety, panic, and even a little bit of depression are just a normal part of the first few weeks of life as a new mom.

Postpartum depression affects 10% of women who give birth, and 80% more women on top of that experience the postpartum "blues." *Postpartum depression* is serious depression after childbirth that is long-lasting and often requires treatment, while women who have the *postpartum blues* experience a milder version of the common depression symptoms—tiredness, worry, and sadness—that typically only last a few weeks. I wouldn't say that I've been experiencing serious depression that requires treatment, but I certainly fall into the 80% of women who get the "blues." I'm constantly worried about doing something wrong, and I feel like I'm on the verge of tears at all times, sometimes for no reason at all. Given that the postpartum blues are so common, knowing that my condition is experienced by *most* women after giving birth, doesn't make it any less difficult. I also didn't expect to feel this way after giving birth, making it even harder to cope with.

I used to think that the postpartum "blues" involved mostly feeling sad that you weren't pregnant anymore. For me, that was only half true. Part of it certainly involves not being pregnant anymore. But, really, the problem is that when I was pregnant, I was surrounded by people who wanted to help me. People constantly asked me if I needed anything. They asked if I was hungry or thirsty. They told me to lie down and take a nap if I was tired. When I was pregnant, people doted on me. They commented on how beautiful I looked (even though I essentially looked like a dilapidated house). They said I was "glowing." They wanted to buy me lunch. Throw me a shower. Feel my belly.

This lasted, of course, until I had the baby. That's when, all of sudden, all of those people just disappeared. Many of them did come to visit a few weeks after the baby was born. For a little while, I had a constant flow of people in and out of the house. Then, they were gone, and what I was left with was only the sound of a crying newborn. There was no one here to ask me if I needed anything. There was no one here to notice that I haven't showered in days and that I desperately needed that nap they offered me months ago. For the first time, the answer to that important question my friends and family used to ask me all the time—*do you need any help?*—was a resounding *yes*, but no one seemed to be there to ask.

For me, being alone has played a big role in the postpartum blues. And it doesn't seem like my experience is all that uncommon. Studies have shown that the amount of social support you have—or the number of people you have in your life that you can turn to for help—is related to whether you will experience symptoms of the postpartum blues (O'hara & Swain, 1996). You are also less likely to experience depression-like symptoms after giving birth if you have a strong marriage or a strong and supportive partner than if you're alone. This is especially true for first-time mothers like me, who are experiencing the difficulties of motherhood for the very first time (Leahy-Warren, McCarthy, & Corcoran, 2012). Furthermore, according to a recent survey of women who gave birth in a New York City hospital, most new mothers think that support from others is absolutely essential after giving birth, and, in fact, these mothers often *expected* to get help without necessarily having to ask for it (Negron, Martin, Almog, Balbierz, & Howell, 2013). These expectations might make being alone even harder to swallow.

The old saying about raising children is that "it takes a village." Unfortunately, most of us don't get one. The American model is for the mother (and not necessarily the father) to take some predetermined amount of maternity leave (alone) and then to decide to either remain home or return to work. Experiencing the postpartum blues myself for the very first time has made me think about whether being alone— even for just a few weeks or months—might make the work of parenting especially difficult on new moms. I'm not the first person to come to this conclusion. Systems of *alloparenting*—situations where people in addition to the child's biological parents share in the parenting responsibilities—do exist in some cultures (Hrdy, 2011). In fact, some researchers and primatologists have suggested that alloparenting is actually the optimal situation for child-rearing, where children are literally raised by a village or at least a large network of caregivers who provide children (and most importantly, mothers) with care and support. Unfortunately, most new moms in the Western world don't experience this kind of parenting situation and face first-time motherhood as a village of one.

On top of being alone, the other half of postpartum blues (at least for me) comes from the fear that you've completely lost the normal part of your life and might never recover it again. In the first few weeks after having Edwin, all I did was nurse him and then try to sleep. I didn't have time for much else—even showering and having a quick meal felt like a challenge. Very quickly, I realized that I'm now handcuffed to this tiny human who depends on me for absolutely everything, and the weight of this responsibility can be utterly overwhelming. Like many women, when I gave birth, I was under the cruel misconception that I would be able to fit this new baby into my life. Turns out that it doesn't work that way, and my life has to change significantly to accommodate the fact that I now have a newborn baby.

For example, a newborn's daily routine (or lack thereof) doesn't exactly fit with mine. Like I said earlier, newborns need a lot of sleep (see Chapter 5). In fact, they spend upwards of two-thirds of the day sleeping. Because of this well-known fact, before I became a mother myself, I thought that new parents must have quite a bit of time on their hands. This certainly has not been my experience so far. Edwin does sleep a lot, but only in blocks of a few hours at a time, and he has absolutely no regard for whether those hours are in the daytime or in the middle of the night. This means that, despite the fact that *he* is getting a lot of sleep, *I* on the other hand, am not. I only get to sleep for about 2–3 hours at a time, which only makes the postpartum blues more difficult (Figure 11.1).

Edwin does spend a small portion of the day awake, but most of that waking time is spent nursing. Nowadays, everyone seems to push new mothers to nurse—doctors, nurses, friends, neighbors, and even celebrities use phrases like "breast is best" to advocate for breastfeeding. The American Academy of Pediatrics' (AAP) recommendation on breastfeeding is that babies should be fed exclusively with breast milk for the first 6 months, and they should continue to be breastfed after the introduction of solid foods for at least until the end of the first year.

Why all the hype? From a scientist's perspective, breastmilk is essentially the perfect food; it is tailor-made for your baby and changes constantly in order to accommodate his growing size and needs. It can sustain a child all on its own for the first 6 months of life (which is why the AAP recommends sticking with it for that long), *and* it even tastes good. Have you ever smelled baby formula? It tastes and smells like nasty chemicals, which is essentially why breastfed babies will often reject it when moms try to make the switch. Food scientists just can't figure out how to inject all of the nutritional value of breastmilk into a baby formula *and* make it taste good. On top of all that, breastmilk

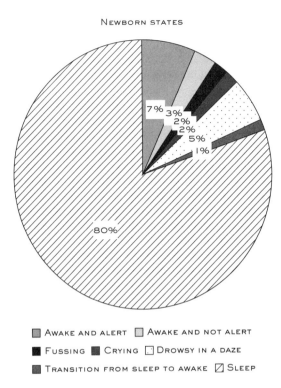

NEWBORN STATES

7% 3%
2%
2%
5%
1%

80%

■ AWAKE AND ALERT □ AWAKE AND NOT ALERT
■ FUSSING ■ CRYING ⬚ DROWSY IN A DAZE
■ TRANSITION FROM SLEEP TO AWAKE ▨ SLEEP

Figure 11.1 | Newborn states. Newborns spend most of their time sleeping or drowsy. They spend the rest of their time awake, either alert or fussing/crying. This varies from baby to baby and changes each month as newborns get older.
Source: Data based on Thoman (1990), chart created by Vanessa LoBue.

is natural, clean, and cheaper than expensive baby formulas. It is also supposed to help babies build immunities, keep them from getting sick, and aid in your recovery from the birth. Hell, I heard that breastfeeding can even help you lose that pesky baby weight since it involves your child literally sucking calories from your body to nourish his own.

For all of these reasons, I decided to breastfeed Edwin. And why wouldn't I? Based on everything I read, everything I've been told, breast certainly seems best. I was told that nursing your child is the most natural thing in the world, and, because of that, I expected it to be easy. It isn't. For me, it's not easy at all, it doesn't feel natural, and it hurts a lot. Every time Edwin latches, it feels like I'm taking knives to my breasts. My nipples are sore and even bled a few times. I can't be separated from Edwin for more than a few of hours; otherwise, my breasts begin to hurt and eventually become engorged. No one else can feed him but me. So it's me waking up every 2 hours all night. It's me that has to stay home from work. I feel like all I do is nurse, that I have little control left over my body, that I will never get a good night's sleep again, and that I will never, ever have my life back.

Because I heard so many positive things about nursing, I was really surprised when I found out how hard it is. In fact, I figured maybe there was something wrong with *me*. Maybe I'm doing it wrong. Maybe my body is defective. If this is so natural, and all women do it, why am *I* having so much trouble? After looking into it a bit more, it turns out that my experience isn't unique. In fact, most women seem to have trouble at first. In a recent study done at the University of California in Davis, researchers asked a large group of new mothers to report on their first 2 months of nursing. They found that *most* women had issues—92% of them—including problems with latching, pain, and anxiety about producing enough milk to feed their newborns (Wagner, Chantry, Dewey, & Nommsen-Rivers, 2013).

I understand wanting to encourage moms to nurse, and perhaps medical practitioners feel that if moms were told directly about how hard it will be, many of them won't bother trying. But it certainly seems that not warning us about how hard it could be might do more harm than good. In fact, the more problems mothers have, the more likely they are to give up on nursing entirely, and most women (about 87% according to one study) give up before reaching the 6-month milestone that the AAP recommends (Wagner et al., 2013). In another study where researchers interviewed women about their experiences breastfeeding, most reported that pushing an unrealistic goal (like nursing exclusively for 6 months) was unhelpful and even undermined their confidence.

The authors of that study concluded that perhaps recommendations on breastfeeding should be modified to consider the individual needs of families instead of pushing moms to strive for standards that they may fail to reach (Hoddinott, Craig, Britten, & McInnes, 2012).

And besides research suggesting that nursing is difficult and stressful for mothers, the research on the benefits of breastmilk aren't as clear-cut as the hype makes them out to be. There is evidence that breastfeeding exclusively for 6 months does help babies fight off sickness, and it is indeed associated with faster recovery time and reduced risk for various types of cancers for the mother (Gartner et al., 2005), and it may even help reduce a mother's risk for heart disease and stroke (Peters et al., 2017). But it's important to point out that all of these studies are correlational; that means we don't know for sure if breastfeeding itself keeps babies and mothers healthy, or instead whether mothers who choose to breastfeed are also more likely to make other healthy lifestyle choices that are actually causing all of the health benefits associated with breastfeeding. It's hard to know for sure.

The bottom line is that breastmilk is likely better for babies than formula, but not in such dramatic ways that moms should beat themselves up if they can't or decide not to do it. Babies raised on formula thrive just like breastfed babies do. But perhaps moving forward, we should be a bit more honest about the difficulties associated with breastfeeding so that it's not so shocking if and when it doesn't come easy for some mothers. If mothers are more prepared for it to be a challenge, we might be less likely to quit if things get hard. Given that it is natural, and it likely will provide several health benefits for both me and my baby, for now, I decided to stick with it, bleeding nipples and all. But again, it's been difficult.

To make matters more difficult, when Edwin isn't asleep or nursing, he spends a lot of his awake-time fussing or crying. Lack of sleep is bad; sore and bleeding nipples is worse; but neither of these are anything compared to enduring the sound of a crying newborn. For a few weeks, it was pretty easy to figure out the problem whenever

Edwin was crying—it was either hunger or gas, which usually came as a pair. He nursed a lot, which meant he burped and pooped a lot (pretty much after every feeding). Although it meant that we had to change his diaper ridiculously often (~10 times a day), it was also a positive indication that breastfeeding was effective. Since you can't see how much milk the baby is drinking when you breastfeed, the only way to know that you're doing it right is if the baby poops and pees regularly and if he gains weight. Edwin didn't have a problem with either. In fact, he had gained almost a pound since birth when we weighed him a week later at the pediatrician's office. Crying was always soothed by either feeding him, by giving him a good burp, or by the sound of rumbling in his diaper. The crying was tough to take, but there was always an easy and logical fix.

By the last week of the first month, this all changed. All of a sudden, Edwin started crying a lot more, and, for the first time, we were unable to find the source of his misery. When I say a lot more, I don't mean for an hour or two at a time; there were nights when he cried for over 3 hours straight. We tried everything—rocking, bouncing, walking, talking, singing—but nothing seemed to work. I know I got lucky with a good pregnancy and birth, but I feel like I'm making up for it now. Inconsolable crying for more than 3 hours a day, for more than 3 days a week, for a period of 3 weeks or more in an otherwise healthy baby is called *colic*. About a quarter of babies have colic, and, unfortunately, we suddenly found ourselves in that unlucky 25%. Listening to my newborn baby scream for 3 hours straight is about the most distressing thing I've ever experienced. I have broken down and cried myself on various occasions when I couldn't console him.

It's important to note that colic refers to the behavior (i.e., long periods of crying), not the condition. Babies cry for a lot of different reasons, and researchers think that some sort of digestive issue like acid reflux or gas usually causes colic. Edwin definitely appeared as if he was in some kind of pain during these crying spells—he arched his back and tensed his muscles and grimaced as he spat up after eating.

Our pediatrician prescribed baby Zantac in case it was reflux (which is very common in newborns due to their underdeveloped digestive system), and she put me on a strict non-dairy diet in case he was having an allergic reaction to cow's milk (which is often what causes reflux in newborns). So, on top of the postpartum "blues," bleeding nipples, and having to listen to my sweet baby cry for hours on end, I was suddenly no longer allowed to eat my feelings—at least not with ice cream, chocolate, cheese, or anything actually worth eating. At least the baby weight is going fast.

Although colic is completely normal and crying itself won't hurt your baby (see Chapter 5), it is incredibly distressing and can have negative consequences for the colicky baby's *parents*. I'm sure we've all had the experience of being forced to listen to a crying baby at a restaurant or on a plane for some period of time. Imagine listening to *your own* baby cry for more than 3 hours straight. It can be very difficult for any parent to take. In fact, babies with colic are more likely to experience physical abuse from their parents, as in cases of *shaken baby syndrome* (SBS), which is head or brain injury caused to an infant from excessive shaking. Researchers have found that the incidence of SBS is related to how much babies cry, suggesting that crying or excessive fussiness itself might cause parents to shake their babies, likely out of frustration or stress (Barr, Trent, & Cross, 2006). Excessive crying is also related to the incidence of postpartum depression in mothers (Akman et al., 2006), so the crying isn't exactly helping me shake those postpartum blues. The point is that sometimes the best treatment for colic is for the *parent* and not necessarily for the baby. For me, sometimes it helps to remind myself that crying itself won't hurt Edwin or to put Edwin in his crib for a few minutes so that I can walk away and clear my head.

So it's been a hard month—wonderful and exciting, but the most difficult month of my life. Maybe I just have thin skin, but I'm going to venture to guess that I'm not alone in this. The big question is, what should we do if we get the postpartum blues, if we have trouble nursing, or we have a baby with colic? As I already mentioned, having a support system helps decrease the risk of postpartum depression, so one thing that new moms can do is look for local parenting groups or even schedule visitors for the first few weeks post-birth to help alleviate the stress. Lots of people love babies, so when they offer to come over, to bring you food, to hold the baby for a few minutes, say *yes*, and don't be shy to embrace any offers for help that come your way. We should also all be aware of the symptoms of serious postpartum depression in case professional help is needed in order to get better. Almost all of us experience some symptoms of depression after giving birth; that means that *none of us* is really alone, and if we look for it, help might not be so hard to find.

And finding help is important. I mentioned in an earlier chapter that anxiety and depression during pregnancy can have negative effects on the fetus (see Chapter 3). Not surprisingly, anxiety and depression *after the baby* is born isn't so great for the newborn either. Infants of mothers who suffer from postpartum depression are more likely to have behavioral problems and form insecure attachments to their mothers compared to infants of non-depressed moms (Murray, 1992), and postpartum depression may have small but real effects on children's cognitive development and IQ (Grace, Evindar, & Stewart, 2003). How could this be, you might ask? There's evidence that depressed mothers spend less time looking at their babies, talking to their babies, and touching their babies when compared to non-depressed mothers (Field, 1995), and they may be less responsive to their babies' facial and vocal signals (Field, Diego, & Hernandez-Reif, 2009). Furthermore, very recent research suggests that a mother experiencing stress can project that stress physiologically onto the baby that she is holding. In other words, stress can be "contagious," and mothers who are tense because of anxiety can project some of their muscle tension onto their babies just by holding them (Waters, West, Karnilowicz, & Mendes, 2017).

Similarly, if you're having trouble breastfeeding, you shouldn't necessarily just give up; again, breast milk is an amazing substance that likely carries several advantages for both you and your baby. But getting support from others for nursing can be helpful. In a recent article by National Public Radio, staff writers interviewed Brooke Scelza, an evolutionary anthropologist from the University of Los Angeles who studies breastfeeding behavior in mothers from various cultures, with a particular focus on a group of women in Namibia called the Himba. In the article, Scelza describes how all Himba women breastfeed—they do it in public, they do it standing up, and they even do it while they're working. What's most noteworthy is that the Himba women (who make breastfeeding look easy) report that they have a lot trouble at first, just like US mothers do. What's different about them and us is that the Himba women typically move in with their mothers in the last trimester and for several months after they give birth, receiving 24/7 help from a seasoned veteran. Other countries in Africa and Asia have similar customs, where new mothers are surrounded by other women—most of whom are also mothers—around the clock for months at a time. These other women not only help care for the baby, but they also share wisdom and support about breastfeeding, helping new mothers get through this new and difficult time (Doucleff, 2017).

This is exactly what helped me get through the first month: Support from my husband and family, as well as constant reaching out and talking to friends who also have children. These friends know exactly what you are going through, and it's these friends (who may not necessarily be your closest friends) who will constantly check in, offer to bring groceries or dinner, and ask how you're doing. They're the ones who can give you tips about nursing and potential strategies to stop your baby from crying. Remember that little club I said I wasn't sure I wanted to be a part of? I understand what being a member of this club means now; I understand why the club is so important and why women go to birthing classes to meet other expecting mothers. These women know *exactly* what you're going through, how difficult it is, how emotional you are, how many questions you have, and they know that you need constant support and encouragement. Most importantly, they know that you need to hear those magic words: "It will get easier." These friends will say it to you, guaranteed. It's not that your childless friends disappear; they want to be there for you, too. But women who are in "the club" know that the weeks following birth are the most difficult of your life, and they will be the ones that will help you get through it. There is an important lesson to be learned here: Don't mock the club, and take all the help that's offered to you. If no one offers, don't be afraid to ask—get help wherever you can find it.

Besides a little help from my friends, the other thing that helped me get through this month was the occasional instances of positive

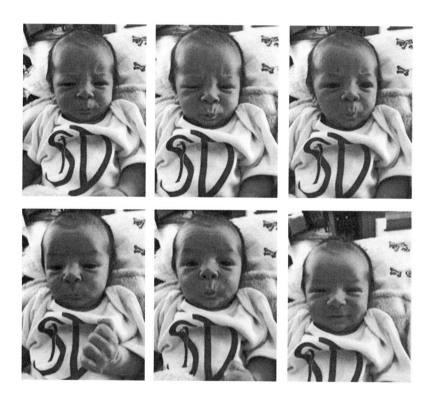

Figure 11.2 | Edwin grapples with one of his daily poops.
Source: Vanessa LoBue.

reinforcement I got from seeing Edwin smile for the first time. He isn't smiling at *me* just yet—he mostly smiles after he farts or poops or in his sleep—but just seeing that toothless grin gives me enough positive energy to endure the next bout of seemingly endless crying. He likely won't smile directly at me until sometime next month, but, for now, it's enough to get me through (Figure 11.2).

12

THE SECOND MONTH

Infant Perception and Touch

As we enter the second month, life with a baby is starting to feel a bit more normal. Breastfeeding has gotten easier compared to the first few weeks, and there is no more bleeding or nipple pain. My breasts still get hard and painful when it's time for feeding, but I've learned how to use it to figure out when to nurse. Despite being easier in the second month, breastfeeding is still by no means easy. There are some days when my breasts get so full that they either spray Edwin in the face when he tries to latch or the milk comes out too fast and he chokes and fusses until it slows down. There are other days when he wants to nurse really often and fusses when the milk doesn't come out fast enough. This month I've learned to identify my *letdown reflex*—the process by which the body releases oxytocin, stimulating the breasts to release milk. It feels kind of like pins and needles. When I haven't fed Edwin in awhile, it happens pretty much right when he latches, and he gets milk immediately. But, if he's eaten recently and wants to eat again, sometimes it takes several minutes to happen, which can be frustrating for both him and for me. The letdown reflex is usually triggered when the baby begins to suckle at the breast. It can also be triggered by hearing your baby cry, seeing his picture, or even just by thinking of him. Normally, this is quite useful, but it can also be embarrassing if it happens in public and you end up with big wet spots on your shirt. I would advise traveling with breast pads (which are like maxi pads for your boobs) if you are nursing and plan to go out in public for a long period of time.

Unfortunately, the crying has not let up. There are still days where Edwin cries for hours and hours, and there is absolutely nothing we can do to get him to stop. It's heart-wrenching, and sometimes I reach my tipping point and start crying myself out of frustration and lack of sleep. Most days, it starts to happen after 5 PM. Some people call this "the witching hour," or the time at the end of the day when your baby cries from the accumulation of daily stimulation. It's like coming home from work and being tired, except that, if you're a baby, "work" is made up of trying to hold your head up and nursing every 2–3 hours. Every day, I dread the coming of the witching hour, and knowing that it's coming doesn't make it easier to get through. The glimmer of good news is that Nick and I have figured out several ways of soothing Edwin so he (sometimes) stops crying, at least for brief periods of time. We've learned how he likes to be rocked, held, and walked around, and what his favorite places are in the house, which can all help to calm him when he's upset.

One really important technique we've been using is *swaddling*, or wrapping a baby very tightly so that he can only move his head. Swaddling has a long cross-cultural history of soothing crying babies and helping them sleep. Descriptions of swaddling in human history go back to biblical accounts of the baby Jesus being swaddled in linens, and it continues to be a long-standing tradition in several parts of Africa and the Middle East. In the past few decades, swaddling has gained popularity in the United States and Europe as well because of research suggesting that swaddled babies sleep longer and cry less than babies who aren't swaddled (van Sleuwen et al., 2007). Although not all of the research indicates *why* swaddling has calming properties, now that I've seen it in action, there are several reasons it's been so effective for us.

First, Edwin loves to be held, so presumably being swaddled tightly makes him feel the same kind of pressure that he feels when he is in my arms or when he was in the womb (see Chapter 7). Most importantly, Edwin, like most newborns, has very little control over his arms and has an easily activated *startle* reflex (which we talked about in Chapter 6). This is problematic when he's sleeping—his own movements startle and wake him up, and sometimes he stretches his arms up in his sleep and lets his clenched fists fall right on his face (effectively punching himself in the nose). When he's swaddled, none of this happens, and he stays asleep for much longer periods of time. Unfortunately, swaddled babies who are lying on their stomachs (as opposed to their backs) are at increased risk for sudden infant death syndrome (SIDS), so doctors recommend that you stop swaddling once they can turn over on their own. We're not there yet (thank goodness) (Figure 12.1).

Another effective method for soothing long bouts of crying has been carrying. Like swaddling, in many African countries, carrying babies all day long is a cultural tradition and often a necessity. Babies are tightly wrapped and strapped to their mothers' (or fathers') backs so that the parents can work. Based on anecdotes about how these African babies could go all day without crying, several researchers in the mid 1980s became interested in looking into the effects of daily carrying on infant crying. In one study, researchers from McGill University asked a group of mothers to carry their infants for 3 hours a day, either in their arms or in an infant carrier, and they asked a second (control) group of mothers to place their babies in front of a mobile for 3 hours a day instead. Infants who were carried cried substantially less than infants who were placed in front of the mobile (Hunziker & Barr, 1986). Importantly, these babies weren't carried *in response* to crying; they were simply carried at random points throughout the day,

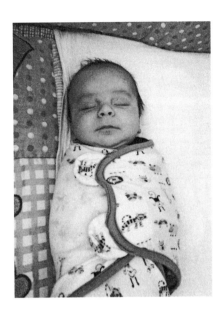

Figure 12.1 | Edwin tightly swaddled and asleep.
Source: Vanessa LoBue.

so carrying infants in general seems to help keep them calm. Edwin responds really well to being carried, especially in an infant carrier or a wrap; it keeps him from getting fussy and it often stops him from crying. The conventional wisdom on carrying (and the advice that the older members of my family keep giving me, unsolicited) seems to be that by carrying infants too much, we "spoil" them. In other words, they get used to being carried all the time and will eventually cry any time you put them down. There is absolutely no evidence that this is the case, and most of the data on carrying suggest that carrying leads to a calm and happy baby. In fact, a very recent study by Darcia Narvaez at the University of Notre Dame found that adults who were held and cuddled as babies were the most likely to be healthy and well-adjusted as adults. In fact, the more they were carried, the better they functioned (Narvaez, Wang, & Cheng, 2016).

One reason carrying might be so effective in reducing crying is that touch has been shown to have a variety of benefits for babies (and moms). Recently, researchers, along with doctors and nurses, have begun to emphasize the importance of skin-to-skin contact between a mother and her newborn. Most doctors try (if possible) to place newborns directly on their mothers' bare chests after they are born. In fact, Edwin was placed on my chest before my doctor was able to deliver my placenta (which is why I missed it!). Skin-to-skin is especially important for premature babies who usually have to spend some amount of time in an incubator before they are held regularly. A classic study by Tiffany Field from the University of Miami School of Medicine reported that premature babies who were given massage therapy while in their incubators gained more weight and were released from the hospital sooner than premature babies who were not given massage therapy (Field et al., 1986). A more recent study reported similar results: Premature babies who received 2 weeks of skin-to-skin contact with their mothers had better stress responses, sleep patterns, and even some better cognitive abilities after the 2-week intervention than premature babies who remained in incubators (Feldman, Rosenthal, & Eidelman, 2014).

Importantly, skin-to-skin isn't just useful for premature babies; in all babies, skin-to-skin contact has been associated with better sleep (Feldman, Rosenthal, & Eidelman, 2014), reduced crying (Ludington-Hoe & Hosseini, 2005; Michelsson, Christensson, Rothgänger, & Winberg, 1996), reduced stress responses (Feldman, Singer, & Zagoory, 2010), and better establishment of a regular breastfeeding routine (Widström et al., 2011). In fact, research has shown that for adults, the simple act of holding hands with a loved one can reduce your stress response (Coan, Schaefer, & Davidson, 2006; more on this later). So, the moral of the story is, a little bit of physical contact can go a long way in reducing crying or stress, even for moms.

Despite the continued bouts of crying, Edwin is much more engaged with his surroundings than he was last month, which is an interesting and fun change. He spends more time awake and alert and is constantly looking around with interest. At first, newborns don't see as well as adults do, but their vision improves dramatically over the first few months of life. This is clear in the second month; Edwin looks directly at objects now, especially lights and fans. He can also track objects as they move, which wasn't something he did in the first month. For example, last month, he wouldn't look at a rattle unless I just happened to place it directly in his line of sight. Now he turns his head toward the sound of a rattle shaking and can follow it with his eyes by turning if it moves out of his field of view (Figure 12.2).

He is also much more interested in people and faces than he was last month. He smiles socially now—in response to people—instead of just in his sleep or after a good poop. He also smiles in response to *my* face in particular. Decades of research has suggested that faces are a really special kind of stimulus for newborns, and, shortly after birth, infants look at faces more than they look at other objects (Johnson & Morton, 1991). In the late 1970s, researchers Daphne Maurer and Philip Salapatek from McMaster University and the University of Minnesota were interested in studying the features of faces that are most attractive to newborns. They recorded eye movements of 1- and 2-month-old infants while they looked at their mother's and at a stranger's face. They found that 1-month-olds looked away from the faces most of the time, and, when they were looking at the faces, they mostly scanned the faces' outer edges (e.g., the hairline) where there is the most contrast in color. The 2-month-olds were much more interested in faces and spent more time looking at them than away from them, especially at their mothers' faces. Furthermore, they spent most of their time looking at the faces' inner features, particularly at the eyes (Maurer & Salapatek, 1976).

A very recent study suggests that humans' attraction to faces develops even earlier than we once thought, perhaps even in the womb. A group of researchers from the United Kingdom used a very clever technique where they projected lights to unborn fetuses

NEWBORN 4 WEEKS 8 WEEKS

3 MONTHS 6 MONTHS ADULT

Figure 12.2 | A photo of Edwin at 2 months, modified to demonstrate an infant's visual acuity (from 24 inches) at birth, 4 weeks, 8 weeks, 3 months, and 6 months, compared to an adult.

Source: Image (by Vanessa LoBue) was modified using Tiny Eyes software (www.tinyeyes.com).

from outside the mother's belly. Remember how I mentioned that, in the third trimester, fetuses can see and will react when you shine a flashlight right into the mother's abdomen? Using this as a basis for their study, the researchers shined different light configurations into expecting mothers' bellies and measured whether their fetuses turned to look at the lights. The researchers found that the fetuses more often turned to look at top-heavy, more face-like configurations, than similar configurations that had more "stuff" on the bottom (Reid et al.,

2017). This suggests that a basic preference for face-like shapes might be something biologically based, and such a preference becomes more specific after birth when newborns gain experience with specific faces (Figure 12.3).

Edwin's preference for my face is certainly evident for the first time this month; he smiles more at me than at other people, and he turns his head to look for my face when he hears the sound of my voice. In the months that follow, faces will likely become his favorite thing to look at, and he will become better and better at identifying the faces of the people most familiar to him. Shortly after birth, newborns quickly learn to differentiate between their mother's face and a stranger's face (Bushneil, Sai, & Mullin, 1989). Newborns also develop the ability to discriminate between various emotional expressions, including happy, sad, and surprised faces, only a few days after birth (Field, Woodson, Greenburg, & Cohen, 1982). By 5 months of age, they can even match

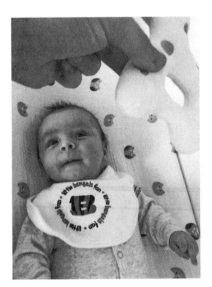

Figure 12.3 | *Left*: Visually tracking a toy. *Right*: Social smile.
Source: Vanessa LoBue.

a photograph of an emotional facial expression (e.g., happy face) with a voice that matches (i.e., happy voice) (Walker-Andrews, 1997).

There is great value in infants' rapidly developing ability to identify different faces and facial expressions given that social interactions are such an important part of our lives. This is especially true from the perspective of a new mother—there's nothing like seeing your baby smile knowingly every time he locks eyes with you. But becoming a face expert so early in life also comes with some unfortunate consequences. For example, infants begin to prefer looking at attractive faces over less attractive faces shortly after birth (Slater et al., 1998). And by the time they turn 1, babies even treat attractive people differently than unattractive people. In a very clever study on this topic, Judith Langlois and colleagues at the University of Texas dressed up a female researcher in a professionally constructed mask and had the researcher play with a group of 12-month-old infants for a short period of time. The researcher either wore an attractive or unattractive mask but wasn't aware of what kind of mask she wore so that the knowledge of how she looked wouldn't bias her behavior. The infants smiled and played more with the researcher when she wore the attractive mask than when she wore the unattractive mask, suggesting that, by the ripe old age of 1, infants are already treating people differently based on how attractive their faces are (Langlois, Roggman, & Rieser-Danner, 1990).

What's even more worrisome is that infants develop a preference for the faces of their own race by 3 months of age (Kelly et al., 2005), and they begin to have trouble distinguishing between two faces of a different race by 9 months of age (Kelly et al., 2007). This phenomenon develops over the course of the first year of life: Up until about 6 months, infants are really good at distinguishing between two faces of any race and even between two faces of another species. For example, if you were to show a 6-month-old and an adult two photographs of faces and asked them to decide whether the photographs were of the same person or of two different people, both the 6-month-old and the adult would be equally good at the task. In contrast, if you show the

6-month-old and the adult pairs of faces of another race, or even faces of other animals (e.g., chimpanzees), only the 6-month-old would get more than half of them correct. It turns out that infants younger than 6 months of age are really good at distinguishing between two faces of any race or species, but adults are only accurate at identifying pictures of their own race and species (Figure 12.4). Unfortunately, by the time these 6-month-olds become 9-month-olds, their ability to distinguish between the faces of any race and species will decline and they will perform just as poorly the adults (Kelly et al., 2007; Pascalis, de Haan, & Nelson, 2002).

This phenomenon is called *perceptual narrowing*. It means that when we are born, our brains are flexible enough to distinguish between a variety of faces, regardless of race or even species; but, as we gain more experience with the faces we see most often, we get better at distinguishing those faces from others, and we lose the ability to distinguish between faces that don't look like the ones we're used to seeing. This sounds bad, but research has shown that if we expose babies to faces of other races regularly, the perceptual narrowing effect disappears. For example, if a child lives in an environment where he is exposed to people of other races, he keeps the ability to distinguish between their faces (Bar-Haim, Ziv, Lamy, & Hodes, 2006). Similarly, if you give babies brief daily exposure to photographs of people of other races, they also keep the ability to distinguish between them. Furthermore, the effect of perceptual narrowing can even be *reversed* if you expose babies to photographs of other-race faces after the 6-month mark (Anzures et al., 2012). The point of all of this is that babies become fast experts at identifying the kinds of faces they see most often, and this expertise or familiarity with certain kinds of faces is what causes face preferences to develop so early. What makes my face so special to Edwin is that it's the one he sees the most every day. But it's times like these that I'm glad we live in a place like New York, where no two faces are ever alike.

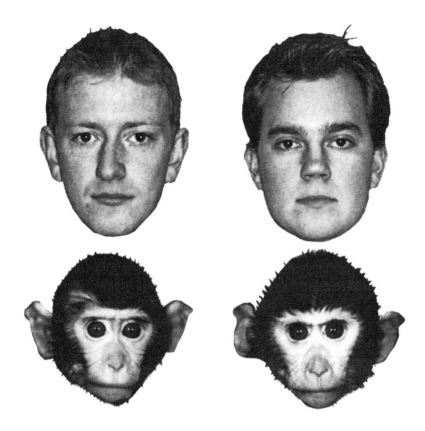

Figure 12.4 | Photos from Pascalis, de Haan, and Nelson (2002). Although it might be easy for you to tell that the photos on the top are of two different men, it is much harder to tell whether the monkey faces on the bottom are of the same or two different monkeys. A 6-month-old baby, in contrast, would have no problem seeing that they are two different monkeys.

Source: Pascalis, O., de Haan, M., & Nelson, C. A. (2002). Is face processing species-specific during the first year of life? *Science, 296*(5571), 1321–1323. Reprinted with permission of AAAS.

Because recognizing various faces and facial expressions is so important for human social interactions, problems with face processing early on in development can be a sign of issues that lie ahead. For example, children and adults with autism spectrum disorder (ASD), who often have problems with social interactions and communication, also show difficulties processing facial expressions at an early age. Recently, researchers from Yale University School of Medicine have found that these problems might even begin in the first year of life. Experimenters showed 6-month-old infants who were genetically at risk for developing ASD (by having an older sibling with an autism diagnosis) different kinds of social scenes, featuring both toys and people. They found that infants who were later diagnosed with ASD looked less at social scenes, particularly at people's faces, when compared to 6-month-olds who didn't later receive an autism diagnosis (Chawarska, Macari, & Shic, 2013). Further research suggests that it's not necessarily that eye contact makes children with autism uncomfortable, but instead, infants who later develop autism might just not be all that interested in social information (Moriuchi, Klin, & Jones, 2016). Altogether, this research suggests that disengagement or disinterest in faces during the first year of life—the time when infants are first becoming experts at face recognition—might predict the development of autism later on in childhood.

Although researchers don't quite know what causes autism, there is strong evidence that it is biologically based. In fact, a group of researchers from Great Britain recently found that ASD is mostly linked to genetics (Colvert et al., 2015). They studied groups of identical twins (who have the same genes) and fraternal twins (who have only some of the same genes) to find out what the likelihood is that if one twin was diagnosed with autism that the second one would be, too. The concordance rate (i.e., the likelihood that both twins have the illness) gives us some insight into the role that genes play in the development of ASD. The researchers found that genetic factors accounted for up to 95% of the incidence of autism in their twin-based population.

Although almost nothing is caused by either genes or the environment alone (not even gender, as we learned in Chapter 4), this study suggests that, in the case of autism, the environment plays only a very small role in who develops it.

To add to the evidence that autism has a biological basis, researchers have also shown that patterns of looking—or not looking—at faces early in infancy vary based on genetic closeness. In a study where researchers showed similar social scenes to more than 300 toddlers with and without an autism diagnosis, identical twins looked at the same places in the scene *91% of the time*; fraternal twins only looked at the same places 31% of the time, and toddlers who weren't related to each other rarely looked in the same place at the same time. These numbers only held for attention to the parts of the face—like the eyes and the mouth—that are most associated with autism, and toddlers with autism in their sample looked less overall at the eyes and the mouth than did toddlers without an autism diagnosis. This study confirms that infants and toddlers with autism show decreased attention to faces in the first few years of life and that these differences in looking might be biologically based (Constantino et al., 2017).

Despite mounting evidence that autism is likely inherited, many parents are still nervous about the risk of autism when it comes to vaccinating. Edwin's first big doctor's visit was this month, along with his first round of vaccinations, starting with two rounds of hepatitis B. Yes, we have chosen to vaccinate. Vaccinating wasn't something that people considered a choice until a few years ago, after British medical researcher Andrew Wakefield and his colleagues published a paper reporting a link between vaccinations (specifically the measles, mumps, and rubella or MMR vaccine) and autism (Wakefield et al., 1998). Wakefield was later accused of making up his data, his paper was retracted, and he lost his job and medical license. But the damage was already done. Vaccination rates in the United States and other countries started to drop, and the incidence of measles and other previously eradicated diseases like whooping cough soared. Since publication of the 1998 paper, countless large-scale follow-up studies have all failed to find a link between vaccinations and ASD (Maglione et al., 2014; Taylor, Swerdfeger, & Eslick, 2014). However, since symptoms for ASD often develop around the same time that infants typically start getting vaccinations, you still hear stories about people claiming that their child got autism from a vaccine, where it was most likely just an unfortunate coincidence. *There is absolutely no evidence that vaccinations of any kind cause autism.* There is, however, very clear evidence that *not* vaccinating makes your infant susceptible to a wide variety of dangerous but completely preventable diseases, including measles, mumps, whooping cough, and chicken pox.

Now that I have a son of my own, I understand why Wakefield's study scared so many people into skipping their monthly vaccines. Everyone wants to do the best they can to protect their children from getting sick, and evidence that vaccinations might come with potentially dangerous side effects can rattle any new parent. The bottom line, based on research, is that vaccinations are highly effective at preventing disease (up to 95%). They do have some potential side effects, but those side effects are relatively rare, generally mild (e.g., fever, headache, joint pain), and there's no evidence that autism is one of them. And again, there's lots of evidence that *not* getting vaccinated is incredibly risky if your child is exposed to a serious and preventable illness, which is becoming an all too immediate reality these days. Perhaps getting the measles or whopping cough doesn't sound that bad, but what happens if the next big outbreak is polio?

13

THE THIRD MONTH

Developing Motor Skills

The third month brought with it some new surprises and some potential difficulties. When we went for our regular doctor's visit, we learned that, despite the many issues I've been having with breastfeeding, Edwin is apparently getting plenty to eat. He now weighs in at over 13 pounds, and he's 50th percentile in weight and 81st percentile in height. His pediatrician said he looked completely healthy. The only thing she was concerned about was his head shape—apparently it is very flat in the back. She called this condition *plagiocephaly*, or flat head. She strongly recommended that we talk to a physical therapist. So, as new and overly anxious parents, we obediently went to see the one she recommended a week later. The physical therapist not only confirmed Edwin's plagiocephaly, but she also said that he had *torticollis*—which means "twisted head"—when she saw his head tilted slightly to the right while sitting in his car seat. Babies with torticollis tilt their heads to one side, typically because the muscles on the other side of the neck are stiffer due to positioning inside the womb or during sleep. The physical therapist recommended that we bring Edwin in for expensive physical therapy weekly for 6–8 weeks to fix both conditions; otherwise, she warned that his motor milestones—things like crawling and walking—might be delayed.

Edwin's head was definitely flat, so the plagiocephaly diagnosis made sense (Figure 13.1). But making a quick torticollis diagnosis without so much as examining my newborn made me a bit skeptical. After all, Edwin was only 2 months old; he barely had the muscle control to hold his head up by himself, so it wasn't all that surprising to me that when sitting in a reclined position, gravity caused his head to tilt to one side. Still, the word "delay" made me nervous enough to look into my options.

It turns out that Edwin's plagiocephaly diagnosis is not at all uncommon, and, in fact, there has been a sharp increase in the frequency of plagiocephaly diagnoses in the past few decades. After searching

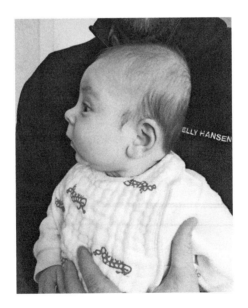

Figure 13.1 | Edwin's "flat head."
Source: Vanessa LoBue.

for statistics about how common it is for pediatricians to recommend testing for plagiocephaly, I found websites citing numbers as high as 50%, suggesting that as many as half of new moms in the United States are now being told to have their babies screened for plagiocephaly.

The rise in plagiocephaly cases in recent decades can be traced to the early 1990s, when the National Institutes of Health first started the "Back to Sleep" campaign. "Back to Sleep," now known as the "Safe to Sleep" campaign, was initiated in order to reduce the incidence of sudden infant death syndrome (SIDS) in the United States. The campaign constituted a massive push from doctors and nurses to encourage parents to put their babies to sleep on their backs (hence the name "*Back* to Sleep") instead of their stomachs. Although researchers don't know for sure, they theorized that one potential cause for SIDS— the unexplained death of an infant during sleep—is that infants have trouble rousing themselves from sleep if they're in need of oxygen. If a newborn is sleeping on his stomach, for example, he may not have the strength to turn his head if he finds himself in a position where oxygen is low. However, if he's on his back, he can easily turn his head if he needs air.

Although the exact cause of SIDS is still unknown, the "Back to Sleep" campaign was very effective, and the rate of SIDS deaths has dropped dramatically since the early 1990s, with 1 in 5,000 SIDS deaths in 1990, compared to 1 in 1,500 in 2014 (Figure 13.2). But there were some strange and unintended consequences of the campaign. Before the early 1990s, parents typically put their babies to sleep on their stomachs to avoid potential suffocation if an infant was to spit up at night (which, by the way, almost never ever happens; see Hunt, Fleming, & Golding, 1997). Once parents started putting their babies to sleep on their backs instead of their stomachs, babies' very soft heads started to look flatter, which is when plagiocephaly started becoming a common diagnosis. Furthermore, babies who spend more time on their backs (as opposed to their stomachs) spend less time pushing up and developing the upper body strength they need to roll over and

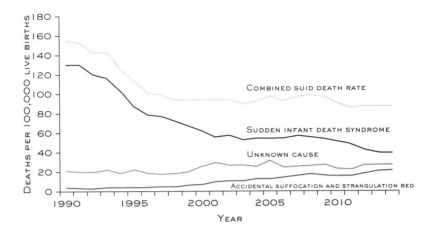

Figure 13.2 | Trends in sudden unexpected infant death by cause, 1990–2014.

Source: CDC Data and Statistics.

crawl. Thus, babies were experiencing a delay in some of their basic motor milestones simply based on their new nightly sleeping position.

On the surface, the idea of delayed motor milestones sounds kind of scary; at least it did for me. In fact, the word *delay* used in any context with regard to your baby probably sounds scary. But the real question is, how concerned should I be if Edwin is late to hit some of his motor milestones, and why is reaching them during a certain timeframe so important? The modern-day motor milestones charts we still see in doctor's offices provide information about the average age you can expect your infant to accomplish various motor feats, like sitting (around 6–7 months), crawling (around 8–9 months), and walking (around 12–13 months). These averages came from re-search by a psychologist named Arnold Gesell from the 1900s. Gesell wanted to track various aspects of infant development, so he took very precise recordings of the ages at which a sample of infants demonstrated various physical behaviors for the first time (Gesell, 1946).

The motor milestones you see on the wall at your pediatrician's office are based on Gesell's research, which is now nearly 75 years old (Figure 13.3).

Although Gesell's important work gave us insight into what we can expect of infants in the first few years of life, calling these averages developmental "milestones" leads to the assumption that all infants must go through them in a predetermined order, that each milestone is required, and that there is no skipping or reverting back to a previous milestone on the chart. It turns out that motor skills don't actually develop this way. First of all, most infants occupy multiple milestones at the same time and revert back to old ones if they are not that good at using the new ones. For example, research by Karen Adolph and colleagues at New York University suggested that babies don't spontaneously start walking one day and then only walk from that day on (Adolph, Robinson, Young, & Gill-Alvarez, 2008). Instead, they might

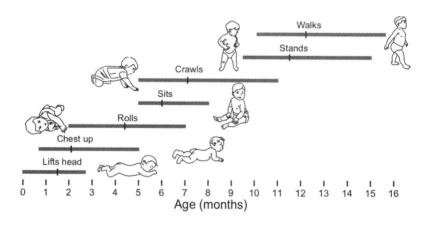

Figure 13.3 | Motor milestones chart.
Source: Adolph, K. E., Karasik, L., & Tamis-LeMonda, C. S. (2010). Motor skill. In M. Bornstein (Ed.), *Handbook of Cultural Developmental Science* (pp. 61–88). New York: Taylor & Francis. Reproduced with permission of Taylor & Francis Group, LLC.

take a few steps one day, then not walk for several days, take a few steps again, and so on. New and inexperienced walkers commonly revert back to crawling or other methods of movement while they are perfecting this new ability. This makes a lot of sense from a practical perspective: Since it takes time to become a skilled walker, novices who are still moving quite slowly might use other more efficient methods of movement if they are in a hurry, perhaps to chase an older sibling or to get their hands on a new toy.

Second, not all of the classic motor milestones are obligatory. For example, another study done more than 100 years ago reported that about 40% of infants in the United States don't crawl in the traditional way (Trettien, 1900). Some infants never crawl and skip straight to walking, while others develop nontraditional ways of crawling instead of doing it the old-fashioned way on their hands and knees. For example, some infants are "army crawlers" (who crawl with their stomachs on the ground), while others are "bum shufflers" (who simply remain seated and pull their bodies along with their hands) while others still are "bear crawlers" (who crawl on their hands and feet) (Adolph & Robinson, 2013). I've seen YouTube clips of infants "inch-worming" across the floor, and even one infant who literally rolled across a room to get from point A to point B. There's absolutely nothing wrong with these weird crawlers—they are simply figuring out the best way to use their bodies to accomplish a goal. In fact, there's nothing wrong with not crawling at all, and there is no evidence that skipping over crawling has any negative long-term effects on development. All typically developing infants eventually abandon all previous methods of locomotion when they learn how to walk.

Third, there is quite a bit of variability in when infants reach each motor milestone based on cultural and generational differences. As mentioned earlier, babies born after 1990 crawl and walk later than babies born before the "Back to Sleep" movement. Babies who are carried or swaddled all day are also likely to crawl or walk later than babies who are free to move around. In contrast, babies who are given extra opportunities to develop their motor skills might crawl or walk sooner than other babies. For example, there are parents in some African countries, India, and the Caribbean who believe that infants should be stretched and exercised daily in preparation for walking. These parents have daily routines that involve massaging and pulling their infants' limbs, helping them practice sitting positions and stepping movements, and even suspending infants from their legs and arms to stretch out their muscles.

Brian Hopkins and Tamme Westra (1988) were interested in whether these daily exercise routines might affect the development of motor milestones. They studied one group of Jamaican mothers living in Great Britain who exercised and stretched their infants every day and a second group of Jamaican mothers who either only massaged their infants or did not partake in any of the traditional exercise routines at all. After 1 month, infants of the first group of mothers had better head control than infants of the second group; after 6 months, infants in the first group were better sitters than infants in the second group (Figure 13.4).

Similarly, Lana Karasik from the College of Staten Island studied the sitting ability of 5-month-old infants in Argentina, Cameroon, Italy, Kenya, South Korea, and the United States and found a lot of variability based on cultural practices. For example, while most of the Kenyan and Cameroonian infants (who spent much of their time on the floor) could sit independently, only a few of the American infants and none of the Italian infants (who spend most of their day with their backs supported) could sit on their own (Karasik, Tamis-LeMonda, Adolph, & Bornstein, 2015). Together, this work suggests that even the most basic motor skills can develop differently based on cultural variations in infant handling. Gesell's milestones were based on a sample of infants from a very narrow demographic (white, middle-class babies from two-parent households in New Haven, Connecticut), discounting the possibility of such cultural variation (Adolph, Karasik, & Tamis-LeMonda, 2010).

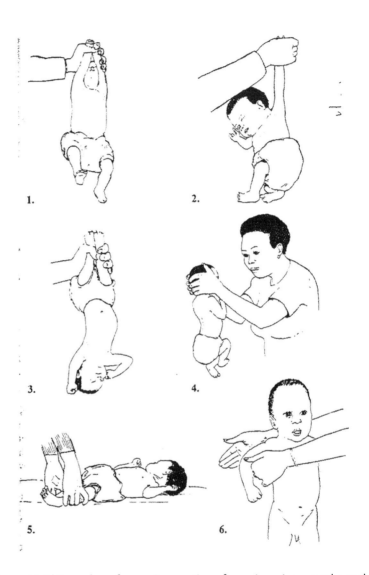

Figure 13.4 | Samples of exercise routines from Jamaican mothers that include (1) holding the baby up by his or her arms, (2) a single arm, (3) legs, and (4) head, and stretching the baby's (5) legs and (6) arms.

Source: Hopkins, B., & Westra, T. (1988). Maternal handling and motor development: An intracultural study. *Genetic, Social, and General Psychology Monographs, 114*, 377–408, reprinted by permission of the publisher Taylor & Francis Ltd.

This kind of variability isn't just specific to different cultures. Different practices within the United States can also lead to differences in the development of motor skills. A now classic study conducted at Harvard University by Philip Zelazo and colleagues showed that even very simple exercises in incredibly young babies could result in the faster development of motor milestones. In the study, a small sample 1-month-old infants were randomly assigned to either receive "active exercise," where they were placed in an upright position, allowing the infants' stepping reflex to take hold and produce a walking motion, or to receive "passive exercise," where they were placed on their backs and parents were told to simply move the infants' legs back and forth for them. Parents in both groups were told to do these exercises for 3-minute sessions, four times a day, every day for 6 weeks. After 6 weeks, infants in the "active exercise" group made more walking motions after the training and eventually walked independently before babies in the "passive exercise" group (Zelazo, Zelazo, & Kolb, 1972).

You might not even need to exercise your baby yourself to change the timing of his or her motor milestones. The simple act of putting them in a walker might affect how soon they walk or crawl and might even affect their developing spatial skills. Although many pediatricians warn against using walkers for safety reasons (e.g., they can be dangerous if infants fall down stairs in such a device), walkers that are used properly and safely might give infants who can't yet walk on their own the experience of using their legs to navigate a room independently. In fact, research has shown that babies who use walkers might begin to understand depth information sooner than babies who lack walker experience (Campos, Bertenthal, & Kermoian, 1992). But, interestingly, infants who use walkers have been found to sit, crawl, and walk independently *after* babies who don't have walker experience, possibly because walkers limit a baby's ability to see and navigate their limbs as they are moving around (Siegel & Burton, 1999).

The point here is that motor "milestones" vary significantly within and across cultures and can be easily manipulated by practice or lack thereof. In fact, for our own peace of mind, perhaps we shouldn't even think about these developments as "milestones" at all; instead, it might be more appropriate to think of them as "achievements" that all of our babies will eventually attain. Again, all typically developing infants will eventually walk despite the fact that the journey to walking might vary from baby to baby. Furthermore, the road to becoming an experienced walker is long, with lots of steps and falls along the way. In fact, research by Karen Adolph and colleagues has shown that infants between the ages of 12 and 19 months take an average of more than 2,000 steps in a single hour of walking, and they fall about 17 times during that same time period (Adolph et al., 2012). That's a lot of walking (and a lot of falling).

Sounds like hard work, but it turns out that babies actually *love* to walk. When an adult walks somewhere, he or she likely has a goal or destination. Even when adults walk for fun, usually there is a goal in mind, like getting some exercise or going outside to enjoy a nice day. This is not necessarily true for babies. Recent research has shown that *most of the time*, babies walk just to walk: They rarely have a particular destination, and they often carry objects around with no particular goal in sight (e.g., Karasik, Adolph, Tamis-LeMonda, & Zuckerman, 2012). They walk just to walk, and they vary greatly in terms of how long it takes them to become competent walkers.

This month, Edwin's important motor "achievement" was reaching: For the first time, instead of staring at the toys hanging from his play mat, Edwin started to reach and bat at them. This is a very typical of a 3-month-old. Next month, he will likely start rolling over from his back to his belly, he will start sitting up on his own sometime between 4 and 7 months, crawling between 6 and 10 months (if he crawls at all), and, finally, I can probably expect him to take his very first steps between 9 to 12 months. Again, the thing to remember about these "achievements" is that there is a lot of variability surrounding them. Another thing to keep in mind is that each achievement might bring with it some important changes in the house, some of them good, some of them bad.

Sitting up independently, for example, frees up a baby's hands to explore objects more easily and might even lead to advances in how babies perceive objects (Soska & Adolph, 2014; Soska, Adolph, & Johnson, 2010). Independent locomotion—like crawling or walking for the first time—provides even more freedom for babies to explore new toys and allows them the flexibility to share objects with you for the first time (Karasik, Tamis-LeMonda, & Adolph, 2011). However, a baby who can crawl or walk also has the sudden capability of getting hurt by eating household plants (which are often poisonous) or by getting hold of sharp objects. Similarly, they will now be at risk for falling off the couch or even down the stairs, and, although experience moving around teaches babies the types of movements that are possible (e.g., a small step) versus impossible (e.g., the distance from the bed to the floor) for their bodies to navigate, it takes several weeks or even months of motor experience for them to learn what's safe and what isn't and that what they learn in one posture (e.g., crawling) does not necessarily translate to another (e.g., walking) (Adolph, 2000). And while some researchers have suggested that infants learn a healthy fear of heights once they start crawling on their own, there is very little data to support this idea; in reality, very few infants are actually afraid of heights (Adolph, Kretch, & LoBue, 2014; LoBue & Adolph, 2019). On top of all that, when babies have the ability to move around on their own, they also gain the ability to break the rules, going places they're not supposed to, and touching things that they shouldn't. Altogether, these changes in motor development can change the family dynamic, and you might find yourself getting angry at your adorable baby more often or perhaps for the very first time (Campos et al., 2000). Given that Edwin is a very large baby with exceptionally heavy legs, I expect for him to reach some of these motor "achievements" a little bit later than other babies. And given all of the social changes that surround a fully mobile baby, a short "delay" is perfectly OK with me.

One caveat worth noting here is that delays in motor development based on differences in positioning, handling, weight, or motor experience are common in otherwise *developmentally typical infants*. Visual or hearing impairments might delay motor development, as babies who are blind, for example, aren't getting the same kind of visual feedback about their movements that seeing babies typically receive. But, again, minor delays are nothing to be worried about as the development of motor skills can vary based on experience and feedback. The only motor delays to worry about are extreme; for example, if your infant shows no signs of reaching for objects by 6 months or no signs of walking by 18–24 months. Significant delays like these warrant seeking a specialist, as they might signal a more serious developmental or neurological condition like Down syndrome or cerebral palsy.

As for motor delays in an otherwise healthy infant, there seems to be a difference of opinion between physical/occupational therapists and psychologists on whether parents should be concerned. Physical and occupational therapists will probably tell you that a delay in motor milestones like crawling could have a negative impact on various aspects of infant development. That's certainly what we were told by our physical therapist. Psychologists (like me) are more likely to tell you that there are little data to support such a contention. Although the only known negative consequence of plagiocephaly is merely aesthetic (i.e., having a flat-looking head), it is possible that untreated torticollis might lead to some neck or muscle problems later on, and there are a variety of approaches parents have taken after receiving these diagnoses.

The most extreme option is to see a physical therapist like our pediatrician recommended. It's an expensive route to take, but parenting is stressful enough without worrying about potential motor delays, so you should do whatever you think will give you peace of mind. I do, however, have to warn you that while there is research showing that therapies for plagiocephaly, like wearing a helmet, can be effective in reducing the flatness of a baby's head (e.g., Couture et al., 2013), there are other studies suggesting that these therapies might not be any different from just letting the problem work itself out on its own. In one of these studies, researchers randomly assigned 5- to 6-month-old infants with plagiocephaly to receive 6 months of helmet therapy or no therapy at all and then examined the flatness of the babies' heads at 24 months. At the end of the study, the babies in the helmet group looked the same as the babies who did not receive any therapy at all, suggesting that helmet therapy may not be so effective (van Wijk et al., 2014). But it's important to note that only about 25% of babies in either group made a full recovery with no signs of a flat head by age 2, so maybe some action is warranted.

A middle-of-the-road approach that many doctors recommend is to simply keep your baby off his back as much as possible during the day and to do "tummy time"—putting him on his stomach to play—a few times a day, so that he can have a chance to practice holding up

Figure 13.5 | Doctor-mandated "tummy time."
Source: Vanessa LoBue.

his head and building the upper body strength he'll need to eventually move around on his own and turn himself over so that he won't be spending so much time on his back. We have decided to go with this approach; we did one session with a physical therapist who showed us some stretches and exercises we could do with Edwin at home to increase his neck and arm strength, including 1 hour of tummy time a day.

So far, Edwin isn't all that fond of tummy time, but he tends to take it with a smile, and hopefully, a few months from now, he will be a full-fledged crawler with a round (or at least less flat) head leading the way. Then again, if he doesn't crawl at all, that's probably OK, too (Figure 13.5).

14

THE FOURTH MONTH

Language Development

I've been hearing from friends (and mommy blogs) that life gets significantly easier once you pass the 3-month mark. In our case, this advice turned out to be true, and we've definitely turned a corner. Edwin is crying significantly less, and when he does, it's much easier to figure out how to make him stop. We've also started sleep training since, as of the beginning of this month, he was still waking up about every 2–3 hours to eat. Our goal is to get him to go 5–6 hours without waking up so that I can get some much-needed rest. As I mentioned in an earlier chapter, there are several different types of sleep training (see Chapter 5). Since infants are quite adept at learning from an early age, many of these sleep training methods are quite effective (Mindell, Kuhn, Meltzer, & Sadeh, 2006), and there is no real evidence that a little bit of controlled crying (in an otherwise healthy infant and loving family) has any negative consequences for development (Price, Wake, Ukoumunne, & Hiscock, 2012). As a result, we have opted to go with a modified version of the Ferber method—developed by Dr. Richard Ferber—which involves putting your infant to bed when he is still awake (even if he cries) so that he can learn to soothe himself to sleep (Ferber, 2006). Parents are advised that they can soothe their babies if they cry, but not to pick them up or feed them during sleep training.

First, we started adhering to a strict bedtime routine that starts at 7 PM; it involves feeding, changing, and swaddling, and then putting Edwin to sleep when he's tired but still awake. After that, we set two goals for when he can eat—1 AM and 6 AM. We decided that if he wakes up before those times, we could comfort him with his pacifier or some gentle rubbing, but we would not pick him up or feed him. He adjusted to the 1 AM feeding immediately, after only one night, and continues to have no problem sleeping from about 7:30 PM to 1 or 2 AM (hallelujah!). But waiting to eat again until 6 AM has proved to be much more difficult. The first night, he woke up at 4:30 and cried for an hour before we had to soothe him back to sleep. It was absolutely miserable to listen to, but by the third night he was only crying for 10 minutes and then going back to sleep on his own. After about 2 weeks, he can make it until 5 AM without crying, but he still wakes up around 4 and needs his pacifier or a little rub down.

This month, there have also been positive changes in Edwin's motor development. He is holding his head up (which is still quite a bit flat) on his own, with a little bobble here and there. He is also batting and grasping at objects for the very first time, which is both fun and exciting to watch. Every day for about 10–20 minutes, we lay him on a play mat facing several attractive toys that hang from above. They make noise every time they move, so accidental touches give him motivation to reach and grasp for them in attempt to repeat the interesting noise. Last month, he simply looked at the toys and smiled at them. This month he can bat at them repeatedly with his hands and can even grab them if he is lucky enough to time his grasp correctly. This week, he also rolled over completely in his crib for the first time. Despite the fact that this is apparently an important motor milestone, it means we might have to stop swaddling him soon, so I'm not all that thrilled about this particular new development.

The biggest change this month has been in Edwin's language—all of a sudden, he talks constantly. He doesn't say any real words, of course, but he coos and babbles endlessly. *Cooing* is making a variety of sounds other than crying, such as gurgles or raspberries, or vowel sounds like "ahhhh." *Babbling* is repeating consonant sounds ("gaga") or stringing together consonant and vowel sounds ("ahgah" or "ahgoo"). He talks to me more than anyone else, and he talks the most when I respond to him, as if he already understands the back and forth of language. He knows to talk to people and animals, but not to objects (with the exception of the occasional stuffed animal) and that language has a rhythm that involves turn taking and imitation (Figure 14.1). Research by Susan Johnson from Ohio State University suggests that the back and forth of communication provides babies with an important hint about what kinds of objects are "alive" and have intentions. Eyes also seem to be an important cue, which might explain why Edwin has a

Figure 14.1 | *Left*: Grasping a toy. *Right*: Talking to stuffed animals.
Source: Vanessa LoBue.

long talk with his stuffed sheep every morning (Figure 14.2) (Johnson, Slaughter, & Carey, 1998).

Babies seem to be prepared to learn language right from birth, and research from Athena Vouloumanos's lab at New York University suggests that even newborns can recognize and prefer to listen to human speech when compared to other types of sounds (Vouloumanos & Werker, 2007). However, this preference isn't specific to humans at first: At birth, newborns will happily listen to human voices as well as the voices of other animals like monkeys over a variety of non-speech sounds. By 3 months of age, infants' preference becomes specific to *human* speech even when compared to the sounds that other animals make (Vouloumanos, Hauser, Werker, & Martin, 2010). Furthermore, by the time they reach 5 months of age, infants not only prefer human speech to all other sounds, but they can also match human speech

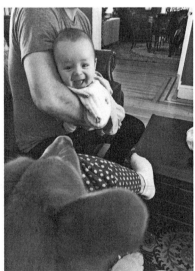

Figure 14.2 | Edwin talking to our dog, Charlotte.
Source: Vanessa LoBue.

sounds with photographs of human faces and monkey "speech" sounds with photographs of monkey faces (Vouloumanos, Druhen, Hauser, & Huizink, 2009). Around the same time, babies start looking more at people's mouths than at their eyes, demonstrating that they are beginning to pay special attention to language cues in the world around them (Lewkowicz & Hansen-Tift, 2012).

How infants are so adept at learning human language is one of the biggest and most widely studied puzzles in all of psychology. Languages are large and complicated symbolic systems, and infants are amazingly good at learning them. Every language has its own set of sounds, or phonemes, that are used to build words. These phonemes are different for different languages, and the sounds in English are not necessarily the same sounds used in other languages. For example, although the sounds /l/ and /r/ are easily distinguishable in the English language, they are not distinct sounds in the Korean language, and often native Korean-speaking adults who are not native English speakers have difficulty distinguishing between them.

Amazingly, infants are born with the ability to distinguish between the sounds in *any world language*. Janet Werker at the University of British Columbia famously documented infants' ability to discriminate between native and nonnative speech sounds. Werker and her colleagues presented 7-month-old infants with sets of English sounds and Hindi sounds (that are not part of the English language). Infants heard a string of sounds repeatedly, such as /la/, /la/, /la/, and so on. When the sound changed—or when the /la/'s suddenly changed to /da/'s—a set of attractive toys cleverly positioned to the infants' right side would light up. Eventually the infants learned that a change in the sound led to a change in the toy display, and they turned their heads to look at the toys in anticipation every time they heard a change in the sound. The researchers used infants' head turns to judge whether they heard the sounds change.

Amazingly, they found that 7-month-olds were easily able to discriminate between both English and Hindi speech sounds, accurately turning their heads every time the sound changed in either language. However, native English-speaking adults were unable to hear the difference between many of the Hindi sounds (Werker, Gilbert, Humphrey, & Tees, 1981). Further studies showed that the ability to perceive all of the phonemes in nonnative languages already begins to decline around 4 months of age and eventually disappears, similar to infants' ability to distinguish between the faces of other species (Werker & Tees, 1983) (see Chapter 12).

In addition to recognizing the sounds that make up language, infants are also faced with the challenge of learning which combinations of sounds make words. Imagine listening to a foreign language; for most of us, it sounds like an ongoing stream of sounds, and it is difficult to pick out which sound combinations are words and which ones are sentences. Jenny Saffran from the University of Wisconsin, along with colleagues Dick Aslin and Elissa Newport, sought to study how infants first break up an ongoing flow of sounds into distinct words. They presented 8-month-olds with a stream of three-syllable nonsense sounds. These sounds either appeared together with some frequency—the way words would appear in the English language—or they only appeared together at random times. The researchers wanted to know whether infants could pull out "words" by simply learning to recognize which sets of three-syllable sounds often appeared together.

After just 2 minutes of listening to a recording of these sounds, the researchers tested infants' learning by presenting them with two "words" (i.e., three-syllable combinations they had heard repeatedly) and one non-word (i.e., a three-syllable combination they hadn't heard before). The infants listened longer to the nonword combinations, demonstrating that they recognized the familiar "words" from the recording. This work suggests that one of the ways infants start to pick out words from an ongoing stream of speech is by recognizing statistical regularity, or combinations of sounds that often go together (Saffran, Aslin, & Newport, 1996). For example, one of the first words infants learn to recognize is their names, likely because they hear "blah, blah,

blah, Edwin, blah, blah, blah, Edwin, blah, blah, blah, Edwin," on a regular basis. Eventually, they recognize that the sounds that make up their names (e.g., "ed-win") come together with some frequency, providing a hint that those sounds make up a word.

Sounds impressive, but infants don't accomplish this feat on their own—their mothers (and fathers) help them out. One way they do this is by talking to infants differently than they talk to adults. Picture yourself talking to a baby. What does it sound like? Your speech is probably slower, high-pitched and exaggerated, with lots of pauses. You might even talk to your pets in a similar way. This is called *motherese*, or infant-directed speech. Motherese is very natural, appearing universally across languages and cultures (Grieser & Kuhl, 1988), and it can even be observed in children when they talk to babies or animals. Importantly, infants *like* listening to motherese and choose to listen to speech samples presented in motherese over those presented in adult-directed speech (Fernald, 1985). Because of its slow and exaggerated nature, motherese makes it easier for infants to pick out words from the speech stream (Nelson, Hirsh-Pasek, Jusczyk, & Cassidy, 1989). Recently, Patricia Kuhl and colleagues at the University of Washington found that the prevalence of motherese in households predicts babbling and future language performance in infants, suggesting that motherese does indeed help infants learn some aspects of language (Ramírez-Esparza, García-Sierra, & Kuhl, 2014).

Parents also help their infants by providing positive feedback for utterances that resemble a phoneme or a word. For example, I (like all new mothers) would love for Edwin to say "Mama." He doesn't even come close, of course, but every time he says something that sounds even remotely like the /ma/ sound, I smile, praise him, and repeat the sound to him. Babies love to see their mothers smile at them, so the smiles act as a positive reinforcement, and eventually Edwin will learn that making the sound /ma/ leads to a very pleasing response from his Mama. Research by Michael Goldstein and colleagues at Cornell University demonstrated that this type of interaction does indeed help infants develop language skills. In one study, mothers were told to reinforce their 8-month-olds' babbles by smiling or moving closer to them. The researchers found that mothers' very simple reinforcements led to more babbling and, most importantly, *better* babbling (sounds that more closely align with English sounds) in their babies (Goldstein, King, & West, 2003). A later study showed that when mothers respond to infants' babbles by repeating similar vocal sounds, infants modified their babbles to match the sounds that their mothers made, also resulting in more mature babbles (Goldstein & Schwade, 2008). I can already see this process in action: Edwin babbles, I smile and repeat his sound with a similar English sound, and then he repeats the sound again to me, better and clearer than before.

Although motherese and positive feedback can help infants with language, these alone do not solve the mystery of why children are so good at learning language, and why they are so much better at it than adults. In fact, there is research suggesting that children are *so* good at learning language that they will develop it themselves if you don't provide them with a means of communication. Anne Senghas from Barnard College found evidence of this in a deaf community of children in Managua, Nicaragua, which, before the 1970s, did not have a school for the deaf. In 1977, a school for the deaf was finally opened, exposing the community's deaf children to each other for the very first time. But the children had hearing parents, and the instructors at the school did not teach the parents any kind of sign language; instead, the instructors focused on teaching the children how to speak and read lips so that they could communicate with the hearing community. Since the children were allowed to communicate by any means possible on the school bus or during recess, Senghas discovered that they created their own rudimentary sign language so that they could communicate *with each other*. Most importantly, it was the youngest students— the students who were new to the school each year—who consistently added structure to the language, forming grammatical rules that mirror those of spoken languages. The children's new language is now called Nicaraguan Sign Language, and it has all of the properties and structure of any other real language (Senghas & Coppola, 2001).

Because of this amazing propensity for language and communication in very young children, many scientists believe that there is a special window of time—known as a critical or *sensitive period*—when a child's brain is especially receptive to learning language-related information. During this period, children are especially good at learning language. But, once they move past the sensitive period (which some hypothesize is around puberty), language learning becomes much harder. Evidence for this theory comes from Jacqueline Johnson and Elissa Newport (1989) from the University of Illinois, who studied second-language acquisition in a group of Korean- and Chinese-speaking immigrants. These immigrants had come to the United States between the ages of 3 and 39 and had been in the United States for a varied number of years. After giving the participants a variety of language fluency tests, the researchers found that it didn't matter how many years the participants had been in the United States; what mattered for English fluency was *when* they had first come to the United States: The younger the age at which they were exposed to English, the better they performed on the fluency tests. Importantly, gains in performance increased until about puberty, but, after that age, it didn't seem to matter when the participants came to the United States or how many years of experience they had with English—they performed poorly across the board—suggesting that learning a language during those critical early childhood years is important for mastery.

One would assume from this research that teaching children a second language early in life would be important for fluency. In fact, although this idea is incredibly intuitive, it is a surprisingly new perspective. The classic view on children who grow up bilingual, for example, is that learning two languages at the same time would be confusing and slow down language development overall. Although learning two new languages at the same time might be confusing (or seemingly impossible) for adults, research suggests that this isn't the case for children. Although children growing up in a bilingual environment lag a bit behind monolingual children in each individual language they are learning, bilinguals catch up, and, if you add up the words they know in both languages, bilinguals look just as competent as monolingual children (Hoff & Core, 2015).

In fact, not only do bilingual children have no problems learning two languages at once, but there are substantial *benefits* associated with growing up bilingual. Children who grown up bilingual, for example, are better at paying attention and switching between tasks (probably because of their ability to switch between languages) than monolingual children (Bialystok, 2011), they are better at taking the perspective of others (Goetz, 2003), they show advantages in certain types of memory (Brito & Barr, 2012), and bilingualism is even thought to be a protective factor against the development of Alzheimer's disease later in life (Bialystok, 2011).

The implication of this research is that forcing children to only speak English instead of their native language may not be the way to go. Twenty years ago, the common wisdom was that children should be encouraged to speak only English in American classrooms, and children who spoke other languages at home should be discouraged from doing so at school. In fact, Proposition 227, or the English Language in Public Schools Statute, was a law instituted in California in 1998 to limit the amount of time children spent speaking other languages besides English in public schools. Based on research demonstrating the benefits of bilingualism for children, rulings like these have been largely reversed in recent years, with a new emphasis on encouraging bilingualism in schools.

Furthermore, there is evidence that being immersed only in English at school can come at the detriment to a child's proficiency in his or her native language. Research by Gisela Jia at Lehman College in New York studied a large group of children and adults who immigrated to the United States from China at various times in their lives. These individuals spoke Mandarin-Chinese as their native language and English as their second language. Jia and her colleagues found that while children who immigrated before the age of 9 were better at learning English than individuals who were older when they came to the United States, it came at the expense of the younger children's fluency in Chinese. In other words, while the younger children made huge strides in learning English, their Chinese suffered. Furthermore, there were cultural factors that contributed to these trends: For example, after some period of time, individuals who came to the United States as children said that English was their preferred language, they were more likely to read books in English than in Chinese, and they were more likely to have English-speaking friends. In contrast, Chinese remained the preferred language for individuals who came to the United States as teenagers or adults, and they were more likely to maintain friendships with other people who also spoke Chinese than they were to make friendships with people who spoke English (Jia & Aaronson, 2003; Jia, Aaronson, & Wu, 2002).

The moral of the story is, in order to be fully bilingual, you need to use *both* languages frequently in your everyday life. If you grow up speaking one language and then abandon that language for something new, chances are you won't fully maintain that first language—even if you learned it as a child. I am the perfect example of this: I grew up speaking both English and Spanish, with fluency in both languages until the age of 8 or 9. At some point, my Cuban grandparents who didn't speak English moved to Florida, limiting my contact with them. Without my grandparents around, I stopped speaking Spanish every day, and, despite the fact that I used to be perfectly fluent, currently my Spanish is embarrassing. Sure, I can still understand it, and my accent is still pretty good, but I am barely conversational, despite the fact that I grew up speaking it daily. So full and consistent immersion in multiple languages is key to becoming a competent bilingual adult.

This means that it might not be worth your time to play tapes of adults speaking other languages to your baby at home if you don't actually speak a second language fluently. It is true that infancy and early childhood is the best time for children to learn more than one language, but it has to be immersive if it's going to stick. Indeed, adults who are immersed in a second language (e.g., by learning Spanish while living in Spain) perform better on second-language proficiency tests than adults who simply learn the same language in the classroom (Linck, Kroll, & Sunderman, 2009). Furthermore, recent research shows that school programs can encourage second-language learning, but these programs need to be intensive.

For example, in a study looking at the success of an early second-language intervention in Spain, researchers gave infants between the ages of 7 and 33 months an 18-week intervention where infants received an hour-long English training session every day while at school. The results showed that, at the end of 18 weeks, infants demonstrated significant gains in English word comprehension and production and in fact produced an average of 74 English words per hour during their normal social interactions at school. Importantly, they also showed the same gains in Spanish (their native language) when compared to other same-aged infants at the same school who didn't receive the English intervention, thus demonstrating that gains in English didn't come at the expense of gains in Spanish (Ferjan Ramirez & Kuhl, 2017). This suggests that second-language programs in schools can be effective, but they need to be intensive and consistent, with language training every day for long periods of time.

If, like most of us, teaching your children a second language isn't something within your reach, there is no need to worry. Your child will develop language naturally just by interacting with the world. But if you want to encourage an avid interest in word learning, there is something you can do. Research suggests that reading to children, even from an early age, can encourage both word learning and early literacy. Recall from Chapter 7 that fetuses who are read to in the third trimester prefer the sound of a familiar story after they are born (DeCasper & Spence, 1986). Pediatricians may not tell you to start reading to your child before it's born, but they will tell you to start shortly after, when your baby is a newborn. In a famous and often-cited study, researchers found that children whose parents talked to them more (using more words on average) had a distinct advantage in school over children of parents who spent less time speaking aloud (Hart & Risley, 1995). In fact, advantages in word production for infants exposed to more words at home have been found as early as 18 months of age (Fernald, Marchman, & Weisleder, 2013). This research is limited, as it was only done in the United States and is not sensitive to the different ways in which people from other cultures might talk (or not talk) to their babies. But, based on this research, pediatricians have reasoned that reading aloud is a great way to get babies exposed to more words at a younger age. In fact, more recent work suggests that children's books contain more unique words than children are generally exposed to in spoken language, so a little bit of book exposure when babies are young might go a long way in terms of introducing them to new words (Massaro, 2015).

The beginnings of language production itself vary from child to child, with some infants producing words in the very first year, while others may not produce words until late in the second year. However, certain kinds of language delays might be red flags for developmental problems and could warrant seeing a specialist. Late talking isn't a problem in and of itself. For most children, comprehending language is much easier than producing it, so as long as children are showing signs that they understand what you are trying to tell them and they are attempting to communicate with you in other ways—by crying, pointing, or grunting—it's likely that they are on track. In one study that looked at 18- to 30-month-old late talkers, researchers found that babies who attempted to communicate—for example, by using gestures—caught up to their nondelayed peers (Hong & Kim, 2005). So if babies are showing that they understand what you're trying to communicate to them and they make attempts to communicate with you—even if it's without words—it's a good sign that they are moving in the right direction. If, however, between the ages of 12 and 30 months, babies are showing very little change in terms of language development, and they are showing little interest in communicating or understanding what you are trying to communicate to them, it might be time to consult your pediatrician about seeing a specialist.

Currently, Edwin has a long way to go with language learning. Infants don't usually produce their first words until later much later in development, likely around 12 months of age or later, but, judging from his early babbling, he might be an early talker as well. First, he will produce single words that belong to important people, such as "mama" or "dada" (although to my chagrin, "dada" will likely come first because it is easier to say), followed by words for favorite toys or foods. *Holophrases* will come next, where infants will use one word to express an entire thought. For example, saying the word "Mama," can mean "come here, Mama," or "Mama, get me that apple," or "Mama, pick me up," and the like. Next will be *telegraphic speech*, or two-word phrases that infants use in place of a sentence, usually without prepositions or articles, for example, "Mama, cookie," or "More milk." Finally, in the next few years, Edwin will learn to string together full sentences including all of the parts of speech. But again, we have a long way to go before we get there. For now, I'm pulling out all the stops (smiling, cooing, praising, repeating) for anything that sounds remotely like "Mama."

15

THE FIFTH MONTH

Infant Emotions

We are now past the 4-month mark, and life with a baby has continued to get easier.

I don't know if pumping has slowed my milk production or if Edwin is just a big eater, but, starting this month, I am no longer producing enough breast milk to satisfy him. To make sure he isn't going to bed hungry, we've been defrosting some of the extra breast milk I've stored in the freezer to top him off, but that supply has started to dwindle as well, so last week we started supplementing his last feeding of the day with formula. Getting him to drink the formula was a big challenge. As I mentioned in a previous chapter, along with many of the difficulties experienced during nursing, when you decide to introduce formula to a breastfed baby for the first time, he often refuses it. Edwin literally gagged when we tried to give him the sample of formula I got from my pediatrician. He gagged and he cried and he refused to drink it. Three different brands of formula later, he finally took one of them with reluctance.

The switch to formula made me see for the first time that although Edwin is not capable of communicating verbally just yet, he is certainly capable of telling me how he feels with an ever-growing range of emotions. When I say he wasn't happy about getting formula, I don't mean he cried or simply looked upset; he was disgusted at first, and then he looked downright *angry*. Imagine anticipating a bottle full of the most delicious thing you can think of, only to find out that the drink you were so looking forward to was instead replaced with something disgusting, like a diet cola. That could easily make anyone angry, even a 4½-month-old.

When do infants develop adult-like emotions? Although we all regularly experience a myriad of emotional responses every day, for centuries, researchers have argued fiercely about exactly what emotions are and when they first develop. Some believe that emotions are housed in dedicated parts of the brain, each one a unique part of our biology. This view was originated in the early 1970s, when researcher Paul Ekman and his colleagues traveled to a remote part of New Guinea to examine whether individuals in an isolated culture would be able recognize facial expressions of adults in the United States. They presented people with a story and showed them photographs of adults from the United States posing for three different facial expressions and asked them to choose which face best represented the emotion in the story (e.g., "His friends have come, and he is happy," or "His mother has died, and he feels very sad"). Subjects from New Guinea who had no prior experience with Americans accurately identified their facial expressions and matched them with the corresponding stories. From this research, Ekman concluded that facial muscle patterns for emotional expressions are universal and consistent across cultures. He identified six specific facial expressions that he called "basic" emotions, and he argued that these six emotions are universally recognizable in most populations. These emotions include sadness, happiness, surprise, anger, disgust, and fear (Ekman, 1992; Ekman & Friesen, 1976).

Research has shown that even infants as young as 1 or 2 months of age are capable of making facial expressions that represent these basic emotions, including fear, disgust, anger, sadness, happiness, and surprise (e.g., Izard, Huebner, Risser, & Dougherty, 1980). Many believe that emotional facial expressions are tightly linked to the experience of the emotion itself, so the fact that even very young infants can make various emotional expressions provides evidence for Ekman's view that our most basic emotions are part of our biology (Figure 15.1).

Other researchers take a more complicated perspective and believe that emotions are a combination of feelings (i.e., physiological responses) and thoughts (i.e., cognitive responses). What we know from research on infant development favors this more complicated view and suggests that emotions are not simply feelings; instead, our thoughts play an important role in the development of emotional experiences and in their expression. At first, newborns do not have the cognitive ability to feel complicated emotions like sadness and anger; instead, their emotional responses are simpler and generally consist of positive or negative feelings, or what we call *affect*. For example, when an infant is uncomfortable or in pain, he can clearly demonstrate his negative affect by crying, but he does not express specific negative emotions like anger, sadness, or fear just yet; instead, he simply reacts negatively to whatever bothers him.

Full-blown emotions are typically *about* something, and to have a specific reaction like sadness or fear in response to a person or event, you have to *know* something about that person or event. It takes some time for infants to develop the cognitive ability to have reactions that are as specific and complex as anger, sadness, or fear. In fact, in the research showing that 1 and 2-month-olds can pose various emotional facial expressions, the expressions were generally evoked somewhat randomly and not in situations where the specific emotion was appropriate, like making a fear face in response to a scary mask (e.g., Camras & Shutter, 2010). In other words, young infants' emotional facial expressions aren't necessarily *about* anything at all.

Figure 15.1 | Children posing for Ekman's six basic emotions plus a neutral face.

Source: LoBue, V. & Thrasher, C. (2015). The Child Affective Facial Expression (CAFE) Set: Validity and reliability from untrained adults. *Frontiers in Emotion Science, 5.*

This suggests that while infants might be capable of making a variety of facial expressions that resemble adult-like emotional expressions, it does not necessarily mean that they are *experiencing* the corresponding emotion.

I can vouch for this myself: Edwin is capable of making facial expressions that look a lot like many of our adult emotional expressions, but they are usually evoked by just taking lots and lots of photos in a row without any specific stimulus or context. In other words, while Edwin can make facial expressions that look like fear, disgust, sadness, happiness, or anger, he usually makes them quickly and at random times, and there's no evidence that he's feeling the emotion that matches the expression on his face (Figure 15.2).

As infants grow older and develop more cognitive abilities, they begin to show a colorful array of more complicated positive and negative emotions, starting with *happiness* or *joy*. Within the first few

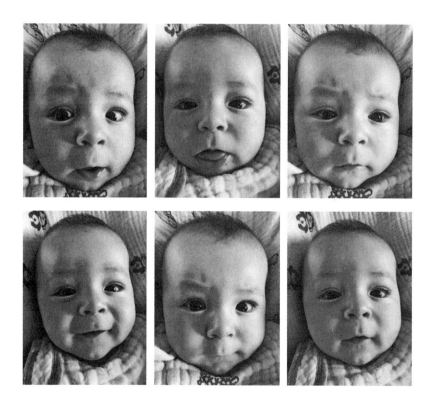

Figure 15.2 | Edwin's many facial expressions. From left to right, top to bottom: Fearful, disgusted, sad, happy, angry, neutral.
Source: Vanessa LoBue.

months of life, infants can express positive affect by smiling. Before the first month, infants usually smile in response to something non-social, and the smiles most often occur during sleep (or, in Edwin's case, after a satisfying poop). *Social smiling*, or smiling in response to people or familiar objects, first happens in the second or third month, and *laughing*—as we found out this month when Edwin let out his first real cackle—develops even later, in the fourth or fifth month. These are the first signs of real joy or happiness. In order for infants to feel happiness, they have to have the cognitive ability to recognize that something is familiar, or conversely, that something is new. Edwin's first smiles were in response to seeing my (a familiar) face. Now he smiles and laughs when I present him with familiar songs or new sounds.

Negative emotions, like positive ones, start out as general affect in response to any discomfort, including gas, sleepiness, or pain. But as infants develop more advanced cognitive skills, negative affect slowly becomes differentiated into distinct and identifiable negative emotions. Like I said, Edwin has been showing fully recognizable signs of *anger* for the first time this month. Think about what you would need to experience in order to feel anger or frustration. It requires the violation of a belief, expectation, or desire. Infants show the first signs of anger when they are either prevented from doing something (e.g., their arms are restrained) or when some series of events that they have learned is interrupted. For example, Edwin has learned that when he is lying on his play mat, his legs can reach the beams above that hold up various toys. When he kicks those beams, the toys move and make unique and interesting sounds. However, when he accidentally misses the beams several times in a row, he shows clear signs of anger and frustration, vocalizing loudly in protest when his toys fail to move.

Research by Michael Lewis and colleagues at Rutgers University has shown a similar pattern in their lab. These researchers taught infants that whenever they pulled on a string, an image of a smiling baby would appear on a screen, accompanied by the "Sesame Street" theme song. After infants learned that pulling the string turned on the slide show, the sneaky researchers turned it off, so that nothing happened when the infants pulled on the string, thus interrupting the fun cause-and-effect that the infants had previously learned (Lewis, Alessandri, & Sullivan, 1990). As you can imagine, they were not pleased; in fact, infants as young as 4 months of age displayed angry facial and vocal expressions in response to the lost contingency.

Clear signs of *sadness* are not evident until slightly later, around 6 months of age. In order to feel sadness, an individual must have some awareness that something valued has been lost. Researchers claim to have documented sad emotional expressions using something call the "still face paradigm" (Lewis & Ramsay, 2005). In this research, mothers are told to smile and interact with their infants as they usually would at home. At some point, the mothers are told to stop the interaction and pose a neutral or "still" facial expression, not responding to or interacting with their infants. At first, the infants continue to smile and bait their mothers to reengage with them, but eventually the infants give up and look away, demonstrating signs of sadness in response to their mothers' lost attention. Other researchers using the "still face" paradigm argue that while infants do attempt to reengage their mothers after the interaction stops, there are no signs of sadness specifically (e.g., Weinberg & Tronick, 1996). The results are still controversial. Edwin certainly tries to get my attention when I look away from him for a short period of time, sometimes even crying at the loss of my gaze, but I've seen no signs of distinct sadness per se, just more general negative affect.

Fear develops even later than sadness, likely because it is more cognitively complex. Fear can be deceptive because, as described in earlier chapters, newborns have an easily elicited startle reflex (see Chapter 6) that is often accompanied by crying, making it easy to conclude that the infant is afraid. However, startle responses are not necessarily the same as fearful responses (although fear can cause an individual to startle more easily). Infants do not begin to show the first signs of fear until around 8 months or later. Just as with happiness, fear requires that an infant recognizes and differentiates things that are familiar from things that are new. However, to feel afraid, the infant must also determine that the new or familiar object or person poses an imminent threat, which generally requires some sort of negative experience with that stimulus.

Classic psychology research and traditional wisdom suggests that infants show their first signs of fear toward strangers. However, while some infants do develop an obvious stranger fear starting around 8 months of age, the traditional belief that *all* infants are afraid of strangers is not quite right, as many or even most infants are not, at least not in all situations. Stranger fear seems to be related to temperament (see Chapter 8), with more sensitive infants commonly showing negative emotional responses to strangers, and more laid back or easy infants possibly showing few signs of fear toward strangers at all.

Stranger fear, or *stranger anxiety* as some researchers call it, is also highly dependent on context. For example, if a stranger enters an infant's home, most infants are unlikely to show any signs of fear whatsoever. However, if the infants are in an unfamiliar place, or their mothers are not there, they are much more likely to show signs of fear at the approach of a stranger (LoBue & Adolph, 2019). Most other fears that infants and young children develop are related to specific negative experiences. A child might develop a fear of the doctor's office after getting a painful shot, or a fear of dogs after being bitten. Likewise, a child could also develop a fear of dogs by watching someone else get bitten by a dog, or by hearing someone say that dogs bite. These fears require that infants learn the relationship between the object (e.g., the dog) and the threatening outcome (e.g., getting bitten). Despite receiving several vaccinations (two rounds of hepatitis B, diphtheria, tetanus, and pertussis), at 4½ months, Edwin has not yet learned that going to the doctor's office usually means he's getting a shot, and he shows no signs of fear when we enter that soon-to-be scary waiting room.

Disgust develops even later than fear. Newborns do experience basic distaste reactions when given something sour to eat or drink (Rottman, 2014). Again, when Edwin tried formula for the first time, he gagged, showing a very typical disgusted facial expression. Distaste—or a negative reaction to tastes and smells—is present even in newborns and is more like a reflex than a true emotion. Full-blown disgust—or the type of disgust we feel when we see blood or insects or hear about a terrible crime—develops much later.

Paul Rozin and his colleagues from the University of Pennsylvania cleverly studied this type of disgust by offering children various drinks and snacks that were contaminated with something that adults would obviously find disgusting. For example, he presented children with a glass of apple juice and offered them a drink. Most children love juice, so they generally responded enthusiastically to his kind offer. But next, he mixed the juice with various objects that most adults would find disgusting and then asked the children again if they wanted to take a sip. For example, he stirred the juice with a comb that the children had previously seen the researcher comb his hair with and then offered them the juice. In the most extreme case, he put a dead grasshopper directly into the juice and asked children if they would take a sip. It wasn't until 6 to 8 years of age that more than half of the kids rejected the contaminated juice. In fact, there was still a portion of 9- to 12-year-olds (~10%) that were willing to drink the juice with a dead grasshopper still floating in it (Rozin, Fallon, & Augustoni-Ziskind, 1985).

In Rozin's study, drinking the juice after it touched a comb or dead insect probably wouldn't have caused the children to get sick. More recent research suggests kids as old as age 8 will eat contaminated food that would not only effectively disgust adults, but that might actually make them sick as well. For example, Jasmine DeJesus, Kristin Shutts, and Katherine Kinzler from the University of Chicago and the University of Wisconsin presented 3- to 8-year-old children with two bowls of applesauce—one that an adult had eaten from with a clean spoon, and another that an adult had eaten from with a contaminated spoon and then sneezed (!!) into. Children were then given the opportunity to eat as much or as little applesauce as they wanted from either bowl. The youngest children (aged 3–5) ate the same amount of applesauce from both bowls, showing no concern over the fact that one of them could be harmfully contaminated. What's most alarming is that although the older children preferred the clean applesauce, many of them still ate *some* of the applesauce from the bowl that had been sneezed in (DeJesus, Shutts, & Kinzler, 2015).

The point of this research (besides the fact that kids are gross) is that most disgust responses are not obvious until middle childhood, suggesting that they are socialized—we learn them from social norms or from other people. At first this might sound like a bad thing, but in the long-run it might be good: People from different cultures have very different opinions about what is disgusting and what is not. In some countries eating grasshoppers is totally normal, while in others it's rare and disgusting to most people. Children have to learn what the traditions of their own cultures are, and it takes quite awhile for them to figure out what is acceptable (and sanitary) behavior versus what some people might be disgusted by. So, it might not be all that strange to find that a toddler regularly samples dog food, or is fascinated by bugs, or tries to play in his own poop. For the most part, children have to learn what's disgusting and what isn't, so they might (or more accurately, they *will*) put a lot of things in their mouths that you might not want them to.

The latest developing emotions are what researchers call the *self-conscious emotions*. These emotions—like guilt, pride, and embarrassment—require the highest level of cognition; specifically, an understanding of the expectations of others and of the social norms that guide a given culture. Some researchers have suggested that a prerequisite for experiencing the self-conscious emotions is a *sense of self*, or the ability to reflect on yourself and your own behavior from the perspective of someone else. The very first evidence that infants have a sense of self appears around 18 months of age, when they first show signs of recognizing themselves in a mirror. Researchers have studied this phenomenon using the classic "rouge test." The test involves putting a bit of lipstick or rouge on an infant's nose and then placing the infant in front of a mirror to observe his or her reaction. Before 18 months of age, infants show no signs of recognizing that it is their own reflection in the mirror. Around a year and a half, however, their reaction looks very different: Infants immediately change their facial expressions and begin rubbing the rouge off their own noses instead of trying to interact with the cute baby in the mirror (Lewis, 1995). Indeed, Edwin loves to look at himself in the mirror, but he thinks he's just looking at a smiley baby and doesn't seem to have any idea that he is in fact that smiley baby. In fact, it will be at least another year before he shows any evidence of recognizing his own reflection in the mirror (Figure 15.3).

So far, Edwin's emotional repertoire includes vast amounts of happiness and joy, mixed in with general negative affect and the occasional bout of anger or frustration. In the next few months, his negative affect will continue to become more specific, and we will see signs of sadness and fear. Although he is fully adept at gagging when I give him something unpleasant to drink, full-blown disgust and the self-conscious emotions will develop even later. At first you might think that such a large repertoire of negative emotions is just that—negative. But, in fact, all emotions are important, and their emergence is just a sign that our babies are now part of the vast array of experiences that the world has to offer. These emotions let them know when something is familiar, when a situation is risky, when they've lost something important, or when they are behaving badly. Although negative emotions like anger and fear might make your baby's (and your) life seemingly more difficult, they also serve as important pieces of information about the social world, and, ultimately, their presence is a sign of your child's cognitive maturity.

But a word of caution: Recall from the previous chapter that infants can understand a lot more than they can communicate. Have

Figure 15.3 | Edwin looking at himself in the mirror at 3 months (*left*) and 6 months (*right*). He doesn't seem to know that it's him yet—he just smiles and tries to play with the cute baby in the mirror. Infants typically do not recognize themselves in the mirror until about 18 months of age.

Source: Vanessa LoBue.

you heard of the "terrible two's?" What makes the two's so terrible is that between the ages of 1 and 2, infants become capable of feeling lots of different kinds of emotions, including happiness, sadness, fear, and anger, but they can't necessarily control those emotions or verbally communicate their feelings. *Emotion regulation* is the ability to control your own thoughts and feelings. Have you ever been at work and had the urge to yell at an incompetent co-worker but had to keep your cool instead? Have you ever been on a date or with a group of friends and had to keep yourself from crying during a cheesy movie? These situations require you to effectively regulate your emotional responses. Over the first year of life, infants generally need *you* to regulate their emotions for them, soothing them whenever they are tired or upset. They get better at soothing themselves over time, but this ability develops slowly over the course of infancy, childhood, adolescence, and even adulthood.

Walter Mischel and his colleagues at Columbia University came up with a clever way to study the development of regulation in children without having to upset them. Instead of making them sad or upset to see if they could calm themselves down, the researchers offered children a very desirable snack but made them wait a long period of time before they were allowed to eat it. Specifically, they offered preschool-aged children two snacks—one that they really wanted (e.g., marshmallow) and one that was less desirable (e.g., cracker). The children were told that the experimenter needed to leave the room for a while, but if the children waited until the experimenter returned, they could have the marshmallow. Alternatively, if the children couldn't wait that long, they could ring a bell and the experimenter would promptly come back. But, if they decided to ring the bell, they would only be given the cracker and would not be allowed to eat the marshmallow. If you've been around children often enough, you can probably guess that this is very difficult for them, and they have a hard time waiting when they are excited. That's exactly what the researchers found— children had a hard time waiting and often had to ring the bell. But they got better at it as they got older, and girls seemed to have an easier time with it than boys (Mischel, Shoda, & Peake, 1988; Mischel, Shoda, & Rodriguez, 1989).

I'm not going to lie to you: Babies are really bad at regulating their emotions. If they can't do something they want to do, or worse, if you stop them from doing something they want to do, they have no other recourse than to show you exactly how they feel about it. They'll respond with frustration, anger, a temper tantrum, and perhaps even a flying sippy cup. What makes matters worse is that their language ability also develops rather slowly, so although they can feel a wide range of emotions at an early age, they have no means by which to tell you how they're feeling. The good news here is that they will get better at this over time. But the most important thing to remember when you feel like you're going to lose control over *your* emotions during the fifth temper tantrum of the day is that children's ability to feel emotions develops before their ability to communicate with you about them and, most importantly, before their ability to control them.

During the first few years, you will probably see a lot of variability in your baby's emotional expressiveness and ability to regulate his or her emotional responses. As I discussed previously (see Chapter 8), from an early age (as early as 3–4 months), babies have their own individual personalities or *temperaments*, which can impact the way they react emotionally to changes in the environment. This is important to keep in mind, as some babies are prone to react to new situations and people with negative emotions. If your baby does respond this way, it might be wise to let her warm up to new situations at her own pace, as pushing her too hard to acclimate to new situations or people might intensify her negative emotional responses. However, if you find that your baby cries in new situations and *never* calms down, or you feel like your child's negative emotional responses are so intense that they keep you from going to new places, it may warrant speaking to a specialist. Such extreme cases of negative emotionality in the first 2 years of life is relatively uncommon, but, as I mentioned earlier, babies who react negatively to *all* new situations, people, or even objects could be at risk for developing social anxiety later in life (Buss, Davidson, Kalin, & Goldsmith, 2004) and might benefit from some kind of intervention or at least some extra sensitive parenting.

Besides differences in emotional development based on temperament, there are also significant cross-cultural differences in emotional expression and regulation. First, very recent cross-cultural research suggests that facial expressions once thought to be basic and universal are actually recognized differently in some cultures. Adults in a group called the Trobrianders of Papua New Guinea, for example, consistently identify faces that we would call "fear" as "anger" (Crivelli,

Russell, Jarillo, & Fernández-Dols, 2016). Furthermore, in a recent study looking at German and Cameroonian children's performance on the marshmallow task I described earlier, researchers found huge cross-cultural differences in the emotional regulation abilities of 4-year-old children. In the task, German children performed much like American children do and had a great deal of trouble waiting to eat the marshmallow. In fact, only 30% of them were able to wait a full 10 minutes until the experimenter returned and needed to use strategies to keep themselves from eating the marshmallow, like fidgeting, singing, or talking to themselves. Cameroonian kids, in contrast *were awesome* at this task. These kids were able to wait twice as long as the German kids, and nearly 70% of them were able to wait the full 10 minutes before eating the marshmallow. Furthermore, they didn't seem to need the same type of strategies that the German kids needed: They were generally relaxed, showed very little movement while they were waiting, and some of them even fell asleep! Can you imagine an American preschooler sitting quietly or falling asleep while waiting to eat a marshmallow that is sitting right in front of them? Why did these researchers find such a big difference? It's not exactly clear, but the researchers believe it has to do with the cultural practices of the small Cameroonian group (called the Nso). The group practices a mainly farming lifestyle, and children are expected to control their negative emotions at a very early age (Lamm et al., 2017). This suggests that perhaps we have something to learn from other cultures in terms of teaching our children to wait to get exactly what they want.

Despite the slow unfolding of Edwin's emotions, *my* emotions have been changing much more rapidly since giving birth. Recent research might help explain these new feelings: It turns out that a new mother's brain actually changes after she gives birth, in ways that might promote caring for her child. Recently, researchers from Autonomous University of Barcelona were curious about whether the brains of new mothers changed after giving birth. Consistent with this idea, they found long-lasting structural changes in the parts of the brain that are most active when the mothers were looking at photographs of their own children. These changes were still present 2 years after the women gave birth. The researchers think that these changes in the brain might be useful in facilitating women's abilities to interpret the facial expressions of their infants, helping them to understand their children's needs and potentially helping them to become responsive mothers (Hoekzema et al., 2016).

I wouldn't say that I'm having more emotions than usual, just that the extremity of each one has a much bigger range, with higher

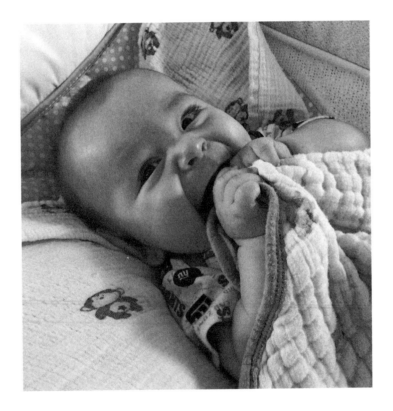

Figure 15.4 | Infant laughter.
Source: Vanessa LoBue.

highs and lower lows than ever before. For example, I was obviously able to feel happiness before Edwin was born. But nowadays, when he smiles, or laughs, or does something new, the joy I feel is bigger than any joy that I've experienced in the past. Unfortunately, this holds for the negative emotions, too: I've felt fear before, but it was nothing like the fear I feel now when I think about Edwin getting hurt or worse. And then there's the *guilt*. I felt particularly guilty this month when mulling over the decision to start supplementing my breast milk with formula, which was multiplied by about 50 when I watched Edwin gag when tasting it for the first time. At this point, I had to remind myself of something a very wise woman once said: "Even if nothing in our birth plan works out . . . if for some reason I am unable to breast-feed . . . it will be OK" (Chapter 9). The logical, less emotional, prebaby version of me from months past was, of course, right. Edwin is now drinking both formula and breast milk, and in fact adding a little bit of formula to our lives turned out to be a huge relief from the constant worry that I wasn't producing enough milk to feed my son. He is happy and he is thriving, the sight of which makes me burst with emotion (Figure 15.4).

16

THE SIXTH MONTH

Cognition and Learning

Given all of the breastfeeding problems we've had since January, this month brought with it an exciting new development—real food. And despite the fact that he doesn't even have teeth yet, Edwin *loves* to eat. Our pediatrician said we could start introducing one new food every day by giving him a single spoonful; if he doesn't have an allergic reaction, he can have as much as he wants from the next day forward. She wisely recommended to start with giving him vegetables and then to introduce fruits. I guess if you start with fruits, some babies might reject green vegetables because they aren't as sweet, and, as we discussed in an earlier chapter, most babies are born with a sweet tooth (see Chapter 7). So far, Edwin doesn't have a problem with any of the flavors we've given him—fruit, vegetable, green, orange, brown, or purple—he loves them all. He slurps up green beans and prunes with the same enthusiasm as apples and bananas. When he knows we have food for him, he gets an intense look on his face and opens his mouth as wide as I've ever seen, quickly swallowing each bite and then opening his mouth again for more.

What can I say, like mother like son.

The most amazing part of introducing food was how quickly he *learned* to eat. Before this month, he really only knew how to drink milk from sucking at a breast or bottle; he had never seen a spoon before and never experienced the heavy consistency of pureed fruits and vegetables. He didn't know what to do with his very first bite and just licked the spoon looking perplexed. But only two bites later, he already had the hang of it, opening his mouth as the spoon approached and using his lips to pull the tasty bit of mush into his mouth (Figure 16.1). The speed at which he learns anything these days is remarkable. He seems to figure out what toys make interesting noises and which ones feel particularly good on his gums and then distinguishes which toy serves each function best. In fact, his motor skills have not yet caught up with his growing cognitive abilities, and he often gets frustrated when his small and still uncoordinated hands fail to produce the action he knows he wants to make.

It's clear that Edwin can learn and remember his favorite toys and his favorite people, like me or Nick or his grandma, but other than that, it's hard to tell what Edwin knows, what he thinks about, and what he

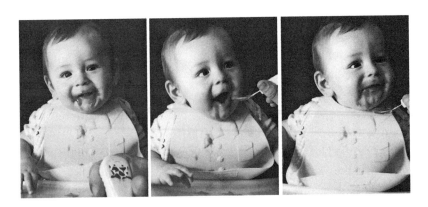

Figure 16.1 | Edwin enjoying his first foods.
Source: Vanessa LoBue.

can remember. Infants can't talk, so they can't tell us how much they've learned or what they can understand. This makes studying infant's cognitive skills, or their general understanding, a very difficult task for scientists. Lucky for us, some very clever researchers of years past have devised ways for the rest of us to surmise what infants know and how they might reason about the world around them.

Jean Piaget—a Swiss scientist who published his work in the 1920s and '30s—was probably the most famous developmental psychologist of all time. He came up with a theory of cognitive development that explains how we come to understand the world from the newborn period through adulthood. According to his theory, in the first month of life, reflexes generally drive infants' behaviors. Between 1 and 4 months, they learn to control these reflexes to guide their own movements. Now, instead of sucking when something happens to be in their mouths, infants have learned to bring their hands to their mouths to suck intentionally. Everything is still about their own bodies in these first few months, and they don't really make the connection between their limbs and the outside world.

Between 4 and 8 months, all of this changes, and infants begin to notice that their bodies can have an effect on their surroundings. Suddenly, toys that the infant previously had no interest in have become new and exciting. Edwin was given a bunch of toys when he was born—including rattles, teethers, and assorted stuffed animals—but showed absolutely no interest in them until this month. Now, every toy I show him grabs his attention, especially toys that make noise. He knows that his body can have an effect on the outside world, and he's interested in shaking, hitting, and mouthing every toy he can get his hands on to explore their new sounds and textures.

According to Piaget, the key to infants' understanding of the world starts around this time, between 4 and 8 months of age, when they start to gain the ability to form mental representations of objects. Having a *mental representation* simply means that an infant can bring to mind something that isn't right in front of them.

For example, I know that my garbage can is sitting outside the back door of my house even though I am in my living room and can't see it. According to Piaget, infants are not born with the ability to mentally represent objects; instead, this ability develops slowly over the first 2 years of life. For infants, once an object is outside of their field of view, it no longer exists: Out of sight out of mind. Piaget called the ability to hold a mental representation *object permanence,* meaning that an object is permanently in existence even when you can't see it. Based on his theory, as soon as you disappear from your infant's field of view, he no longer knows that you exist, even if he just watched you walk into the next room. That doesn't mean your baby can't recognize that you are familiar—it just means that he can't bring you to mind when you're not right in front of him. This would certainly explain why peek-a-boo is so much fun for babies—to them, when you cover up your face and then uncover it, it literally disappears and then reappears again seconds later out of nowhere. Sounds like a pretty great magic trick if you're a 6-month-old (Piaget, 1993).

You might be asking yourself, how could Piaget know for sure whether infants can bring absent objects to mind? Piaget had a very clever way of testing his hypothesis; he simply showed infants a very attractive object—perhaps a favorite toy—and then hid it under a blanket right in front of them. You'd expect that if someone hid your favorite possession under a blanket right in front of your face, you'd simply lift up the blanket to reclaim it. But, Piaget found that, before 8 months of age, babies don't search for hidden objects. In fact, they behave as if the objects never existed in the first place. If you have an infant younger than 8 months, you can see this for yourself at home: Simply show your baby a toy that he really likes, then completely cover it up with a cloth while he is still looking at it. What you'll probably find is that the baby will simply look away, as if the object is now gone for good—a kind of *que sera sera* attitude. It's not that they didn't see you hide the toy; it's as if it's just not there anymore.

Most researchers agree that Piaget's experiments work, and they are easy to replicate almost a century after he first designed them. Again, you can try this at home with your own baby and it is almost guaranteed to work out just like it did for Piaget in the 1920s. In fact, he based his whole theory of cognitive development on a series of mini experiments just like this one that he did at home with his own kids. What researchers disagree about is whether Piaget's experiments actually demonstrate that infants aren't capable of holding mental representations, and, in fact, most modern-day psychologists think that Piaget may have underestimated what infants can do. For example, there are a lot of reasons why infants might not search for a hidden object that have nothing to do with mental representations: Maybe they aren't coordinated enough to lift the blanket to get the toy, or maybe they aren't so good at planning their actions; maybe they aren't motivated enough to put in the effort to uncover a hidden object, or maybe their attention span isn't quite there yet to follow through.

Regardless of the reason, several researchers have provided evidence that infants under 8 months of age do in fact mentally represent things that they can't see. Rachel Keen (then Rachel Clifton) and her colleagues at the University of Massachusetts at Amherst, for example, asked whether infants would reach for objects they couldn't see if they didn't have to pick up a cloth or blanket first. They introduced 6½-month-olds to two objects that each made a distinct sound—a small rattle and a big hula-hoop. The infants spent some time in the lab playing with each object so that they could learn which sound belonged to the rattle and which sound belonged to the hula-hoop. After the infants had some time to familiarize themselves with the two objects, the researchers turned off the lights in the lab. They then presented the infants with each object in the dark, shaking them to remind the infants of what sounds they made. After hearing each sound, the infants reached out to grab the objects, demonstrating that they *knew* the objects were there even though they could not be seen. Most importantly, the infants reached with one hand if they heard the rattle and with two hands if they heard the hula-hoop. This suggests that even though the infants couldn't see the objects, they had a mental image of what each one looked like that helped them to guide their reaching (Clifton, Rochat, Litovsky, & Perris, 1991).

Other researchers designed experiments that made it even easier for infants to show that they had mental representations, eliminating the need to reach for objects altogether; infants were simply required to look at what the experimenters showed them. Renee Baillargeon from the University of Illinois, for example, simply showed infants a wooden plank that rotated 180 degrees back and forth on a table. The infants watched the plank rotate, initially looking eagerly at this new and interesting event, but eventually getting bored and looking away. Once they got bored, the real experiment began. The infants watched as Baillargeon put a second wooden plank in the path of the first. Then, the infants watched as the logical thing happened: The first plank began to rotate, it hid the second plank from view as it reached 90 degrees, and then it stopped rotating when it hit the second plank. Next, the infants saw something impossible: This time, when the first plank began to rotate to where the second plank stood in its way, it just continued to rotate the full 180 degrees, as if the second plank was never there.

Baillargeon was interested in something very simple: Would the infants be more interested in looking at the possible event, where the first plank stopped rotating as it hit the second plank; or would they be more interested in the impossible event, where the first plank rotated through as if the second plank disappeared when it was no longer in view? She found that infants as young as 3½ months of age looked longer at the impossible event. Baillargeon interpreted this finding as evidence that the infants expected the first plank to stop when it hit the second, and they were intrigued when it just rotated through, suggesting that the infants could mentally represent the second plank even when it wasn't in view (Baillargeon, 1987).

This research, and several experiments that followed, suggests that perhaps infants do have mental representations of objects before

Piaget said they would. When trying Piaget's object permanence experiment at home with Edwin, it worked just as he said it would: I hid Edwin's favorite toy (Sophie the giraffe) under a burp cloth. Edwin did not lift the cloth to search for Sophie (as Piaget predicted he wouldn't), *but* he did whimper when he realized that she was gone. Does this mean that he could bring Sophie to mind even though she was hidden? It's not really that clear, because again, Edwin can't tell me what he's thinking just yet. Piaget would say no, that Edwin no longer knew Sophie was there, despite the whimper. According to Piaget, infants do not have full object permanence until they are 18 months of age and can show clear evidence of what he called *deferred imitation*. Imitation is simply what it sounds like—when someone can repeat the actions of another. Deferred imitation is when someone can repeat the actions of another even when the action is not happening right in front of them: For example, when Piaget watched his daughter have a temper tantrum that she had seen a neighboring child display the day before.

Whether infants are born with the ability to form mental representations, whether this ability develops sooner in the first year of life than Piaget initially predicted, or whether Piaget was right in suggesting a long developmental trajectory for object permanence, by the second half of the second year it is crystal clear that infants can imitate actions that they've seen previously, telling us for sure that they can mentally represent both objects and actions. The next developmental step in Piaget's theory is the ability to hold and manipulate *multiple* mental representations at the same time—an ability that develops (according to Piaget) between 2 and 7 years of age. Holding multiple representations at the same time is required for taking another person's perspective or for understanding that people might have different views of the world.

The classic way researchers have examined whether children can hold multiple representations is through the *Sally-Anne* task (Figure 16.2). In the task, researchers present children with two dolls, one named Sally and one named Anne. Next, the children watch as the Sally doll plays with a marble, puts the marble in a basket, and then leaves the room. While Sally is gone, the Anne doll takes the marble from the basket and moves it to a box. The researchers ask the children where Sally will look for the marble when she comes back. The obvious answer is that she'll look in the basket. But in order for children to answer the question correctly, they have to simultaneously

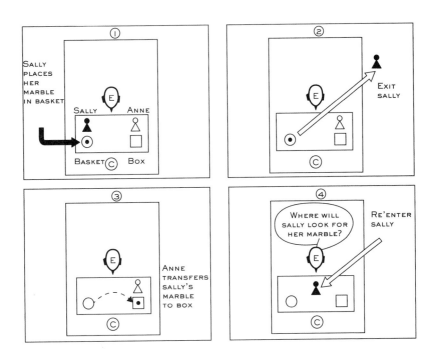

Figure 16.2 | Sally-Anne task. In the task, researchers present children with two dolls, one named Sally and one named Anne. Next, the children watch as the Sally doll plays with a marble, puts the marble in a basket, and then leaves the room. While Sally is gone, the Anne doll takes the marble from the basket and moves it to a box. The researchers ask the children where Sally will look for the marble when she comes back.

Source: Reprinted from Baron-Cohen, S., Leslie, A. M., & Frith, U. (1985). Does the autistic child have a "theory of mind?" *Cognition, 21*, 41, with permission of Elsevier.

represent that (1) Sally thinks the marble is in the basket but (2) that it is really in the box. Three-year-olds most often get this question wrong; they usually say that Sally thinks the marble is in the box. Why? Because according to Piaget, they can only hold one representation in their minds at a time, the current one being the actual state of affairs (the marble is in the box) (Baron-Cohen, Leslie, & Frith, 1985).

The ability to reason about the mental states of others is called *Theory of Mind*. This ability develops over the preschool years. During this time, children have problems taking the perspective of others or switching back and forth between multiple perspectives at once. In other words, you can't really blame a kid if he has trouble reasoning about how another kid might feel if a favorite toy got snatched away. Again, Piaget would say that the problem here is the inability to hold multiple representations at once. Many modern researchers disagree and would say that the problem might be about children's general knowledge or immature language ability. In experiments designed with so much language involved (like the Sally and Anne scenario), perhaps it's not surprising that children fail. Research has shown that in studies with fewer language requirements, much younger children can infer the mental states of others.

For example, Felix Warneken and Mike Tomasello (2006, 2007) from the Max Planck Institute in Leipzig presented infants with a playroom. While in the playroom, the infants watched as an experimenter tried and failed to achieve a goal. For example, the experimenter might drop a marker on the floor and then reach for it repeatedly, each time failing to pick it up. The research question was simple: Do the infants understand the intention (or mental state) of the researcher? Infants as young as 14 months of age did indeed understand the researcher's intention, and they responded by helpfully picking up the marker and handing it to the researcher. This suggests that even infants as young as 14 months of age might be able to reason about another person's point of view, which is much earlier than Piaget first proposed.

The final step in Piaget's cognitive ladder is the ability to hold abstract representations, or to think hypothetically. According to Piaget, we don't reach this final step until we are 11 or 12, or perhaps even later in adolescence. Before this age, Piaget proposed that children are bound to concrete thinking and have trouble reasoning about abstract concepts like love or gravity. As you can imagine, modern researchers have once again argued about the many ways in which Piaget might have underestimated children's abilities with abstract concepts as well. In fact, the debate over Piaget's theory is still alive and well in psychological science despite the fact that he died three decades ago and that his theory is nearly a century old.

Overall, Piaget thought of infants as "baby scientists" and found that they often learn by experimenting with the world around them independently. As a scientist myself, I can tell you firsthand that, on occasion, we do learn new things by experimenting with the world on our own. But most scientists make their most important discoveries while working with other (smarter) scientists. Consistent with this idea, another famous psychologist and contemporary of Piaget's named Lev Vygotsky agreed that infants could learn by experimenting with the world on their own, but suggested that perhaps they could learn *more* by interacting with other people, especially other people who are smarter than them (Vygotsky, 1980). He talked about the *zone of proximal development,* which is what children can learn on their own, versus what they might achieve with the help of a parent (Figure 16.3). Within the zone, he said that parents *scaffold* supportive behaviors to help children learn, much like the scaffolding on buildings provides support while they are growing taller.

You can think of scaffolding as simply modeling or reinforcing a behavior for a child. It happens quite naturally when parents and children are interacting, and often parents don't even know that they're doing it. For example, you can often see scaffolding when a mother is talking to her baby. It goes something like this: Baby makes a sound, mom smiles and repeats the sound more clearly and louder, and seeing

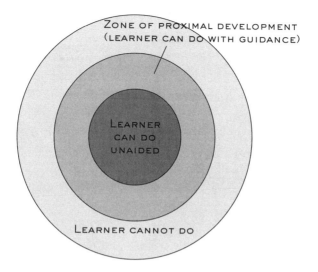

ZONE OF PROXIMAL DEVELOPMENT
(LEARNER CAN DO WITH GUIDANCE)

LEARNER
CAN DO
UNAIDED

LEARNER CANNOT DO

Figure 16.3 | Vygotsky's zone of proximal development. The middle circle illustrates what infants can do on their own, followed by what they can do with some help, and, finally, what they cannot yet do, even with the guidance of others.

mom smile acts as a reinforcement for the baby, encouraging him to make the sound again, but this time more clearly than before. Earlier I mentioned a study by Michael Goldstein and colleagues who studied how moms shape their babies' language learning. This is an example of scaffolding: After the researchers trained moms to reinforce their 8-month-olds by simply smiling and moving closer whenever their babies babbled, their babies babbled more, and they babbled better (see Chapter 14).

Parents are pretty good at doing this naturally, and research suggests that when given a problem-solving task to complete as a pair, parents skillfully give their 2-year-olds hints and instructions when needed, while at the same time also giving them space to explore and spend time off-task (Conner, Knight, & Cross, 1997). This kind of thing is called *guided play*, or play that involves the participation and guidance of a parent (Weisberg, Hirsh-Pasek, Golinkoff, Kittredge, & Klahr, 2016). As Vygotsky would have guessed, research on guided play has shown that children can often learn more with the help of a parent than by exploring a task on their own. For example, one study reported that children learn more about engineering from building a skyscraper with blocks when their parents asked simple open-ended questions (Haden, Cohen, Uttal, & Marcus, 2016). Children also learn more about how a new toy works when parents ask them to explain how they think it might work (Legare & Lombrozo, 2014). It's important to note here that parents don't have to do too much; asking questions and dropping hints is useful, but providing too much information through direct instruction may not be. Indeed, children learn more by exploring on their own than by watching an adult do something for them (Sobel & Sommerville, 2010), and they explore more if parents don't give them instructions about how to use a new toy (Bonawitz, Shafto, Gweon, Goodman, Spelke, & Schulz, 2011).

The moral of the story is that children can learn by playing the "baby scientist" and experimenting with the world on their own, but there are cases where they might learn more by playing with someone who's smarter than they are—someone like you. Again, this doesn't mean you have to think really hard about what you're going to say when playing with your child; parents scaffold behaviors naturally in the course of their everyday interactions. And who knows: Asking simple questions and providing a few helpful hints along the way might give kids the little push they need to reach their full "scientific" potential.

Edwin has a long way to go in terms of cognitive development, but, in the meantime, I'm happy to know that I'm helping his journey by simply playing with him every day. He might be well on his way toward forming mental representations of objects and people, but it will be a while before he can hold multiple representations at the same time and a long while before he can think in the abstract. That's fine by me: One important feature that having a Theory of Mind affords us is the ability to lie or to report a state of affairs that is different from reality. I am in absolutely no rush for my sweet little baby who can't even talk yet to turn into a tiny human who is capable of stealing from our cookie jar (representation 1) and then telling me that he didn't do it (representation 2). I guess it's bound to happen eventually though—he does love food.

17

THE SEVENTH MONTH

MEDIA AND SCREEN USE

Well, it's finally happened—this month, we said goodbye to nursing for good. The last time we checked in on the state of my breasts, Edwin was still nursing, but mostly in the middle of the night and in the morning and only accepting the bottle during the day. In the past few weeks, he's decided to refuse the breast in the middle of the night and in the morning and will only take the bottle. Since I'm not about to get up at 3 AM to give him a bottle *and then* pump, I was going about 9 hours without pumping or nursing. The missed night feeding caused my milk supply to quickly plummet to almost nothing, so with him eating real food and accepting formula, we decided it was finally time to say goodbye to breast milk. We made it a whole 6 months, so I should be happy and proud and probably relieved to finally be done—and I am. But I'm also a little bit sad that I won't have any more of those late night bonding moments with Edwin anymore. It's a bittersweet farewell, but I am happy to have my body back.

Edwin is almost sitting up by himself and becoming increasingly mobile, enjoying the ease with which he can now prop himself up on his belly and roll around in his crib. Sometimes I will put him to bed on his back on one side of the crib facing north only to find that, when I wake up, he is on his belly at the opposite end of the crib facing south. If he hears someone coming into his bedroom, he can roll over and prop himself up on his belly to get enough height to peek at who's there. It's clear that he wants to move around on his own pretty badly, so we got him a walker. Again, some doctors will tell you that walkers are a no-no because they have caused injury to lots of infants who have walked right down a flight of stairs, walker and all. We don't have stairs that could easily hurt him on the first floor, so we decided there was little risk in letting him explore (see Chapter 13).

The other new development this month is that he's suddenly very interested in screens, including the television, our smartphones, and laptops. He stares at the TV any time it's on, no matter what the content is, and he will even crane his neck to get a look at the screen if he's facing the opposite direction. He reaches for my cell phone whenever the screen turns on and desperately throws his body in the directly of my laptop if it's on the couch with him (Figure 17.1). The American Academy of Pediatrics (AAP) put out a policy report in 2011 recommending that children under the age of 2 should not watch any television. They updated their policy in 2016, recommending now that infants under 18 months of age stay away from screens as much as possible unless it is to video chat with grandparents or other relatives (Council on Communications, 2016).

They cite several reasons for these recommendations. First, they argue that although "educational" television programming has been shown to have positive learning outcomes for preschool-aged and older children, there is no evidence that it has such benefits for children under the age of 2. Second, they say that television takes time away from other important activities, like creative play. Third, they claim that there are negative consequences of watching too much television, including aggressive behavior, sleep problems, and an inability to concentrate in school. Finally, they argue that even having television

Figure 17.1 | Edwin, much more interested in my iPhone than in his toys.
Source: Vanessa LoBue.

on in the background can be distracting to both children and parents, keeping parents from interacting with their children and keeping children from concentrating on other activities.

A year ago when I first got pregnant, I would have said no problem—my kid isn't going to watch TV *at all*, let alone in the first 2 years of his life. I used to judge parents at restaurants whose kids' faces were buried in tablets or hand-held video games. I used to scoff at mini-vans with built-in DVD players and swear that my future perfect children would choose a book over a movie. I take back my premature judgment. Now that I have a kid of my own, I'm starting to see why parents put on a movie at dinnertime or give their kids an iPhone to keep them quiet at a restaurant. I would, of course, love to entertain my child 24 hours a day, 7 days a week. That's the ideal isn't it? To keep them engaged in an educational and intellectually stimulating activity every waking hour of the day? Unfortunately, this is just not realistic for most parents, especially working parents who need at least a small slice of time during the day to get something done, like making dinner or simply having a cup of coffee in the morning.

In fact, in a survey of more than 300 parents on their infants' screen time habits, only about 9% kept with the AAP's policy and had a "no-television" rule for their babies (Barr, Danzinger, Hilliard, Andolina, & Ruskis, 2010). According to Common Sense Media, children under the age of 8 in the United States spend about 2 hours a day with screen media, including television, DVDs, computers, video games, and mobile devices. Furthermore, while 58% percent are read to every day, 65% watch television every day, and 36% of these children live in households where television is on *all day long*. Many of these children have a television in their own bedrooms—including 45% of 5- to 8-year-olds, 37% of 2- to 4-year-olds, and even 16% of 0- to 1-year-olds (Common Sense Media, 2013). So, with the popularity of screen-based media in most households today, it is virtually impossible to keep our children from being exposed to it. What's a parent to do?

Research does have some answers. First, let's talk about the content of children's media. I was really shocked to find out this month how many children's television shows there are nowadays that are "educational." Just by flipping through PBS or the Disney Channel, I was incredibly impressed by how much science, math, and music content is burgeoning on children's television shows. I put "educational" in quotes because most shows tout educational content, but it is not always clear whether children learn from them. Does having educational content mean that children really learn from watching TV? The answer is that it depends.

There is evidence that preschool-aged children can learn from educational media. A new study by Melissa Kearney and Phillip Levine from the National Bureau of Economic Research examined the long-term of effects of watching *Sesame Street* from the time when the show first aired in 1969. The researchers found that children who lived in areas that had access to the show were less likely to fall behind in school. Importantly, this was especially true for children living in socioeconomically disadvantaged areas (Kearney & Levine, 2015). Learning benefits have also been reported for other educational programs besides *Sesame Street* (Linebarger, Kosanic, Greenwood, & Doku, 2004; Wright et al., 2001), so it does appear that children can learn from TV.

However, there are some important caveats to this work. First, children do not necessarily learn from every television show they watch. In fact, research has shown that watching noneducational, general-audience shows predicts *lower* academic skills in preschool-aged children (Wright et al., 2001). Second, as the AAP points out, there is very little or even no evidence that *infants* can learn from educational media, which is in part what led to their recommendation of no TV for children under the age of 2. Finally, the fact that children can learn from educational media doesn't mean that they wouldn't learn *more* from engaging in other activities. For example, in one study examining whether a popular educational DVD could effectively teach infants new words (as advertised), the researchers found that infants learned virtually nothing from watching the DVD. On top of that, they reported that babies learned the highest number of new words in a condition where they didn't watch the DVD at all, and parents were instructed to just teach their infants each of the new words themselves (DeLoache et al., 2010).

Two additional studies on the same topic also found that babies ranging from 12 to 25 months do not learn new words from educational DVD's aimed at teaching babies words (Richert, Robb, Fender, & Wartella, 2010; Robb, Richert, & Wartella, 2009), and, in fact, one of these studies reported that the only thing that actually predicted infants' word production was the amount of time they were read to each day (Robb et al., 2009). Studies show that babies also imitate less and remember less from demonstrations they see on screens than from face-to-face interactions with a live model (Barr, 2013), suggesting that screens may have a lot less to offer in terms of educational value for infants than the media itself might suggest.

And most infant-directed media does indeed claim to have educational value. In a recent analysis of 58 infant-directed television programs targeted at children aged 0–3, researchers found that *most* of these programs make some sort of claim about the educational benefits of the show (Fenstermacher et al., 2010). One of the conclusions we can draw from this research is that, despite widespread claims of the educational value in television shows, we should have very few expectations about what infants under the age of 2 can gain from watching television. This shouldn't be surprising, given that infants are not verbal and are likely to have a difficult time understanding what television *is*, let alone interpret the content of a children's TV show. In fact, research by Judy DeLoache and colleagues at the University of Virginia has shown that 9-month-old infants don't understand two-dimensional displays like photographs or videos, and grasp and pat them as if they were real three-dimensional objects (DeLoache, Pierroutsakos, Uttal, Rosengren, & Gottlieb, 1998; Pierroutsakos & Troseth, 2003). Edwin does this all the time: He explores images in the books we read to him as if he's trying to grab Elmo right off the pages, and every night he pets the dragonflies on his crib bumper as if they were real.

What photos and books and screens all have in common is that they are *symbols* for something else: They represent something that isn't really there. Classic research that Judy DeLoache did several decades ago suggests that children have quite a difficult time understanding symbols. She found this out by mistake, which I know because I was her graduate student for 7 years, and she shared this story with me during my time under her mentorship. As a young budding researcher, Judy wanted to study children's memory, and she came up with a task that she thought would be a piece of cake for preschool-aged children. She built a scale model of her lab—sort of like a dollhouse, but with only one room—and showed it to children. She then hid a tiny Snoopy doll in the small model of the room, and asked whether the 2 ½- and 3-year-old children could find a larger version of the Snoopy doll in the identical full-sized lab room. As she expected, 3-year-olds had no problem acing this task, and, after watching Judy hide the tiny Snoopy doll in the small model room, they easily pranced into the identical lab and found the big Snoopy doll hidden in the exact same place. What was so surprising was that 2½-year-olds completely failed the task. Like the 3-year-olds, they watched as Judy hid the small Snoopy doll in the scale model, but when they wandered into the full-sized lab room they looked completely confused, searching everywhere they could think of without finding the doll. The kicker is, they had no problem *remembering* where little Snoopy was hidden in the model: After failing to find big Snoopy in the full-sized room, all of the 2½-year-olds were easily able to successfully remember where little Snoopy was hiding in the little room (DeLoache, 1987).

After some thinking, Judy realized that perhaps the younger children weren't failing because they had problems remembering where big Snoopy was hidden; perhaps they failed because they couldn't see the relationship between the small model room and the larger full-sized room that it represented. In other words, they were unable to use the model as a *symbol* for the larger room in order to correctly locate big Snoopy. To test out her hypothesis, she figured that if 2½-year-olds really failed because they couldn't see the relationship between the small and the big room, perhaps they would succeed if they somehow thought the small model room *was* the big room. How would you convince children of that, you might ask? Judy decided to tell 2½-year-olds that she could *shrink* the larger room into its miniature version. She reasoned that if children thought the small room was just a shrunken version of the large room, there was no need to use it as a symbol—it wasn't a symbol anymore, it was just the very same room.

She did this by introducing 2½-year-old children to a "shrinking machine" (which was really an old oscilloscope that she got from the physics department). She told children that the machine could make big things little and little things big. She then showed them a troll doll—called Terry the Troll—and told them that they could use the shrinking machine to shrink Terry. She turned the machine on and then took the children into the next room where they could hear the shrinking machine working (i.e., making various noises played from a nearby cassette tape). While the children were listening, a sneaky experimenter switched full-sized Terry with a mini-version of him so that when Judy let the children back into the room, it appeared as if the machine had indeed shrunk Terry. After a few rounds of making Terry big and then little again, Judy introduced the children to a large room (Terry's room; made of plastic piping and cloth). She then hid Terry somewhere in his room (e.g., under a pillow, in a drawer, or in a basket), turned the shrinking machine on, and again led the children out of the room. While listening to the machine work, those sneaky experimenters moved the large version of the room behind a curtain and replaced it with a small identical model, with mini Terry hidden in the same place Judy had previously hidden big Terry. When the children came back into the room, this time, they had no problem finding Terry. The experiment was a success, and Judy found that 2½-year-olds—who failed to find big Snoopy after seeing him hidden in a small scale model of a large lab space—had no problem finding the big and small versions of Terry the Troll when they thought that the small version of Terry's room *was* the big version (just shrunken down; Figure 17.2). This suggests that children, at least under the age of 3, have trouble seeing the relationship between something symbolic, like a model room, a photograph, or something depicted on a screen and the actual real-life object that those symbols represent (DeLoache, Miller, & Rosengren, 1997).

It takes quite a while for children to fully understand the way symbols work, which means it also takes them a while to realize that what they see on TV isn't real. John Flavell and his colleagues at Stanford University presented 3- and 4-year-olds with a film of balloons being inflated on a television screen. He then asked the children whether the balloons would come floating out into the room if he took off the top of the TV. The 4-year-olds responded as if the experimenters were crazy, and they clearly knew that objects depicted on the screen were not real, but a substantial portion of the 3-year-olds thought that the balloons

Figure 17.2 | The shrinking machine and Terry the Troll from Judy DeLoache's shrinking room study. In the study, Judy convinced 2½- and 3-year-old children that she had a shrinking machine that could shrink full-sized Terry the Troll (*left*) to mini Terry (*right*).

Source: DeLoache, J. S., Early understanding and use of symbols: The model model. *Current Directions in Psychological Science, 4(4)*, 112, reprinted with permission of SAGE Publications, Inc.

might indeed fly out of the top of the TV if the experimenters removed it (Flavell, Flavell, Green, & Korfmacher, 1990). Altogether, this work suggests that really young children—particularly infants and children under the ages of 2 or 3—are not likely to understand the content of what they're seeing when they're looking at a television screen.

One more thing worth mentioning about the content of children's television is that watching violent or aggressive behavior on TV can lead to aggressive behavior in children. I know that this has been presented as a controversial issue in the media, but the research is quite clear: Watching violent behavior on television can make your child behave more aggressively. Alfred Bandura and his colleagues at Stanford University asked whether children can learn aggressive behaviors by watching aggressive displays on TV all the way back in the 1960s. In the study, preschool-aged children watched a video of an adult playing with a Bobo Doll, which is essentially a blowup doll with sand at the base that wobbles back and forth when touched. The adult depicted in the video sat on Bobo and punched him, kicked him, and hit him on the head with a toy mallet. Later, the children were invited to play with the very same Bobo doll they saw in the video, along with various other toys. Not surprisingly, children who watched the adult play aggressively with Bobo imitated the behaviors they saw in the video— they were more likely than other children to punch, kick, and hit the Bobo doll. On top of that, these children also played more aggressively with the other toys in the room, including toy guns. So it wasn't just that children were imitating the behaviors they saw; watching the aggressive video resulted in these children playing more aggressively *overall* (Bandura, Ross, & Ross, 1963).

To sum up, if you're going to let your kids watch TV, content is important. There are so many educational programs marketed for kids these days that parents don't need to turn to adult-centered programming or shows that contain aggression or violent behavior. But, if you have a child under the age of 2, there's not much that can be gained from watching TV, and, in fact, one study showed that for every hour that infants under the age of 2 watched TV, there was a 17-point drop in a standard language test (Zimmerman, Christakis, & Meltzoff, 2007). The TV itself is not what caused the language deficit; as the AAP points out, it's the fact that TV is replacing other more enriching activities—playing, talking to parents, interacting with other children—that is likely causing the effect (Figure 17.3).

It's also important to note that having the television on in the background distracts kids from other activities, like playing with toys or talking to parents. Research suggests that its distracting nature also reduces the quality of children's play (Schmidt, Pempek, Kirkorian, Lund, & Anderson, 2008). Even newer work shows that babies play less when their *parents* are distracted by screens; instead of concentrating on playing, babies spend their time trying to regain their parents' attention when the parent is distracted by a screen (Myruski et al., 2018). Screens can distract parents from teaching their children effectively as well. In a recent study from Temple University and the University of Delaware, researchers brought mothers and their 2-year-olds into the lab and asked mothers to teach their toddlers two brand new words. While the mothers were attempting to teach their children one of the two words, the researchers made sure that they were interrupted by their cell phones. The researchers found that 2-year-olds only learned new words when their mothers were not distracted by their phones during the teaching portion of the study, regardless of the number of times the mother presented their toddlers with the new word. In other words, it didn't matter how many times the mother said the new word out loud—if they were interrupted by their cell phones, their toddlers had a hard time learning (Reed, Hirsh-Pasek, & Golkinkoff, 2017). This suggests that screens can be distracting to both children and parents if they interrupt other activities.

Despite the obvious negatives of screen-time use, newer screen technology can also provide us and our babies with important opportunities if we use it properly. For example, smartphones and touchpads are now giving us the chance to communicate with far away relatives

Figure 17.3 | Mesmerized by dancing Grover.
Source: Vanessa LoBue.

face-to-face for the very first time. With FaceTime and other video chat platforms, infants are now afforded with the opportunity to meet and speak with family members like grandparents, aunts, uncles, and cousins that they wouldn't normally get to see more than once a year (or less). You might be wondering at this point whether babies can figure out that they can interact with people that they see on a screen via FaceTime. The answer seems to be yes. In a recent study by researchers at Lafayette College, children aged 12–25 months were taught different kinds of words and actions using video chat. Half the infants interacted with a live person on FaceTime, whereas the other half just saw prerecorded videos of the same person demonstrating the same words and actions (just not live). After a week of interacting with their new video chat friend, infants who saw the live person on FaceTime recognized that person and learned more words and actions than did infants who just saw a prerecorded video. This suggests that not only can infants actively engage with FaceTime or video chat, but they might even be able to learn from these interactions, as long as they are live (Myers, LeWitt, Gallo, & Maselli, 2017).

Now that I'm a parent, people have been asking me a lot about what I think of screen time—most of them with a nervous twitch, hoping that I won't tell them that they are terrible parents for letting their kids watch 20 minutes of cartoons every day. Based on research and on my personal desire to stay sane, I think a good rule of thumb is to ask yourself, "What is screen time replacing?" Does watching _Seseme Street_ in the morning for 10 minutes replace an agitated interaction with a half-awake, unengaged parent who can subsequently function better by having that 10 minutes to herself? Does watching a DVD in the car on a long road trip replace an hour and a half of crying or fighting with a sibling? In cases where screens are replacing something that is not otherwise educational or enriching for the child, or if it is giving you enough energy to be the wonderfully engaged parent that you know you can be, I don't think there's anything wrong with a little bit of screen time, given that the content is appropriate (e.g., child directed, non-violent), and it is very, very limited for children under the age of 2. It is a completely different issue altogether if a child is spending hours and hours in front of the TV or an iPad instead going outside to play with his friends, reading a book, doing homework, engaging with family members, or simply talking with you. If this is the case, then thinking about some stricter rules for screentime might be warrented.

Edwin is nearly 7 months old and way too young to understand anything he sees on a screen, so his screentime is pretty limited. But I've already found that he loves watching the characters from _Seseme_

Street dance and sing, so I have no problem playing him very short clips from the *Sesame Street Songs* channel on YouTube during car trips, plane rides, or instances where he's too cranky to do anything but cry. Sometimes a few minutes of watching Elmo sing and dance with Usher is just what he needs to calm down and just what I need to keep it together. Parenting is hard work, and it's a 24-hour job, so we shouldn't feel bad about taking a little time out once in awhile.

18

THE EIGHTH MONTH

ATTACHMENT

Our farewell to nursing came just in time: This month Edwin finally sprouted his first tooth (which I imagine wouldn't feel great latched onto a nipple), which was quickly followed by his second. He's been "teething" for about 4 months now, gnawing on anything he can get his hands on while producing buckets of drool in the process. He's worn a bib nonstop for what seems like forever. Finally, this month, two little dots of white started rising out of his gums, and the gnawing that he does on his toys started to leave a mark. He's also completely sitting up by himself and (after another painful bout of sleep training) is *finally* sleeping through the night. As the end of my maternity leave is quickly nearing, this is all happening at exactly the right time. Unfortunately, the first signs of *separation anxiety* are also beginning to sprout, which might make the transition to going back to work a little bit harder.

Separation anxiety is when a child has a negative emotional response to being separated from his mother. As I mentioned before, Edwin has a pretty easy temperament so he's been fine with anyone holding him and has generally smiled in response to strangers.

This is still true most of the time, but lately when we are in a new place with a large number of new people, he gets a bit cranky if he's not with me or Nick. Some babies who have more difficult or slow-to-warm-up temperaments have a much stronger reaction to being held by strangers, with the most anxious babies being moved to tears at the approach of someone new. Separation anxiety is said to be the first sign of infant *attachment*. Attachment is an infant's relationship to his caregiver or, most commonly, to his mother. Some people have described attachment as an infant's *love* for his mother, but something like love is really difficult to pin down in infants. Instead, to study the development of attachment in the first few years of life, researchers look at how babies react when their mothers leave the room, or by how much babies cling to their mothers in a new situation, or by how comforted babies are when their mothers soothe them.

The traditional view of why babies become attached to or begin to love their mothers is because their mothers are usually the ones who feed them. It turns out that this explanation isn't quite right. A famous researcher named Harry Harlow from the University of Wisconsin studied attachment in baby rhesus monkeys in the 1950s and discovered that baby monkeys don't necessarily attach to just anything that feeds them. He discovered this by separating baby monkeys from their mothers at birth and giving them two new "mothers" to interact with. One of the new "mothers" was a monkey doll made of wire with a bottle attached to it and the other "mother" was a monkey doll made of cloth. The wire "mother" was able to feed the baby monkeys, while the cloth "mother" was comforting to the touch. Harlow observed how much time the baby monkeys spent with each of their new "mothers" and where the baby monkeys turned to for support when presented with something new or scary. Surprisingly, he found that the baby monkeys only spent time with the wire mother when they wanted to eat, and they spent the rest of their time clinging to the cloth mother. Most importantly, when Harlow presented the baby monkeys with a new situation or a scary toy, they immediately ran to the cloth mother for comfort (Harlow, 1958).

Obviously, we would never do an experiment like this with human babies; it isn't ethical to separate a baby from his mother for long periods of time for research purposes (in fact, it's doubtful that Harlow's studies with monkeys would be considered ethical today). But, a decade later, a psychologist named Mary Ainsworth from Johns Hopkins University and the University of Virginia thought of a way to study attachment in infants and developed an experiment she called the "strange situation." She named it the strange situation because it's . . . well . . . *strange*, at least from the perspective of an infant. In the study, mothers were invited to bring their 12-month-old babies to a lab space to sit together and play with a group of toys. After a few minutes, a new experimenter (a stranger) entered the room and sat down near the baby. After a few more minutes, the baby's mother was told to stand up and leave the room, leaving the baby alone with the stranger. Finally, the mother returned to the room a few minutes later. Ainsworth was interested in what babies would do when the stranger entered, when their mothers left, and, most importantly, when their mothers returned.

By looking at these simple behaviors, Ainsworth was able to classify infants into one of four attachment styles. Most babies were "securely attached" (~65%); they were happy to play in a new place when their mothers were around, they were distressed or at least noticed when their mothers left the room, and they were comforted when their mothers came back, embracing her happily. Babies that she called "insecure/avoidant" were indifferent to their mothers' presence; they weren't alarmed when she left the room, and they didn't seem to care when she came back. The "anxious/resistant" babies clung to their mothers the entire time they were in the room, were really upset when she left, but couldn't be comforted when she returned. In fact, some of them seemed somewhat *angry* with her for leaving in the first place. The last group, called "disorganized/

disoriented" did not fit neatly into any of the other categories, showing a mix of approach and avoidance responses to their mothers and generally looked confused throughout the study (Ainsworth, 1979; Karen, 1990).

Although this research was originally done nearly 50 years ago and was specific to children in the United States, it highlights that the process of attachment isn't necessarily related to who feeds the baby; instead, it's related to mothers' sensitivity to their infants' needs and their subsequent responsiveness. Infants of responsive mothers learn that when they are upset, their mothers will be there to comfort them. This is an incredibly important developmental process in the first few years of life when it's vital for infants to explore the world around them in order to learn new things. During this time, mothers act as a secure base for exploration, making infants feel safe to experiment with the world since they have a dependable caregiver nearby to help if something goes wrong. This is why Ainsworth referred to a healthy attachment as a "secure attachment": Securely attached infants feel confident enough in their mothers' presence to explore new situations; they feel less confident when she leaves the room, but her return immediately restores their confidence and they can continue to explore the world freely.

So, although this new phase where Edwin doesn't like being separated from me can be inconvenient, it is a normal part of a healthy attachment. And a healthy attachment is important: While having a secure attachment has all sorts of positive outcomes like a healthy self-esteem and positive social relationships, insecure attachments predict various psychological problems like anxiety later in development (e.g., Lewis-Morrarty et al., 2015). Generally, a lack of any kind of preference for mom over strangers is often seen as a sign of trouble. In fact, children who grow up without an attachment figure or a primary caregiver tend to show a behavior called *indiscriminate friendliness*, where they treat everyone the same way—they are willing to walk away with a stranger, get in anyone's car, or hold anyone's hand, however strange or familiar the person (Gleason et al., 2014). This might sound pretty good at first, especially if you have a super clingy child, but when you think about it, a child who doesn't distinguish between his or her primary caregiver and a total stranger is incredibly problematic, and this behavior usually only characterizes children who have been raised in some sort of social deprivation, like in an orphanage.

Despite the enduring charm of famous orphan stories like Batman or Oliver Twist, orphanages are no longer common in the United States, and they began to disappear around the 1950s, when many countries started to favor foster care over institutionalized care. But orphanages do still exist more prominently in some countries. In the 1960s, the Romanian government, for example, adopted policies outlawing both abortion and contraception, which led to a massive increase in the country's birth rate. A few decades later, in attempt to pay back some of Romania's debt, austerity measures were put in place to ration food, making the struggle for families supporting several children even worse. One result of these policies was a large number of abandoned children—estimated at 170,000—living in Romanian orphanages under incredibly poor conditions (Zeanah, Humphreys, Fox, & Nelson, 2017). Notably, these children did not often have a primary attachment figure; they were generally housed in rooms with large numbers of children who were all cared for by a single person and not necessarily the same person every day. You can imagine that besides the devastating effects caused by poverty alone, the lack of a primary attachment figure could have detrimental effects on the children's social well-being.

To study the long-term effects of institutionalized care on attachment and on child development more generally, in 2000, a group of researchers founded the Bucharest Early Intervention Project—a research program aimed at studying the long-lasting effects of early deprivation in Romanian orphanages and how children raised in these orphanages might benefit from being placed in foster care. The study started with 136 children between the ages of 6 and 31 months living in orphanages, and half were randomly assigned to move to high-quality foster care. The researchers have now been studying the long-term differences between the group that remained institutionalized and the group that was moved to high-quality foster care for more than 10 years.

First, it may not surprise you to learn that the children who remained in orphanages did not fair well when compared to the children who were placed in foster care; they experienced deficits across almost all of the areas the researchers studied, including physical development, brain development, IQ, and social functioning. The children who were removed from the orphanages and placed in foster care actually caught up to children in Romania who never lived in an orphanage in many ways, and the younger they were when they were removed from institutionalized care, the better they did (Zeanah et al., 2017). So, early interventions for children who spend much of their infancy in impoverished environments can indeed be effective.

However, what's most relevant here is that where children often suffered most was in the domain of attachment, and it is also where many of the improvements were observed when children were placed in the foster system. First, children who were placed in foster care soon after birth were much more likely to have secure attachments between the ages of 3 and 4 years than children who remained in institutionalized care (Smyke, Zeanah, Fox, Nelson, & Guthrie, 2010). Furthermore, researchers found that attachment security to the new foster family served as a protective factor against the development of various psychological disorders. In other words, children who were in the foster care group and formed secure attachments to their new caregivers were the least likely to develop anxiety, depression, and other psychological problems when compared to the institutionalized children and the foster care children who hadn't developed a secure attachment relationship (McGoron et al., 2012; McLaughlin, Zeanah, Fox, & Nelson, 2012). Further studies have confirmed this trend in more typically developing infants: If infants with insecure attachments then receive highly responsive parenting, they show improvements in social competence later in development (Belsky & Fearon, 2002).

However, despite the fact that some improvements were observed in children who were moved from orphanages to foster care, there were also ongoing negative long-term effects of institutionalized care. For example, children in both the institutionalized group and in the foster care group continued to show signs of indiscriminate friendliness with strangers even at the age of 4 and 5 years (Gleason et al., 2014), suggesting that not having a primary attachment figure from early in life can cause problems with future attachments in the long term.

Since most infants in the United States are no longer raised in orphanages, you might ask what causes typical infants—who live in a home with some kind of primary caregiver—to develop an insecure attachment? Since I've become a new mom, I've found that parent-centered media often cautions about the various ways you might destroy your attachment relationship with your infant: by letting them cry for small amounts of time via sleep training, by leaving them with a babysitter overnight, or even by telling them about Santa Claus. There is no evidence to back up any of these claims (for example, see Chapter 11). What really causes an infant to develop an insecure attachment is having a mother or primary caregiver who is unresponsive to the infant's needs for *an extended period time*. For example, infants and preschoolers of mothers who suffer from chronic depression are more likely to develop an insecure attachment when compared to children of non-depressed mothers (Martins & Gaffan, 2000; Teti, Gelfand, Messinger, & Isabella, 1995). Similarly, having an insecure or disorganized attachment is related to childhood instances of maltreatment and neglect (Baer & Martinez, 2006). Again, interventions focused on developing maternal sensitivity have been effective in promoting better attachment security (Bakermas-Kranenburg, Van Ijzendoorn, & Juffer, 2005), so if you're concerned, talking to a specialist can likely help.

Theoretically, an infant's initial attachment to his or her mother provides a model for attachment relationships with other people, like friends, extended family, and eventually a romantic partner. But there is something special about having a primary attachment figure in those first few years. Without the presence of a mother or father or other primary attachment figure, infants don't know how to develop trust with some people and not with others, and they don't have a secure place that makes them feel that they can explore and take risks. Recently, researchers have found evidence to suggest that early attachment relationships shape the way fear and other emotions develop in the brain (Gee et al., 2014). To do this, they focused on the amygdala—the part of the brain that is activated when we experience emotions like fear. They found that when children are presented with something new or scary, their amygdala's are less active when their mothers are present than when their mothers are absent. This suggests that a child's mother might act as a buffer from activating that part of the brain most associated with fear, giving children the freedom to explore new things in the comfort of their mother's presence. As further evidence for this point, researchers have also found that the amygdala is activated more readily in children who grow up in foster care and typically grow up without a mother figure (Gee et al., 2013), again suggesting that a mother's presence can affect a child's developing brain, potentially protecting it from experiencing fear in the face of something new or challenging. These effects seem to lessen as children approach adolescence (Gee et al., 2014), suggesting that as the amygdala (and the child) matures, the need for his or her mother's presence as a secure base for exploration becomes less important.

Although an infant's mother is usually his most prominent attachment figure, infants have attachments to lots of other people, too, including their fathers, grandparents, nannies, and others. In fact, attachment doesn't end in infancy—everyone has attachment figures, even adults. Imagine yourself at a party filled with people you don't know (strangers, if you will). What is the first thing you do? If you've come alone, it's likely that you'll look for someone you know in the crowd. Once you've spotted your friend getting a drink in the corner, you immediately feel better as you approach them. Maybe you're like me—a little shy and introverted—and you wouldn't even attempt to go to a party alone. I would bring someone (probably my husband) with me. In fact, the very idea of having Nick with me in a strange place immediately puts me at ease. This is because my mother isn't my only attachment figure; I'm also attached to my father, my brother, and I'm very attached to my husband. All of these people can provide comfort in times when I'm feeling anxious.

When I was a graduate student at the University of Virginia, Nick and I were subjects in my friend Jim Coan's research that focuses on how being around a loved one might help reduce anxiety in new or threatening situations. For the study, Jim put me in an functional magnetic resonance imaging (fMRI) machine, which is a giant magnet that can record images of the brain. The machine is a highly claustrophobic, tube-like mechanism that you lie in and look at a small screen while researchers scan your brain. I didn't really know what the experiment was going to be about at the time, only that it was a study about relationships and that Nick had to come with me to the lab. Once I was not so comfortably situated in the fMRI machine, the experiment started and directions appeared on a small screen on the ceiling of the scanner. They said that in a series of trials, I would either see a green circle or a red "x." If I saw a green circle, the trial would simply end after a few seconds. If I saw a red "x," there was a 25% chance that I would receive an uncomfortable electric shock a few seconds later.

For about 5 minutes, the experiment went on just as the instructions said it would. Then I heard Jim's voice through a speaker tell me that, for the next set of trials, someone I didn't know would come in the room and hold my hand. From inside the scanner I couldn't see the person's face, but it appeared that a man about my age was walking into the room and coming over to hold my hand through the next set of trials. After another 5 minutes, the man left and I heard Jim's voice again. This time he told me that, for the last set of trials, Nick was going to come in and hold my hand. The door opened again, and, even though I couldn't see his face, I could tell that it was Nick who was now walking over and picking up my hand. Immediately I felt the anxiety of seeing the dreaded red "x" slip away.

After the study was over, Jim told me that he wasn't interested in how I responded to the shock itself; instead, he was interested in how my brain reacted to the *anticipation* of being shocked—what was happening in my brain between seeing the red "x" and feeling the shock. Specific parts of our brain are activated when we anticipate something bad happening or in the presence of something threatening in the environment. Jim found that the brain's reaction to the anticipation of something threatening (like an electric shock) is lessened when your spouse is holding your hand. So when Nick was holding my hand, my brain (and clearly my body) was more relaxed when I saw that red "x" than when I was holding a stranger's hand or no hand at all. Jim found the same result in a full sample of 16 couples, and the happier the couples were together, the greater the effect (Coan, Schaefer, & Davidson, 2006). This means that physical contact with a loved one (or attachment figure) during a stressful time can decrease the brain's stress response. So, when you're feeling anxious, physical contact with an attachment figure might be just what you need to take the edge off.

We are lucky that Edwin's separation anxiety is pretty minimal so far and only seems to kick in when there are a lot of strangers in a loud and crowded room. That doesn't mean that he doesn't love me as much as babies who do cry when handed to strangers; it just means that he is responding according to his temperament, approaching novel situations and people with minimal negative emotion. Babies vary widely in their personal style of emotional responding, and there is no right or wrong way to handle new people and new situations.

Figure 18.1 | An infant with his primary attachment figure.
Source: Vanessa LoBue.

All babies, regardless of temperament, grow to love their mommies, or whoever their primary caregiver might be. Hopefully, when we hand him off to the nanny next month, Edwin will smile just like he does when he greets most strangers (Figure 18.1). At least one of us should be smiling, right?

19

THE NINTH MONTH

EARLY CHILDCARE

In September, everyone goes back to school, and, if you're a teacher or a professor (or both), back to school also means back to work. That means that my time at home with Edwin—12 weeks of maternity leave plus a summer with no teaching commitments—was coming to an end. Unfortunately for most parents, going back to work after having a baby likely happens much sooner. According to the Family and Medical Leave Act (FMLA), full-time employees in the United States are entitled to up to 12 weeks of maternity leave. That sounds nice, but those 12 weeks often come without pay and health benefits, and it only holds for full-time employees; part-timers aren't entitled to anything. Furthermore, FMLA only applies to *women* who have children—men generally don't get the same benefits and usually have to go back to work almost immediately. Of 10 friends who recently had babies, I was the only one who got the full 12 weeks with full pay and benefits. Compared to what other countries offer, these US policies are grossly insufficient: According to a recent survey of 185 different countries by the International Labor Organization, all but three had mandatory time off with pay for women—Oman, Papua New Guinea, and the United States were the only ones that didn't (Addati, Cassirer, & Gilchrist, 2014). In fact, many countries had mandatory paid leave for *men* as well.

According to a recent report from the Center for American Progress, almost two-thirds (64.4%) of moms work, compared to only one-fourth (25%) in 1970 (Glynn, 2016). So, even with paid maternity leave, working women all face the inevitable day when they have to leave their babies in someone else's care. For me, it came exactly 8 months after he was born: On the first day of September, I had to hand my baby off to another woman to care for. That morning, our new nanny came to pick up Edwin at 6:45 AM so that I could head into the office for the first time in months. There was a lot of fussing and crying, but not by Edwin—by me. Edwin was fine. He smiled at his brand-new caregiver when she walked up to the house, just like he smiles at everyone else. As she took him from my arms, I nervously read down a list of his feeding and nap schedules, adding some tidbits here and there about how to get him to sleep, or what mood he's typically in when he wakes up. A few minutes later she drove away with my baby, and I drove to work by myself.

This all sounds really melodramatic, I know. If I were you, I'd be rolling my eyes at me, too. But this is really what it felt like, and I had no idea that I would feel such strong emotions when it came time to go back to work. Like I've said many times now, I *love* my job. For the past 8 months, I've missed my students, I've missed teaching, and I've missed writing—I've even taken on the task of writing a book to keep my mind busy. During some of Edwin's episodes of inconsolable crying, I fantasized about what it would be like to be in my quiet office instead of with my screaming baby. I had jealous feelings toward Nick, who got to go back to work after 6 weeks while I stayed home all by myself with the baby, and I even found myself wishing from time to time that Nick would have been the one to stay at home so that I could go back to work. I never once felt bad about having these thoughts—that is, until the night before the nanny came to pick Edwin up for the first time. All of sudden, I felt an overwhelming rush of guilt for feeling those things and sadness that I didn't savor every single minute that I had with my little boy before I had to start missing out on most of his day.

The hardest decision for Nick and me when I went back to work was choosing what kind of childcare we wanted. Should I stay home? Should we hire a nanny? Should Edwin go to daycare? How do we decide? This is a decision that all families with children have to make. For me, not working wasn't an option, so I outlined the pros and cons of both daycare and a nanny.

On one hand, if you hire a nanny, you are paying for one on-one-care (in most cases), and you can be sure that your child is getting a lot of personalized attention throughout the day. You also get flexibility in terms of scheduling, whereas in a daycare, there are only a set number of hours and days that are available. But nannies can be expensive; the average cost for a nanny in the United States is $705 per week, whereas daycare on average costs more like $972 per month (Kimball, 2016). Furthermore, there is no licensing or certification process by which nannies can be held accountable. Websites like care.com or sittercity. com (which is the one we used) allow potential nannies to upload information from background checks or CPR certifications that can help you find a nanny that fits your needs or qualifications.

On the other hand, daycares offer care for a number of infants and children at the same time, so your child is not getting one-on-one attention per se, but most daycares have to go through a lengthy certification process so you can be sure that they are held accountable to certain standards. They are also more reliable, and you don't have to worry about your nanny getting sick and canceling your childcare for the entire day. They also provide your child with other children his or her own age to play with, giving children important social experience interacting with peers. However, in some regions, daycares can be incredibly expensive as well, especially daycares that take infants, and many of the good ones have long waiting lists. Furthermore, many families can't afford either option, because, when you get down to it, both are incredibly expensive, especially when you have multiple children, and moms might feel like it's cheaper and more efficient to just stay at home instead of handing their entire paycheck over to childcare (Figure 19.1).

In addition to the obvious costs and limitations of daycares, they are also incubators for germs, and it is likely that your child will come home sick quite frequently as a result of being exposed to other germ-infested children on a daily basis. Not all germs are bad, of course. In a

A Nanny Versus Daycare: Important Differences to Consider

Daycare	Nanny
More affordable	Higher cost
Many caregivers	Single caregiver
Socialization	Personalized attention
Reliable (open during working hours)	Potential for tardiness (need for sick days)
Holiday closures	Flexible schedule
Will not take care of sick children	Will take care of sick children with mild illness
Supervision	No supervision of nanny
Licensed and regulated	No regulation
Requires drop offs/pick ups	Convenient (watches child in home)
Different environment	Familiar environment
Exposure to many illnesses	Less illness
Most will include some early childhood education/preschool	Will need to also enroll in preschool
Many will include diverse activities (gym times, music, art)	Parent will need to separately enroll in any supplemental classes

Figure 19.1 | Differences to consider when deciding between a nanny and daycare.
Source: Data from Kimball (2016).

recent book, researchers from the University of British Columbia argue that interacting with a variety of germs on a daily basis is important for building healthy immune systems. They came to this conclusion by examining the bacteria babies had in their bodies and the relationship between the presence of these bacteria and the child's health several years later. They found that babies who had the most variety of bacteria in their bodies at 3 months of age were the *least* likely to develop asthma and allergies as children several years later. The title of their book—*Let Them Eat Dirt*—says it all: It's not only okay for children to get a little dirty sometimes, but it might also be a healthy choice (Finlay & Arrieta, 2016).

I know it seems like a good idea to cover your hands (and your child's) in antibacterial soap all the time in order to keep the environment as germ-free as possible, but it could be that getting a little dirty once in awhile might actually be a lot better for your children's health. The truth is that most of the bacteria we interact with during our daily lives are completely safe. However, although we should be encouraging our children to play outside (something children do less now than they did 20 years ago), not all environments are equally safe. The kinds of bacteria that are actually harmful and can indeed make us sick—like the bacteria found in feces or urine or the bacteria *Salmonella*—are most often found in places like playgrounds and daycare centers. In fact, researchers think that playground sand was to blame for a large *Salmonella* outbreak in Australia in 2007–2009.

One obvious thing to do if you plan to send your child to daycare (and this is my personal recommendation even if you don't) is to make sure his or her vaccinations are up to date and to get yearly flu shots for the whole family. Additionally, if your child is under the weather, keeping him home for a day or two until he's feeling better can protect other children from getting sick as well. But the reality is, we aren't going to be able to be there all the time to wipe our children's runny noses and make sure they cover their mouths when they cough, and we aren't going to be able to protect them from other kids who don't wipe their noses or cover their mouths and then share toys with our kids. At some point, we have to hope that our children will learn strategies for keeping themselves healthy, especially if they're going to be around other children at daycares or preschools.

Unfortunately, germs are tiny biological substances that you can't see, so they aren't all that easy to reason about, especially for young children. And research suggests that while preschool-aged children can list some accurate reasons of how someone might get sick, they also list lots of inaccurate ones, including telling lies and behaving badly. They also think that things like mental illnesses, cancer, and a broken leg are just as contagious as a cold (Bares & Gelman, 2008; Fox, Buchanan-Barrow, & Barrett, 2010; Legare, Wellman, & Gelman, 2009). They will happily eat applesauce that has been sneezed in and even drink juice that has a dead bug floating inside (DeJesus, Shutts, & Kinzler, 2015; Rozin, Fallon, & Augustoni-Ziskind, 1985; see Chapter 15), so helping them understand what can and can't make you sick seems like a tall order.

Does this mean we should just forego daycare for the nanny option? Unfortunately for babies, there isn't much we can do besides vaccinate and cross our fingers that their little immune systems will fight the good fight. But my own research suggests that we might be able to teach children as young as 3 or 4 some healthy behaviors if we teach them the right things about germs and how they're transmitted.

In my own lab, we found that children aged 4–7 who knew that playing with a sick person might make them sick were the ones who avoided touching potentially contaminated toys. What's most important here is that even the youngest kids in our study who already knew that playing with a sick person could make them sick later on avoided touching a sick experimenter's toys. This suggests that even kids as young as 4 and 5 are capable of learning how germs spread; most of them just haven't yet (Blacker & LoBue, 2016). Altogether, this and other research suggests that kids don't really learn much if you just spout out lists of healthy do's and don'ts (Au, Chan, Chan, Cheung,

Ho, & Ip, 2008). Telling them to "wash your hands before you eat" or "cover your mouth when you cough" aren't all that effective in changing children's behavior unless you explain *why* these behaviors might be useful. If we want our kids to actively engage in these healthy behaviors and to apply them to new situations, we have to explain how germs might make us sick, how germs can move from one person to another, and how they could be transferred from people to objects or even food. Until our kids do learn how to protect themselves against getting sick, we probably just have to grin and bear the seemingly endless colds and runny noses, especially if we choose to go with the daycare option.

After a long search over the summer, we decided to go with a nanny. Part of our decision was purely based on finances—believe it or not, a nanny was significantly cheaper than a daycare in our area. Furthermore, we found a particular nanny who we already love. She is a mother of three who left her job several years ago to stay at home to raise her family. Now that her kids are in school, she was looking for something to do during the day until her own kids got home. She had a full background check, was CPR certified, and had lots of experience caring for infants in her home. She was already fully equipped with everything Edwin needs, including a car seat, high chair, stroller, crib, a basement full of toys, and a smile that could warm a sasquatch. I knew as soon as I met her that if Edwin couldn't be with me, I wanted him to be with her.

During our search for childcare, we came across a local Montessori daycare/preschool that has programs starting at 18 months of age. Edwin is obviously too young to attend now, but we decided that either next fall or the fall after, this is where he will likely go and where he will stay until he's ready for kindergarten. If you've never heard of Montessori, you're not alone—I only heard about it for the first time as a graduate student (in a program tailored to learning about child development). Montessori is a specialized educational approach developed by Dr. Maria Montessori in Italy in the early 1900s. Montessori schools operate differently from typical public and private schools in the United States; Maria Montessori believed that children learn best by working independently with their hands and not by listening to lectures. As a result, Montessori classrooms function very differently from typical American classrooms where a group of students of the same age sit in desks and listen to a teacher give lessons. In a Montessori classroom, you're likely to see children of mixed ages (usually within 3 years of each other) explore a highly organized classroom space with minimal formal guidance from teachers.

I know what you're thinking—this sounds all hippy dippy with kids running around naked and throwing poop at each other—but, in fact, Montessori classrooms are extremely structured, just not in the standard way. Instead of highly structured lectures given by the teacher, Montessori learning is guided by highly structured materials that children can choose to explore; children are only allowed to interact with these materials in a set number of ways that each encourage them to learn specific concepts, like how to count by 10's or how calculate the volume of a cylinder.

Montessori education is based on the idea that children learn best by doing and not by passively listening, which is a concept that has much support from research (and would be endorsed by Piaget). However, while children in Montessori schools have been shown to outperform children in public schools on several measures of learning (e.g., Lillard & Else-Quest, 2006), it is difficult to say why this is the case. For example, it could be that the parents who choose Montessori over public schools are more educated or have more money, which can often account for differences in school performance. Furthermore, although there are some Montessori schools for older children, Montessori education is generally tailored to young children, so many Montessori students eventually switch to a local private or public school at some point in their education. We chose Montessori because Nick's mother founded a Montessori school where she taught for more than 35 years; Nick and his four sisters all went to school there, as did several of their children, so Montessori education is already a family tradition. Edwin will likely go there next year or the year after, and stay there until kindergarten, but will he then switch to the local public elementary school.

Obviously, we've given this a lot of thought—Edwin isn't even 9 months old yet and we have the next decade of his academic life already planned out. Providing our son with good quality education is important to us, and for good reason. I'm sure you've heard a lot about the effects of good schooling on later development. What you may not have heard is that how children perform in kindergarten predicts how they will perform throughout their academic years. Many places are encouraging parents to send their children to preschool at an early age as well, as attending high-quality local daycares and preschools have positive effects on children's performance in kindergarten. "High quality" usually means that there is a low teacher-to-child ratio in the classroom, that teachers are highly trained and responsive to children's needs, and that the curriculum is professionally developed. Research suggests that children who attend childcare centers that have these qualities are happier than other children, they perform better on language and cognitive tests, and they have more advanced social skills than other children (Vandell, 2004).

These benefits are especially strong for children growing up in low-income households. Elliot Tucker-Drob from the University of Virginia made a strong case for this point by studying pairs of twins who either attended or did not attend a high-quality preschool (Tucker-Drob, 2012). If you recall from an earlier chapter, I explained that researchers often study groups of identical twins (who have the same genes) and fraternal twins (who have only some of the same genes) to find out what the likelihood is that if one twin shows some characteristic that the other one will show it, too. The *concordance rate* (i.e., the likelihood that both twins have the characteristic) gives us some insight into the role that genes and the environment each play in development (see Chapter 12).

A large part of intelligence, for example, is often attributed to genetic factors; that is, unless you live in a poor neighborhood. For children from low-income families, the disadvantaged environment can wash away some of the positive effects of genes, meaning that being in a disadvantaged environment can set you back in a way that not even brilliant genes can overcome (Turkheimer, Haley, Waldron, D'Onofrio, & Gottesman, 2003). In his sample, Elliot found that going to preschool provides some protection from these effects: While the effect of the environment was less than 50% in math and reading scores if low-income children went to preschool, the environment accounted for 72–73% of the variability in math and reading scores in children who did not attend preschool. This suggests that going to a high-quality preschool reduces the potential negative impact of the environment for children who grow up in poor neighborhoods.

So sending your children to a high-quality daycare has some significant benefits and might benefit some children more than others, such as children who might not have access to resources for learning at home or who might need a head start on some of the skills they might get from daycare before entering preschool or kindergarten. Another potential reason it might be a good idea to send your child to daycare is for socialization. This might be especially important for infants with a reactive or difficult temperament that might make them more prone to develop shyness later in development (see Chapter 8). Research does suggest that children who have a reactive or difficult temperament demonstrate lower levels of aggression after spending time in daycare. Furthermore, daycare also has a positive effect on children's shyness over time if they have a difficult temperament as infants, but only if their experiences interacting with their peers at daycare are relatively positive. In fact, there is evidence that positive interactions with peers at daycare can make any child—regardless of temperament—less shy over time, so the individual experiences of each child within a daycare also matter (Almas et al., 2011).

The moral of the story here is, don't feel bad if you have to go back to work and send your child to daycare. Attending a high-quality childcare program, even full-time, is associated with all sorts of positive outcomes for kids. Furthermore, sending your kids to a good daycare program is not associated with attachment problems, so there's no evidence that they'll love you less for it (Vandell, 2004). This isn't to say that you should never choose a nanny over daycare or choose to stay home over going back to work—there are a lot of benefits to these options as well; in both of these scenarios, your child will get one-on-one care for most of the day, and the adult-to-child ratio is one of the most important factors in determining how good a daycare or pre-school is in the first place. Furthermore, there are studies showing that children who stay at home with a parent instead of attending daycare have higher grade point averages (GPAs) as adolescents, so staying at home has its benefits as well (e.g., Bettinger, Hægeland, & Rege, 2014). In the end, you have to make a choice that fits with your family's needs, whether it is a nanny, childcare, or staying at home. And, regardless of what you choose, it might make you feel better to know that having a secure attachment with your child is what best predicts his or her social and cognitive functioning, regardless of what kind of childcare you choose—even if the quality of the childcare program is not so great (NICHD Early Childcare Research Network, 2001).

Despite my decision to go back to work, I completely understand now why a lot of mothers decide to leave their jobs after spending some time at home with their children. The fact that Edwin is going to be spending all but 3 waking hours of his time with his nanny instead of with me on a daily basis is downright crippling at times. How am I going to feel if he takes his first step while I'm at work? Or says his first word? Or scrapes his knee for the first time, and I'm not there to comfort him? He's already gone on his first slide and his first swing without me, and we've only just begun. But the reality is that I can't have a full-time job and expect to be there for all of these firsts; I can't have it both ways; I can't have my full-time baby and my full-time job, too.

The idea that women can "have it all" has been popular in the media lately. It's a concept I've been thinking about a lot as a woman with a career and now a new baby. What does "having it all" really mean anyway? I think it's supposed to mean that you can have a family and have a full-time job, too. If that's what having it all means to you, then sure, you can have it. But to me, "having it all" means having a successful full-time job while also being at home all the time with my baby so that I don't miss a single second of his life. That version of "having it all" isn't so easy, and, I'm sorry ladies, but we can't have *that*. In fact, I think the phrase is a bit toxic: Women are already expected to have full-time careers, be perfect full-time mothers, *and* keep up our general appearance while juggling these two incompatible lives. I don't think we should be putting this kind of undue pressure on ourselves or on each other; I don't care how energetic, motivated, or wealthy you are—you can't choose to be a full-time stay-at-home mom *and* have a full-time career—we just can't have both. Heck, the idea of having time to take a 10-minute shower and blow dry my hair sounds like a luxury on some days.

Although we can't necessarily "have it all," we do have choices. If we choose to be full-time moms, then we don't get to have the kind of careers we might have planned for—we don't get to be doctors or lawyers or college professors—and you know what? That's OK. Being a full-time mom *is* a career, and I can tell you that on most days it's 100 times more work than my actual career, which isn't exactly a walk in the park. If we instead choose to have a full-time job, we don't get to be full-time moms, and we have to rely on babysitters, nannies, and daycares to help us raise our kids. Guess what—that's OK, too. Many of us don't have the luxury of being able to afford to stay home all the time, or we value our jobs too much to leave them, so we hire help and go on working. Either way, we all have to make a choice—we don't get to have it all—and either choice is OK.

After 2 weeks of working and leaving Edwin with his nanny every morning, I was starting to feel a bit better about *my* choice to go back to work. In fact, I was so busy catching up from my time away that I didn't have any time during the day to think about what I was missing out on, and I was so happy to see Edwin when I got home in the evening that I was too preoccupied to think about work. This, of course, isn't the same from day to day; on some days, I have a hard time concentrating at work and yearn to go home; on other days, I'm so wrapped up in thinking about work that I have a hard time being present with my baby. And, like I said, we've only just begun: there are going to be more ups and downs, more crying, more laughing, more firsts, more seconds, and maybe even another baby.

In the Introduction to this book—which I wrote long before I was pregnant or a new mother—I mentioned a phenomenon that women experience when they have children that I called the "postnatal glow." To refresh your memory, it's how mothers seem to forget all of the gruesome details about their pregnancy and labor, the difficulties of having a newborn, the crying, the lack of sleep, the stress, and instead just tell you about the joys of motherhood. I mentioned reasons why this might be and even cited you some research suggesting that nature might stack the deck so that we forget all of the bad in favor of the good. Now I know for sure that the science, as always, is right. For some reason, forgetting all of the difficulties that go along with pregnancy and first-time motherhood is easier than remembering. Even now, as I read through the previous chapters of this book, I have to remind myself of the hardships I faced at certain points of Edwin's development—the weight gain, the contractions, the postpartum blues, the nursing problems, the crying, and on and on and on. Most of these troubles have already melted away, and when I think of Edwin, I can only help thinking of the smiling and the laughter (Figure 19.2). It is indeed nature's clever way of tricking us into having more children; otherwise, who'd do this all over again?

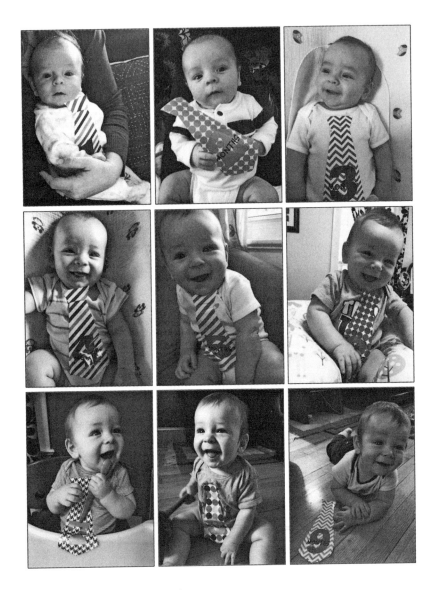

Figure 19.2 | Edwin, 9 months out.
Source: Vanessa LoBue.

I would. See you next time.

20

AFTERWORD

It's been about 2 years since I stopped documenting my monthly parenting experiences with Edwin and just fell into being a regular old parent. He's 2½ now, he's speaking in full sentences, going to preschool (the Montessori school I mentioned in Chapter 19), and potty training for the very first time. As I go through this book to make final edits and update the research, I'm reminded of the details of my journey into first-time parenthood and I'm yet again surprised at how much I'd forgotten already. Besides reading my own thoughts and feelings on these pages, there is something new that is also a powerful reminder of my experience—I'm pregnant again.

I'm 37 now, and, despite the fact that my pregnancy is considered "high risk," my symptoms are exactly the same—I'm tired and hungry all the time and spending a lot of time in the bathroom. I'm even having another boy, and I'm due in January, again. I'm growing faster this time, so even before the end of the first trimester it was difficult to keep the news from my friends and colleagues; it's almost as if my body remembers what it's like to be pregnant (despite the fact that my brain has forgotten) and fell back into it like an old habit. The only major difference so far between my second pregnancy and my first is that I can't just nap whenever I want to, I don't get to eat as I please, and my work schedule is much tighter because I have a toddler who needs to be picked up from school, who needs to nap and eat regularly as well, and who is in love with his mommy's attention, making the whole pregnancy much more exhausting the second time around. But I'm taking with me some valuable lessons that will likely make the second time different from the first in many ways.

First, I've learned that everything gets easier with time. I remember sitting in bed nursing Edwin in the middle of the night during those first few months postpartum and wondering helplessly whether things would get easier and frankly not knowing exactly if and when it would happen. Now I know that it will, and, in fact, I know that it continues to get easier every day. One of the things that makes everything a lot easier in the first few years is communication. Edwin went through a massive change in language ability between the ages of 18 months and 2½ years. During this time, I was *floored* to see how many new words he produced each day. And with every new word, communication between us became easier.

For a long time, Edwin had about 20 words in his repertoire, and then, all of a sudden, I heard him spout out a countless number of brand-new words every day. He started repeating and remembering everything he heard us say (which wasn't always convenient when a curse word slipped out). His pronunciation wasn't perfect—which was adorable and sometimes embarrassing, especially when he would swap the /r/ sound in favor of the /c/ sound in words like "rock"—but the meaning was there. Researchers have reported a phenomenon called the "vocabulary spurt" or "word explosion" during the second year of life (e.g., Woodward, Markman, & Fitzsimmons, 1994). It's a controversial issue for researchers, and while some have provided evidence of a huge vocabulary increase during this time period, others report more steady growth. I always found the latter to be more believable, but Edwin's language development certainly felt like more of an explosion than a period of steady growth, with a staggering change between 1 and 2 years of age. Again, he is speaking in full sentences now, he tells stories about what happened in the past and what he's going to do in the future, he sings songs and even knows all of his letters. This is truly remarkable compared the mere 20-word vocabulary he had less than a year ago. And now I don't have to guess the meaning of every cry or whimper; Edwin can tell me how's he feeling with a growing number of words and expressions.

Second, I've already learned that despite a parent's expectations, infants have a very distinct personality from the very beginning, and there's only so much you can do to push them to be something that doesn't quite fit with that personality. Again, infants have their own unique temperament that is evident from 4 month of age (see Chapter 8). What I wasn't expecting was that, along with his unique temperament, Edwin also has unique preferences for toys and activities that were evident within the first 12 months of life.

For example, he started playing with gender-stereotyped toys from a very early age. As I mentioned earlier, gender-stereotyped behaviors usually start around 2½ or 3, when children start talking about their own gender (see Chapter 4). It was a mission of mine to keep his clothes and toys as gender-neutral as possible before then so that Edwin could decide which toys he wanted to play with without gender-stereotypes getting in the way. Despite my best intentions, Edwin's gender-stereotyped behavior started much sooner than I expected it would, and he began to prefer stereotypical "boy" toys pretty early on. In fact, in my effort to keep him from gender-stereotyped toys, at some point the poor kid was only playing with our dog's toys because all he wanted to do was play with balls. His first word was "ball," followed by "car" followed by "dada" (to my dismay, "mama" didn't even make the top 10). After a while, I just gave up and gave him the toys he wanted—all boy toys, all the time, by the time he was 18 months of age. The point isn't that gender-stereotyped behaviors start earlier than research suggests; it's that *Edwin* had his own distinct preferences for what he liked and what he didn't at an early age, despite how hard his mom tried to guide him. I expect that this won't be the only time I try to steer him one way to find that he turns around and goes another.

This isn't something to worry about, of course—we all have our own personalities and preferences—which brings me to my third lesson: There's *always* something to worry about, so might as well try to worry less. Again, I'm 37 now, which makes my new pregnancy more high risk and brings with it a lot more anxiety. On top of my age, now we have the Zika virus and a surge of Lyme-disease carrying ticks infesting our area, so it feels like there's always something new to be afraid of. Parenting is a scary business and the fear is always there. But I've found that worrying less makes me a better mom; it means I can have more fun with my son and that he is free to explore more as well.

One specific thing I'm hoping to worry less about this time around is nursing. I have decided to try to nurse again, despite all of the difficulties I had the first time. The main reason I'm doing it all over again is that Edwin rarely gets sick, and he has no known allergies. In fact, whenever we see his pediatrician for well visits, she greets him with "Hey, it's the boy who never gets sick!" I can't say that this is a direct result of my time nursing, but we know from research that children who are breastfed do tend to get sick less and are less prone to developing allergies than children who are formula-fed. So, despite all of the trouble I had, I don't regret it for a second, and I will do it again for my second son. Furthermore, letting go of the worry over whether I'm doing it right and whether my son will have enough milk might help.

We actually continued to have eating problems well past nursing that were in part driven by anxiety. In fact, eating became quite a battle once we weaned Edwin from formula at 12 months. Despite the fact that he loved to eat solid food as a baby, once he became mobile he hated to sit down and eat, mostly because he wanted to be active and move around all the time. He started refusing most foods, and I was constantly worried that he wasn't getting enough to eat. A wonderful friend and colleague—Lisa Oakes from the University of California, Davis—recommended I read a book called *Child of*

Mind: Feeding with Love and Good Sense, by Ellyn Satter (Satter, 2000). Satter explains that, for toddlers, eating is a power struggle, and children want to have control over how much food goes into their bodies. She also provides mothers with a simple rule: You are responsible for providing your children with food and a safe place for them to eat it; your children are responsible for deciding how much to eat, and *if any.* In other words, you don't have to be a short-order chef and make your child 10 different options until he finally eats something (which I was doing). Instead, your job is to put food on the table and let your children decide independently how much they should eat. Children need time to grow accustomed to new flavors, and, in fact, on average you have to expose children to a new food up to 15 times before they decide that they like it (Ventura & Worobey, 2013). Satter was right: As soon as we let Edwin take control of how much he ate, he became an excellent eater, and we can now take him to any restaurant and always find something on the menu that he will eat. Being more relaxed about meal times effectively made Edwin a better eater, and it made me a better and more relaxed mom.

Finally, I've learned that everyone parents a little bit (or maybe even a lot) differently, and there is no single "right" way to do it as long as your children are healthy and safe. In fact, we all need to be a little more mindful about judging the way other parents make decisions just because we make different ones. In a brave new world where people can express their opinion to hundreds or even thousands of strangers with a mere click of a button, "mom shaming" is all around us. Now that I'm a mom, I see it everywhere, all the time. It can be obvious, like when someone posts a photo of a mom on social media, and users feel the urge to chime in to criticize her every move. But most mom shaming takes more subtle forms, like a judgmental glance from a passerby or an "innocent" comment about something you forgot at home. Although it feels most infuriating when it comes from people who don't have children, most mom shaming comes from us—other moms. We shame moms when they choose to nurse in public or when they choose not to nurse at all; we shame moms for going back to work and for choosing to stay home; we shame moms for sleep training their children and for not teaching them how to soothe themselves at night; we even glare at moms in restaurants or on airplanes for letting their children play on screens so that the poor overtired and overstressed woman can have 5 minutes of peace and quiet.

I know, it sounds mean and you might be thinking that you'd never, ever judge another mother for her parenting choices, but we are *all* guilty of mom shaming. Even if we don't do it directly and aggressively on social media, we do it with our eyes, and we do it with our thoughts. We do it when we think a fellow mom is making a bad choice for her child's well-being. But, it's important to remember that the shamed mom is likely acting in a way that *she thinks is best for her child.* The truth is, in the end, what we all want is what's best for our kids. As parents, we are all on the same team, we're in the same club, and we all want our children to be safe, healthy, and happy.

As Nick, Edwin, and I approach the next chapter in our lives, we will revisit some old experiences and make some new adjustments. Edwin will keep growing and, in the next few months, will have to learn to make room for a new baby brother in his developing cognitive and emotional life. Likewise, I will have to reshuffle work and family life—something that I've learned is a dynamic, difficult, ever-changing balance that will never quite feel perfect. This brings me to the moral of this whole story: Parenting is really hard. Really, really, really, astronomically hard. We can never truly realize another parent's struggles or the reasoning behind their decisions, but, despite the fact that some of the experiences I describe here will play out differently for you, what we all share is that parenting is difficult for everyone—even an expert in infant and child development. We all need support, encouragement, and comfort to do it well and to buffer those inevitable feelings of

Figure 20.1 | Edwin, age 2½, preparing for an important new beginning.
Source: Vanessa LoBue.

anxiety, guilt, fear, and even shame that come with being a new parent. To make life easier on each other and on ourselves, we should relish the fact that we have choices, we should celebrate the different ones each of us makes, and we should know that they all come from same place—a place of love for our children (Figure 20.1).

ACKNOWLEDGMENTS

While some people decide to concentrate on staying healthy and stress-free when pregnant and on maternity leave, I decided to write a book, and it took a village to make it happen. First, I would like to thank my publisher, Oxford University Press, for being willing to take a chance on a first-time author—Andrea Zekus in particular for believing in my proposal and Courtney McCarroll and Abby Gross for seeing it through to publication. I would also like to thank my book agent, Giles Anderson, for helping me figure out how to get a book published and how to market myself as an author. He encouraged me to start a blog, which is now published monthly on *Psychology Today*. I always knew I loved to write about science, but I didn't know how much I loved writing about science for other moms until Giles encouraged me to start doing it regularly. I don't think I'll ever stop.

Next, I'd like to thank the people who have educated me about the science of infancy and motherhood, starting with my mentors, Judy DeLoache and Karen Adolph. Judy and Karen taught me everything I know about child development, how to ask scientific questions, and how to communicate science to a variety of audiences. They are two of my favorite women (and moms) in the world, and I would not be who I am if it wasn't for them. They taught me how to think, how to talk, and how to write, and for that, I will be forever grateful. To my fellow baby scientists and academic mamas for providing some of the inspiration for what's written in this book—especially Lana Karasik for providing detailed feedback—thanks for not only being great moms, but for also being brilliant and inspiring scientists.

I'd like to thank my mom friends ("the club") for helping me get through my first 9 months as a parent, and my non-mom friends for constantly putting up with my family circus during dinners out, vacations, and social events, and for treating my children like their own. Thanks to Dr. Catherine Goodstein for providing me with excellent prenatal care and support and for bringing my first son safely into this world, and to her colleagues Drs. Caitlin Fiss and Laura Schiller for delivering my second and for saving my life in the process. To our nanny Dana and her "boys" (Dave, Ryan, Jason, and Eric)—thank you for giving my sons a second family in your home and for giving me an endless amount of peace of mind. I don't know what we would do without you.

Last, but not least, I'd like to thank my family. First, my wonderful sisters-in-law—Jenni, Carrie, Sadie, and Becca—and their families; you guys make dealing with in-laws look easy. I'm so glad to have you and your families in my life, and especially in Edwin's and Charlie's. To my parents, Xonia and Frank, and my brother Mike, who are the greatest grandparents and uncle I've ever seen: Not only do you provide Edwin and Charlie with immeasurable love and support, but you've also provided me with a model for what a loving family should look like; I only hope I can somehow give my sons a fraction of what you've all given me over the years. Finally, to my husband Nick, and my sons Edwin and Charlie: Everything I do every day is inspired by you. Thank you for being there, always, every day, no matter what.

REFERENCES

Adams, S., Kuebli, J., Boyle, P. A., & Fivush, R. (1995). Gender differences in parent-child conversations about past emotions: A longitudinal investigation. *Sex Roles, 33,* 309–323.

Adams, S. S., Eberhard-Gran, M., & Eskild, A. (2012). Fear of childbirth and duration of labour: A study of 2206 women with intended vaginal delivery. *BJOG: An International Journal of Obstetrics & Gynaecology, 119,* 1238–1246.

Addati, L., Cassirer, N., & Gilchrist, K. (2014). *Maternity and paternity at work: Law and practice across the world.* Geneva: International Labour Organization.

Adolph, K. E. (2000). Specificity of learning: Why infants fall over a veritable cliff. *Psychological Science, 11,* 290–295.

Adolph, K. E., Cole, W. G., Komati, M., Garciaguirre, J. S., Badaly, D., Lingeman, J. M., . . . Sotsky, R. B. (2012). How do you learn to walk? Thousands of steps and dozens of falls per day. *Psychological Science, 23,* 1387–1394.

Adolph, K. E., Karasik, L., & Tamis-LeMonda, C. S. (2010). Motor skill. In M. Bornstein (Ed.), *Handbook of cultural developmental science* (pp. 61–88). New York: Taylor & Francis.

Adolph, K. E., Kretch, K. S., & LoBue, V. (2014). Fear of heights in infants? *Current Directions in Psychological Science, 23,* 60–66.

Adolph, K. E., & Robinson, S. R. (2013). The road to walking: What learning to walk tells us about development. In P. Zelazo (Ed.), *Oxford handbook of developmental psychology* (Vol. 1, pp. 403–443). New York: Oxford University Press.

Adolph, K. E., Robinson, S. R., Young, J. W., & Gill-Alvarez, F. (2008). What is the shape of developmental change? *Psychological Review, 115,* 527–543.

Ahadi, S. A., Rothbart, M. K., & Ye, R. (1993). Children's temperament in the US and China: Similarities and differences. *European Journal of Personality, 7,* 359–378.

Ainsworth, M. S. (1979). Infant–mother attachment. *American Psychologist, 34,* 932–937.

Akman, I., Kuşçu, K., Özdemir, N., Yurdakul, Z., Solakoglu, M., Orhan, L., . . . Özek, E. (2006). Mothers' postpartum psychological adjustment and infantile colic. *Archives of Disease in Childhood, 91,* 417–419.

Allen, E. (2012). *Laboring well: A labor nurse shares insights from 10,000 births.* Longboat Key, FL: Elizabeth Allen an imprint of Telemachus Press.

Almas, A. N., Degnan, K. A., Fox, N. A., Phillips, D. A., Henderson, H. A., Moas, O. L., & Hane, A. A. (2011). The relations between infant negative reactivity, non-maternal childcare, and children's interactions with familiar and unfamiliar peers. *Social Development, 20*, 718–740.

American Academy of Pediatrics Council on Communications and Media. (2011). Media use by children younger than 2 years. *Pediatrics, 128*, 1040–1045.

Anders, T. F., Halpern, L. F., & Hua, J. (1992). Sleeping through the night: A developmental perspective. *Pediatrics, 90*, 554–560.

Anderson, A. N., Wohlfahr, J., Christens, P., Olsen, J., & Melbye, M. (2000). Maternal age and fetal loss: Population based register linkage study. *British Medical Journal, 320*, 1708–1712.

Anzures, G., Wheeler, A., Quinn, P. C., Pascalis, O., Slater, A. M., Heron-Delaney, M., . . . Lee, K. (2012). Brief daily exposures to Asian females reverses perceptual narrowing for Asian faces in Caucasian infants. *Journal of Experimental Child Psychology, 112*, 484–495.

Au, T. K. F., Chan, C. K., Chan, T. K., Cheung, M. W., Ho, J. Y., & Ip, G. W. (2008). Folkbiology meets microbiology: A study of conceptual and behavioral change. *Cognitive Psychology, 57*, 1–19.

Aznar, A., & Tenenbaum, H. R. (2013). Spanish parents' emotion talk and their children's understanding of emotion. *Frontiers in Psychology, 4*.

Baer, J. C., & Martinez, C. D. (2006). Child maltreatment and insecure attachment: A meta-analysis. *Journal of Reproductive and Infant Psychology, 24*, 187–197.

Baillargeon, R. (1987). Object permanence in 3½ and 4 ½-month-old infants. *Developmental Psychology, 23*, 655–664.

Bakermans-Kranenburg, M. J., Van Ijzendoorn, M. H., & Juffer, F. (2005). Disorganized infant attachment and preventative interventions: A review of meta-analysis. *Infant Mental Health Journal, 26*, 191–216.

Blacker, K., & LoBue, V. (2016). Behavioral avoidance of contagion in childhood. *Journal of Experimental Child Psychology, 143*, 162–170.

Bandura, A., Ross, D., & Ross, S. A. (1963). Imitation of film-mediated aggressive models. *The Journal of Abnormal and Social Psychology, 66*, 3.

Barclay, K., & Myrskylä, M. (2016). Advanced maternal age and offspring outcomes: Reproductive aging and counterbalancing period trends. *Population and Development Review, 42*, 69–94.

Bares, C. B., & Gelman, S. A. (2008). Knowledge of illness during childhood: Making distinctions between cancer and colds. *International Journal of Behavioral Development, 32*, 443–450.

Bar-Haim., Y., Ziv, T., Lamy, D., & Hodes, R. M. (2006). Nature and nurture in own-race face processing. *Psychological Science, 17*, 159–163.

Barker, T. V., Reeb-Sutherland, B. C., & Fox, N. A. (2014). Individual differences in fear potentiated startle in behaviorally inhibited children. *Developmental Psychobiology, 56*, 133–141.

Baron-Cohen, S., Leslie, A. M., & Frith, U. (1985). Does the autistic child have a "theory of mind"? *Cognition, 21*, 37–46.

Barr, R. (2013). Memory constraints on infant learning from picture books, television, and touchscreens. *Child Development Perspectives, 7*, 205–210.

Barr, R., Danziger, C., Hilliard, M. E., Andolina, C., & Ruskis, J. (2010). Amount, content and context of infant media exposure: A parental questionnaire and diary analysis. *International Journal of Early Years Education, 18*, 107–122.

Barr, R. G., Trent, R. B., & Cross, J. (2006). Age-related incidence curve of hospitalized shaken baby syndrome cases: Convergent evidence for crying as a trigger to shaking. *Child Abuse & Neglect, 30*, 7–16.

Beebe, K. R., Lee, K. A., Carrieri-Kohlman, V., & Humphreys, J. (2007). The effects of childbirth self-efficacy and anxiety during pregnancy on prehospitalization labor. *Journal of Obstetric, Gynecologic, & Neonatal Nursing, 36*, 410–418.

Belsky, J., & Fearon, R. M. P. (2002). Early attachment security, subsequent maternal sensitivity and later child development: Does continuity in development depend on continuity of caregiving? *Attachment & Human Development, 4*, 361–387.

Bem, S. L. (1989). Genital knowledge and gender constancy in preschool children. *Child Development, 60*, 649–662.

Bertrand, M., Goldin, C., & Katz, L. (2010). Dynamics of the gender gap for young professionals in the financial and corporate sectors. *American Economic Journal: Applied Economics, 2*, 228–255.

Bettinger, E., Hægeland, T., & Rege, M. (2014). Home with mom: The effects of stay-at-home parents on children's long-run educational outcomes. *Journal of Labor Economics, 32*, 443–467.

Bialystok, E. (2011). Reshaping the mind: The benefits of bilingualism. *Canadian Journal of Experimental Psychology/Revue canadienne de psychologie expérimentale, 65*, 229.

Bian, L., Leslie, S. J., & Cimpian, A. (2017). Gender stereotypes about intellectual ability emerge early and influence children's interests. *Science, 355*(6323), 389–391.

Blackstone, A., & Stewart, M. D. (2016). "There's more thinking to decide" how the childfree decide not to parent. *The Family Journal, 24*, 296–303.

Blair, P. S., Sidebotham, P., Pease, A., & Fleming, P. J. (2014). Bed-sharing in the absence of hazardous circumstances: Is there a risk of sudden infant death syndrome? An analysis from two case-control studies conducted in the UK. *PLoS One, 9*(9), e107799.

Blass, E. (1990). Suckling: Determinants, changes, mechanisms, and lasting impressions. *Developmental Psychology, 26*, 520–533.

Boismier, J. D. (1977). Visual stimulation and wake-up sleep behavior in human neonates. *Developmental Psychobiology, 10*, 219–227.

Bonawitz, E., Shafto, P., Gweon, H., Goodman, N. D., Spelke, E., & Schulz, L. (2011). The double-edged sword of pedagogy: Instruction limits spontaneous exploration and discovery. *Cognition, 120*, 322–330.

Brito, N., & Barr, R. (2012). Influence of bilingualism on memory generalization during infancy. *Developmental Science, 15*, 812–816.

Bushneil, I. W. R., Sai, F., & Mullin, J. T. (1989). Neonatal recognition of the mother's face. *British Journal of Developmental Psychology, 7*, 3–15.

Buss, K. A., Davidson, R. J., Kalin, N. H., & Goldsmith, H. H. (2004). Context specific freezing and associated physiological reactivity as a dysregulated fear response. *Developmental Psychology, 40*, 583–594.

Campos, J. J., Anderson, D. I., Barbu-Roth, M. A., Hubbard, E. M., Hertenstein, M. J., & Witherington, D. (2000). Travel broadens the mind. *Infancy, 1*, 149–219.

Campos, J. J., Bertenthal, B. I., & Kermoian, R. (1992). Early experience and emotional development: The emergence of wariness of heights. *Psychological Science, 3*, 61–64.

Camras, L. A., & Shutter, J. M. (2010). Emotional facial expressions in infancy. *Emotion Review, 2*, 120–129.

Carpenter, R., McGarvey, C., Mitchell, E. A., Tappin, D. M., Vennemann, M. M., Smuk, M., & Carpenter, J. R. (2013). Bed sharing when parents do not smoke: Is there a risk of SIDS? An individual level analysis of five major case–control studies. *BMJ Open, 3*(5), e002299.

Chawarska, K., Macari, S., & Shic, F. (2013). Decreased spontaneous attention to social scenes in 6-month-old infants later diagnosed with autism spectrum disorders. *Biological Psychiatry, 74*, 195–203.

Cheng, Y. W., Shaffer, B. L., Nicholson, J. M., & Caughey, A. B. (2014). Second stage of labor and epidural use: A larger effect than previously suggested. *Obstetrics & Gynecology, 123*, 527–535.

Clifton, R. K., Rochat, P., Litovsky, R. Y., & Perris, E. E. (1991). Object representation guides infants' reaching in the dark. *Journal of Experimental Psychology: Human Perception and Performance, 17*, 323.

Coan, J. A., Schaefer, H. S., & Davidson, R. J. (2006). Lending a hand social regulation of the neural response to threat. *Psychological Science, 17*, 1032–1039.

Colvert, E., Tick, B., McEwen, F., Stewart, C., Curran, S. R., Woodhouse, E., . . . Ronald, A. (2015). Heritability of autism spectrum disorder in a UK population-based twin sample. *JAMA Psychiatry, 72*, 415–423.

Common Sense Media. (2013). *Zero to eight: Children's media use in America in 2013.* Retrieved from www.commonsensemedia.org

Conner, D. B., Knight, D. K., & Cross, D. R. (1997). Mothers' and fathers' scaffolding of their 2-year-olds during problem-solving and literacy interactions. *British Journal of Developmental Psychology, 15*, 323–338.

Constantino, J. N., Kennon-McGill, S., Weichselbaum, C., Marrus, N., Haider, A., Glowinski, A. L., . . . Jones, W. (2017). Infant viewing of social scenes is under genetic control and is atypical in autism. *Nature, 547*(7663), 340–344.

Council, O. C. (2016). Media and young minds. *Pediatrics, 138*(5).

Couture, D. E., Crantford, J. C., Somasundaram, A., Sanger, C., Argenta, A. E., & David, L. R. (2013). Efficacy of passive helmet therapy for deformational plagiocephaly: Report of 1050 cases. *Neurosurgical Focus, 35*(4), E4.

Crivelli, C., Russell, J. A., Jarillo, S., & Fernández-Dols, J. M. (2016). The fear gasping face as a threat display in a Melanesian society. *Proceedings of the National Academy of Sciences, 133,* 12403–12407.

Davidson, R. J., & Fox, N. A. (1982). Asymmetrical brain activity discriminates between positive and negative. *Science, 218,* 1235–1237.

Davidson, R. J., & Fox, N. A. (1989). Frontal brain asymmetry predicts infants' response to maternal separation. *Journal of Abnormal Psychology, 98,* 127–131.

DeCasper, A. J., & Spence, M. J. (1986). Prenatal maternal speech influences newborns' perception of speech sounds. *Infant Behavior and Development, 9,* 133–150.

DeJesus, J. M., Shutts, K., & Kinzler, K. D. (2015). Eww she sneezed! Contamination context affects children's food preferences and consumption. *Appetite, 87,* 303–309.

Delbaere, I., Verstraelen, H., Goetgeluk, S., Martens, G., De Backer, G., & Temmerman, M. (2007). Pregnancy outcome in primiparae of advanced maternal age. *European Journal of Obstetrics & Gynecology and Reproductive Biology, 135,* 41–46.

DeLoache, J. S. (1987). Rapid change in the symbolic functioning of very young children. *Science, 238,* 1556–1557.

DeLoache, D. S., Chiong, C., Sherman, K., Islam, N., Vanderborght, M., Troseth, G. L., . . . O'Doherty, K. (2010). Do babies learn from baby media? *Psychological Science, 21,* 1570–1574.

DeLoache, J. S., Miller, K. F., & Rosengren, K. S. (1997). The credible shrinking room: Very young children's performance with symbolic and nonsymbolic relations. *Psychological Science, 8,* 308–313.

DeLoache, J. S., Pierroutsakos, S. L., Uttal, D. H., Rosengren, K. S., & Gottlieb, A. (1998). Grasping the nature of pictures. *Psychological Science, 9,* 205–210.

Dominguez-Bello, M. G., Costello, E. K., Conreras, M., Magris, M., Hidalgo, G., Fierer, N., & Knight, R. (2010). Delivery mode shapes the acquisition and structure of the initial microbiota across multiple body habitats in newborns. *Proceedings from the National Academy of Sciences, 107,* 11971–11975.

Doucleff, M. (2017). Secrets of breast-feeding form global moms in the know. National Public Radio, June 26, 2017.

Ekman, P. (1992). Facial expressions of emotion: New findings, new questions. *Psychological Science, 3,* 34–38.

Ekman, P., & Friesen, W. V. (1976). *Pictures of facial affect.* Palo Alto, CA: Consulting Psychologists' Press.

Entwisle, D. R., & Baker, D. P. (1983). Gender and young children's expectations for performance in arithmetic. *Developmental Psychology, 19,* 200–209.

Falgreen Eriksen, H., Mortensen, E., Kilburn, T., Underbjerg, M., Bertrand, J., Støvring, H., . . . Kesmodel, U. (2012). The effects of low to moderate prenatal alcohol exposure in early pregnancy on IQ in 5-year-old children. *BJOG, 119,* 1191–1200.

Feldman, R., Rosenthal, Z., & Eidelman, A. I. (2014). Maternal-preterm skin-to-skin contact enhances child physiologic organization and cognitive control across the first 10 years of life. *Biological Psychiatry, 75,* 56–64.

Feldman, R., Singer, M., & Zagoory, O. (2010). Touch attenuates infants' physiological reactivity to stress. *Developmental Science, 13,* 271–278.

Fenstermacher, S. K., Barr, R., Salerno, K., Garcia, A., Shwery, C. E., Calvert, S. L., & Linebarger, D. L. (2010). Infant-directed media: An analysis of product information and claims. *Infant and Child Development, 19,* 556–557.

Ferber, R. (2006). *Solve your child's sleep problems: Revised edition: new, revised.* Simon and Schuster.

Ferjan Ramirez, N., & Kuhl, P. (2017). Bilingual baby: Foreign language intervention in Madrid's infant education centers. *Mind, Brain, and Education.*

Fernald, A. (1985). Four-month-old infants prefer to listen to motherese. *Infant Behavior and Development, 8,* 181–195.

Fernald, A., Marchman, V. A., & Weisleder, A. (2013). SES differences in language processing skill and vocabulary are evident at 18 months. *Developmental Science, 16*(2), 234–248.

Field, T. (1995). Infants of depressed mothers. *Infant Behavior and Development, 18,* 1–13.

Field, T., Diego, M., Dieter, J., Hernandez-Reif, M., Schanberg, S., Kuhn, C., . . . Bendell, D. (2004). Prenatal depression effects on the fetus and the newborn. *Infant Behavior and Development, 27,* 216–229.

Field, T., Diego, M., & Hernandez-Reif, M. (2009). Depressed mothers' infants are less responsive to faces and voices. *Infant Behavior and Development, 32,* 239–244.

Field, T. M., Schanberg, S. M., Scafidi, F., Bauer, C. R., Vega-Lahr, N., Garcia, R., . . . Kuhn, C. M. (1986). Tactile/kinesthetic stimulation effects on preterm neonates. *Pediatrics, 77,* 654–658.

Field, T. M., Woodson, R., Greenberg, R., & Cohen, D. (1982). Discrimination and imitation of facial expressions by neonates. *Science, 218 (4568),* 179–181.

Finlay, B. B., & Arrieta, M. C. (2016). *Let them eat dirt.* New York: Algonquin Books.

Flavell, J. H., Flavell, E. R., Green, F. L., & Korfmacher, J. E. (1990). Do young children think of television images as pictures or real objects? *Journal of Broadcasting & Electronic Media, 34,* 399–419.

Fox, C., Buchanan-Barrow, E., & Barrett, M. (2010). Children's conceptions of mental illness: A naïve theory approach. *British Journal of Developmental Psychology, 28,* 603–625.

Fox, N. A., & Davidson, R. J. (1986). Taste-elicited changes in facial signs of emotion and the asymmetry of brain electrical activity in human newborns. *Neuropsychologia, 24,* 417–422.

Fox, N. A., & Davidson, R. J. (1987). Electroencephalogram asymmetry in response to the approach of a stranger and maternal separation in 10-month-old infants. *Developmental Psychology, 23,* 233–240.

Fox, N. A., Barker, T. V., White, L. K., Suway, J., & Pine, D. S. (2013). Commentary: To intervene or not? Appreciating or treating individual differences in childhood temperament–remarks on Rapee. (2013). *Journal of Child Psychology and Psychiatry, 54,* 789–790.

Fox, N. A., & Helfinstein, S. M. (2013). The contribution of temperament to the study of social cognition. In M. Banaji & S. Gelman (Eds.), *Navigating the social world: What infants, children, and other species can teach us* (pp. 49–53). New York: Oxford University Press.

Fox, N. A., Rubin, K. H., Calkins, S. D., Marshall, T. R., Coplan, R. J., Porges, S. W., . . . Stewart, S. (1995). Frontal activation asymmetry and social competence at four years of age. *Child Development, 66,* 1770–1784.

Franks, M. E., Macpherson, G. R., & Figg, W. D. (2004). Thalidomide. *The Lancet, 363*(9423), 1802–1811.

Gartner, L. M., Morton, J., Lawrence, R. A., Naylor, A. J., O'Hare, D., Schanler, R. J., & Eidelman, A. I. (2005). Breastfeeding and the use of human milk. *Pediatrics, 115,* 496–506.

Gee, D. G., Gabard-Durnam, L. J., Flannery, J., Goff, B., Humphreys, K. L., Telzer, E. H., . . . Tottenham, N. (2013). Early developmental emergence of human amygdala–prefrontal connectivity after maternal deprivation. *Proceedings of the National Academy of Sciences, 110,* 15638–15643.

Gee, D. G., Gabard-Durnam, L., Telzer, E. H., Humphreys, K. L., Goff, B., Shapiro, M., . . . Tottenham, N. (2014). Maternal buffering of human amygdala-prefrontal circuitry during childhood but not during adolescence. *Psychological Science, 25,* 2067–2078.

Gesell, A. (1946). The ontogenesis of infant behavior. In L. Carmichael (Ed.), *Manual of child psychology* (pp. 295–331). New York: John Wiley.

Gleason, M. M., Fox, N. A., Drury, S. S., Smyke, A. T., Nelson, C. A., & Zeanah, C. H. (2014). Indiscriminate behaviors in previously institutionalized young children. *Pediatrics, 133,* e657–e665.

Glynn, J. S. (2016). Breadwinning mothers are increasingly the US norm. Center for American Progress, December 19, 2016. https://www.americanprogress.org/issues/women/reports/2016/12/19/295203/breadwinning-mothers-are-increasingly-the-u-s-norm/

Goetz, P. J. (2003). The effects of bilingualism on theory of mind development. *Bilingualism: Language and Cognition, 6,* 1–15.

Goldstein, M. H., King, A. P., & West, M. J. (2003). Social interaction shapes babbling: Testing parallels between birdsong and speech. *Proceedings of the National Academy of Sciences, 100,* 8030–8035.

Goldstein, M. H., & Schwade, J. A. (2008). Social feedback to infants' babbling facilitates rapid phonological learning. *Psychological Science, 19,* 515–523.

Gottlieb, G. (1980). Development of species identification in ducklings: VI. Specific embryonic experience required to maintain species-typical perception in Peking ducklings. *Journal of Comparative and Physiological Psychology, 94,* 579–587.

Grace, S. L., Evindar, A., & Stewart, D. E. (2003). The effect of postpartum depression on child cognitive development and behavior: A review and critical analysis of the literature. *Archives of Women's Mental Health, 6,* 263–274.

Grieser, D. L., & Kuhl, P. K. (1988). Maternal speech to infants in a tonal language: Support for universal prosodic features in motherese. *Developmental Psychology, 24,* 14.

Gugusheff, J. R., Ong, Z. Y., & Muhlhausler, B. S. (2013). A maternal "junk-food" diet reduces sensitivity to the opioid antagonist naloxone in offspring postweaning. *The FASEB Journal, 27,* 1275–1284.

Guyer, A. E., Benson, B., Choate, V. R., Bar-Haim, Y., Perez-Edgar, K., Jarcho, J. M., . . . Nelson, E. E. (2014). Lasting associations between early-childhood temperament and late-adolescent reward-circuitry response to peer feedback. *Development and Psychopathology, 26,* 229–243.

Guyette, J. P., Charest, J. M., Mills, R. W., Jank, B. J., Moser, P. T., Gilpin, S. E., . . . Gaudette, G. R. (2016). Bioengineering human myocardium on native extracellular matrixnovelty and significance. *Circulation Research, 118,* 56–72.

Haden, C. A., Cohen, T., Uttal, D., & Marcus, M. (2016). Building learning: Narrating and transferring experiences in a children's museum. *Cognitive development in museum settings: Relating research and practice,* 84–103.

Halim, M. L., Ruble, D., Tamis-LeMonda, C., & Shrout, P. E. (2013). Rigidity in gender-typed behaviors in early childhood: A longitudinal study of ethnic minority children. *Child Development, 84,* 1269–1284.

Hamilton, B. E., Martin, J. A., & Ventura, S. J. (2011). Births: Preliminary data for 2010. *National Vital Statistics Reports, 60,* 1–25.

Harlow, H. F. (1958). The nature of love. *American Psychologist, 13,* 673–685.

Hart, B., & Risley, T. R. (1995). *Meaningful differences in the everyday experience of young American children.* Baltimore, MD: Paul H Brookes Publishing.

Hasegawa, J., Farina, A., Turchi, G., Hasegawa, Y., Zanello, M., & Baroncini, S. (2013). Effects of epidural analgesia on labor length, instrumental delivery, and neonatal short-term outcome. *Journal of Anesthesia, 27,* 43–47.

Heinrichs, M., Meinlschmidt, G., Wippich, W., Ehlert, U., & Hellhammer, D. H. (2004). Selective amnesic effects of oxytocin on human memory. *Physiology & Behavior, 83,* 31–38.

Hepper, P. G., Shahidullah, S., & White, R. (1991). Handedness in the human fetus. *Neuropsychologia, 29,* 1107–1111.

Hinkle, S. N., Mumford, S. L., Grantz, K. L., Silver, R. M., Mitchell, E. M., Sjaarda, L. A., . . . Schisterman, E. F. (2016). Association of nausea and vomiting during pregnancy with pregnancy loss: A secondary analysis of a randomized clinical trial. *JAMA Internal Medicine, 176,* 1621–1627.

Hoddinott, P., Craig, L. C., Britten, J., & McInnes, R. M. (2012). A serial qualitative interview study of infant feeding experiences: Idealism meets realism. *BMJ Open, 2,* e000504.

Hoekzema, E., Barba-Müller, E., Pozzobon, C., Picado, M., Lucco, F., García-García, D., . . . Ballesteros, A. (2016). Pregnancy leads to long-lasting changes in human brain structure. *Nature Neuroscience, 20,* 287–300.

Hoff, E., & Core, C. (2015, May). What clinicians need to know about bilingual development. *Seminars in Speech and Language, 36*(2), 89–99.

Honaker, S. M., Schwichtenberg, A. J., Kreps, T. A., & Mindell, J. A. (2018). Real-world implementation of infant behavioral sleep interventions: Results of a parental survey. *The Journal of Pediatrics, 199,* 106–111.

Honda, A., Choijookhuu, N., Izu, H., Kawano, Y., Inokuchi, M., Honsho, K., . . . Ohinata, Y. (2017). Flexible adaptation of male germ cells from female iPSCs of endangered Tokudaia osimensis. *Science Advances, 3,* e1602179.

Hong, G. H., & Kim, Y. T. (2005). A longitudinal study of predictors for expressive vocabulary development of late-talkers. *Communication Sciences & Disorders, 10,* 1–24.

Hook, E. B., & Lindsjo, A. (1978). Down Syndrome in live births by single year maternal age interval in a Swedish study: Comparison with results from a New York State study. *American Journal of Human Genetics, 30,* 19–27.

Hopkins, B., & Westra, T. (1988). Maternal handling and motor development: An intracultural study. *Genetic, Social, and General Psychology Monographs, 114,* 377–408.

Howie, P. W., Forsyth, J. S., Ogston, S. A., Clark, A., & Florey, C. D. (1990). Protective effect of breast feeding against infection. *BMJ, 300*(6716), 11–16.

Hrdy, S. B. (2011). *Mothers and others.* Harvard University Press.

Huh, S. Y., Rifas-Shiman, S. L., Zera, C. A., Edwards, J. W. R., Oken, E., Weiss, S. T., & Gillman, M. W. (2012). Delivery by caesarean section and risk of obesity in preschool age children: A prospective cohort study. *Archives of Disease in Childhood, 97,* 610–616.

Hunt, L., Fleming, P., & Golding, J. (1997). Does the supine sleeping position have Any adverse effects on the child?: I. Health in the first six months. *Pediatrics, 100,* e11–e11.

Hunziker, U. A., & Barr, R. G. (1986). Increased carrying reduces infant crying: A randomized controlled trial. *Pediatrics, 77,* 641–648.

Hutchison, J. E., Lyons, I. M., & Ansari, D. (2018). More similar than different: Gender differences in children's basic numerical skills are the exception not the rule. *Child Development.*

Huttunen, M. O., & Niskanen, P. (1978). Prenatal loss of father and psychiatric disorders. *Archives of General Psychiatry, 35,* 429–431.

Izard, C. E., Huebner, R. R., Risser, D., & Dougherty, L. (1980). The young infant's ability to produce discrete emotion expressions. *Developmental Psychology, 16,* 132.

Jacobsson, B., Ladfors, L., & Milsom, I. (2004). Advanced maternal age and adverse perinatal outcome. *Obstetrics and Gynecology, 104,* 727–733.

Jia, G., & Aaronson, D. (2003). A longitudinal study of Chinese children and adolescents learning English in the United States. *Applied Psycholinguistics, 24*, 131–161.

Jia, G., Aaronson, D., & Wu, Y. (2002). Long-term language attainment of bilingual immigrants: Predictive variables and language group differences. *Applied Psycholinguistics, 23*, 599–621.

Johnson, J. S., & Newport, E. L. (1989). Critical period effects in second language learning: The influence of maturational state on the acquisition of English as a second language. *Cognitive Psychology, 21*, 60–99.

Johnson, K., Caskey, M., Rand, K., Tucker, R., & Vohr, B. (2014). Gender differences in adult-infant communication in the first months of life. *Pediatrics, 134*, e1603-e1610.

Johnson, M. H., & Morton, J. (1991). *Biology and cognitive development: The case of face recognition*. Oxford: Basil Blackwell.

Johnson, S., Slaughter, V., & Carey, S. (1998). Whose gaze will infants follow? The elicitation of gaze-following in 12-month-olds. *Developmental Science, 1*, 233–238.

Jones, N. A., Field, T., Lundy, B., & Davalos, M. (1996). One-month-old infants of depressed mothers and right frontal asymmetry. *Infant Behavior and Development, 19*, 529.

Kagan, J. (1997). Temperament and the reactions to unfamiliarity. *Child Development, 68*, 139–143.

Kahn, M., Fridenson, S., Lerer, R., Bar-Haim, Y., & Sadeh, A. (2014). Effects of one night of induced night-wakings versus sleep restriction on sustained attention and mood: A pilot study. *Sleep Medicine, 15*, 825–832.

Kaplan, L. A., Evans, L., & Monk, C. (2008). Effects of mothers' prenatal psychiatric status and postnatal caregiving on infant biobehavioral regulation: Can prenatal programming be modified? *Early human development, 84*, 249–256.

Karasik, L. B., Adolph, K. E., Tamis-LeMonda, C. S., & Zuckerman, A. L. (2012). Carry on: Spontaneous object carrying in 13-month-old crawling and walking infants. *Developmental Psychology, 48*(2), 389–397.

Karasik, L. B., Tamis-LeMonda, C. S., & Adolph, K. E. (2011). Transition from crawling to walking and infants' actions with objects and people. *Child Development, 82*, 1199–1209.

Karasik, L. B., Tamis-LeMonda, C. S., Adolph, K. E., & Bornstein, M. H. (2015). Places and postures: A cross-cultural comparison of sitting in 5-month-olds. *Journal of Cross-Cultural Psychology, 46*, 1023–1038.

Karen, R. (1990). Becoming attached. *The Atlantic Monthly, 265*, 35–70.

Kearney, M. S., & Levine, P. B. (2015). *Early childhood education by MOOC: Lessons from Sesame Street* (No. w21229). Washington, DC: National Bureau of Economic Research.

Kelly, D. J., Quinn, P. C., Slater, A. M., Lee, K., Ge, L., & Pascalis, O. (2007). The other-race effect develops during infancy. *Psychological Science, 18*, 1084–1089.

Kelly, D. J., Quinn, P. C., Slater, A. M., Lee, K., Gibson, A., Smith, M., . . . Pascalis, O. (2005). Three-month-olds, but not newborns, prefer own-race faces. *Developmental Science, 8*, F31–F36.

Kesmodel, U., Bertrand, J., Støvring, H., Skarpness, B., Denny, C., & Mortensen, E. (2012). The effect of different alcohol drinking patterns in early to mid pregnancy on the child's intelligence, attention, and executive function. *BJOG, 119*, 1180–1190.

Kesmodel, U., Falgreen Eriksen, H., Underbjerg, M., Kilburn, T., Støvring, H., Wimberley, T., & Mortensen, E. (2012). The effect of alcohol binge drinking in early pregnancy on general intelligence in children. *BJOG, 119*, 1222–1231.

Kimball, V. (2016). A nanny versus daycare: Is there a right choice? *Pediatric Annals, 45*, e36–e38.

Kisilevsky, B. S., Hains, S. M. J., Lee. K., Xie, X., Huang, H., Ye, H. H., . . . Wang, Z. (2003). Effects of experience on voice recognition. *Psychological Science, 14*, 220–224.

Koren, G., Madjunkova, S., & Maltepe, C. (2014). The protective effects of nausea and vomiting of pregnancy against adverse fetal outcome—a systematic review. *Reproductive Toxicology, 47*, 77–80.

Lamm, B., Keller, H., Teiser, J., Gudi, H., Yovsi, R. D., Freitag, C., . . . Vöhringer, I. (2017). Waiting for the second treat: Developing culture-specific modes of self-regulation. *Child Development.*

Langlois, J. H., Roggman, L. A., & Rieser-Danner, L. A. (1990). Infants' differential social responses to attractive and unattractive faces. *Developmental Psychology, 26*, 153–159.

Leahy-Warren, P., McCarthy, G., & Corcoran, P. (2012). First-time mothers: Social support, maternal parental self-efficacy and postnatal depression. *Journal of Clinical Nursing, 21*, 388–397.

Leboyer, F. (1975). *Birth without violence.* New York: Alfred Knopf.

Lee, K. S., Ferguson, R. M., Corpuz, M., & Gartner, L. M. (1988). *American Journal of Obstetrics and Gynecology, 158*, 84–89.

Legare, C. H., & Lombrozo, T. (2014). Selective effects of explanation on learning during early childhood. *Journal of Experimental Child Psychology, 126*, 198–212.

Legare, C. H., Wellman, H. M., & Gelman, S. A. (2009). Evidence for an explanation advantage in naïve biological reasoning. *Cognitive Psychology, 58*, 177–194.

Leung, M. Y. M., Groes, F., & Santaeulalia-Llopis, R. (2016). The Relationship between age at first birth and mother's lifetime earnings: Evidence from Danish data. *PloS One, 11*(1), e0146989.

Lewis, M. (1995). Embarrassment: The emotion of self exposure and evaluation. In J. P. Tangney & K. W. Fischer (Eds.), *Self-conscious emotions: The psychology of shame, guilt, embarrassment, and pride* (pp. 198–218). New York: Guilford Press.

Lewis, M., Alessandri, S. M., & Sullivan, M. W. (1990). Violation of expectancy, loss of control, and anger expressions in young infants. *Developmental Psychology, 26*, 745.

Lewis, M., & Ramsay, D. (2005). Infant emotional and cortisol responses to goal blockage. *Child Development, 76*, 518–530.

Lewis-Morrarty, E., Degnan, K. A., Chronis-Tuscano, A., Pine, D. S., Henderson, H. A., & Fox, N. A. (2015). Infant attachment security and early childhood behavioral inhibition interact to predict adolescent social anxiety symptoms. *Child Development, 86*, 598–613.

Lewkowicz, D. J., & Hansen-Tift, A. M. (2012). Infants deploy selective attention to the mouth of a talking face when learning speech. *Proceedings of the National Academy of Sciences, 109*, 1431–1436.

Lillard, A., & Else-Quest, N. (2006). The early years: Evaluating Montessori. *Science, 313*(5795), 1893–1894.

Linck, J. A., Kroll, J. F., & Sunderman, G. (2009). Losing access to the native language while immersed in a second language: Evidence for the role of inhibition in second-language learning. *Psychological Science, 20*, 1507–1515.

Linebarger, D. L., Kosanic, A. Z., Greenwood, C. R., & Doku, N. S. (2004). Effects of viewing the television program *Between the Lions* on the Emergent literacy skills of young children. *Journal of Educational Psychology, 96*, 297–308.

Liu, C. M., Hungate, B. A., Tobian, A. A., Serwadda, D., Ravel, J., Lester, R., . . . Price, L. B. (2013). Male circumcision significantly reduces prevalence and load of genital anaerobic bacteria. *MBio, 4*(2), e00076–13.

LoBue, V. (2009). More than just a face in the crowd: Detection of emotional facial expressions in young children and adults. *Developmental Science, 12*, 305–313.

LoBue, V. (2010). And along came a spider: Superior detection of spiders in children and adults. *Journal of Experimental Child Psychology, 107*, 59–66.

LoBue, V., & Adolph, K. E. (2019, in press). Fear in Infancy: Lessons from strangers, heights, snakes, and spiders. *Developmental Psychology*.

LoBue, V., Buss, K. A., Taber-Thomas, B. C., & Pérez-Edgar, K. (2017). Developmental differences in infants' attention to social and non-social threats. *Infancy, 22*, 403–415.

LoBue, V., & DeLoache, J. S. (2008). Detecting the snake in the grass: Attention to fear relevant stimuli by adults and young children. *Psychological Science, 19*, 284–289.

LoBue, V., & DeLoache, J. S. (2011). Pretty in pink: The early development of gender-stereotyped color preferences. *British Journal of Developmental Psychology, 29*, 656–667.

LoBue, V., & Pérez-Edgar, K. (2014). Sensitivity to social and non-social threats in temperamentally shy children at-risk for anxiety. *Developmental Science, 17*, 239–247.

LoBue, V., & Thrasher, C. (2015). The Child Affective Facial Expression (CAFE) Set: Validity and reliability from untrained adults. *Frontiers in Emotion Science, 5*.

Ludington-Hoe, S. M., & Hosseini, R. B. (2005). Skin-to-skin contact analgesia for preterm infant heel stick. *AACN Clinical Issues, 16*, 373.

Luke, B., & Brown, M. B. (2007). Elevated risks of pregnancy complications and adverse outcomes with increasing maternal age. *Human Reproduction, 22,* 1264–1272.

Maccoby, E. E. (1988). Gender as a social category. *Developmental Psychology, 24,* 755–765.

Maglione, M. A., Das, L., Raaen, L., Smith, A., Chari, R., Newberry, S., . . . Gidengil, C. (2014). Safety of vaccines used for routine immunization of US children: A systematic review. *Pediatrics, 134,* 325–337.

Martin, C. L., & Ruble, D. (2004). Children's search for gender cues: Cognitive perspectives on gender development. *Current Directions in Psychological Science, 13,* 67–70.

Martin, J. A., Hamilton, B. E., Osterman, M. J. K., Curtin, S. C., & Matthews, T. J. (2015). Births: Final data for 2013. *National Vital Statistics Reports: Centers for Disease Control and Prevention, National Center for Health Statistics, National Vital Statistics System, 64,* 1–65.

Martins, C., & Gaffan, E. A. (2000). Effects of early maternal depression on patterns of infant-mother attachment: A meta-analytic investigation. *Journal of Child Psychology & Psychiatry, 41,* 737–746.

Mascaro, J. S., Rentscher, K. E., Hackett, P. D., Mehl, M. R., & Rilling, J. K. (2017). Child gender influences paternal behavior, language, and brain function. *Behavioral Neuroscience, 131,* 262–273.

Mason, M. A., Stacy, A., & Goulden, M. (2002-3). *University of California Work and Family Survey.* Berkeley: University of California.

Massaro, D. W. (2015). Two different communication genres and implications for vocabulary development and learning to read. *Journal of Literacy Research, 47,* 505–527.

Maurer, D., & Salapatek, P. (1976). Developmental changes in the scanning of faces by young infants. *Child Development,* 523–527.

McGoron, L., Gleason, M. M., Smyke, A. T., Drury, S. S., Nelson, C. A., Gregas, M. C., . . . Zeanah, C. H. (2012). Recovering from early deprivation: Attachment mediates effects of caregiving on psychopathology. *Journal of the American Academy of Child & Adolescent Psychiatry, 51,* 683–693.

McKenna, J. J., & McDade, T. (2005). Why babies should never sleep alone: A review of the co-sleeping controversy in relation to SIDS, bedsharing and breast feeding. *Paediatric Respiratory Reviews, 6,* 134–152.

McLaughlin, K. A., Zeanah, C. H., Fox, N. A., & Nelson, C. A. (2012). Attachment security as a mechanism linking foster care placement to improved mental health outcomes in previously institutionalized children. *Journal of Child Psychology and Psychiatry, 53,* 46–55.

Medina, A. M., Lederhos, C. L., & Lillis, T. A. (2009). Sleep disruption and decline in marital satisfaction across the transition to parenthood. *Families, Systems, & Health, 27,* 153–160.

Meltzer, L. J., & Mindell, J. A. (2007). Relationship between child sleep disturbances and maternal sleep, mood, and parenting stress: A pilot study. *Journal of Family Psychology, 21*, 67–72.

Mennella, J. A., Jagnow, C. P., & Beauchamp, G. K. (2001). Prenatal and postnatal flavor learning by human infants. *Pediatrics, 107*, e88–e88.

Michelsson, K., Christensson, K., Rothgänger, H., & Winberg, J. (1996). Crying in separated and non-separated newborns: Sound spectrographic analysis. *Acta Paediatrica, 85*, 471–475.

Miller, C. C. (2014). The motherhood penalty vs. the Fatherhood Bonus. *The New York Times*, September 6, 2014. https://www.nytimes.com/2014/09/07/upshot/a-child-helps-your-career-if-youre-a-man.html

Miller, D. I., & Halpern, D. F. (2014). The new science of cognitive sex differences. *Trends in Cognitive Sciences, 18*, 37–45.

Mindell, J. A., Kuhn, B., Meltzer, L. J., & Sadeh, A. (2006). Behavioral treatment of bedtime problems and night wakings in infants and young children. *Sleep, 10*, 1263–1276.

Mischel, W., Shoda, Y., & Peake, P. K. (1988). The nature of adolescent competencies predicted by preschool delay of gratification. *Journal of Personality and Social Psychology, 54*, 687–699.

Mischel, W., Shoda, Y., & Rodriguez, M. I. (1989). Delay of gratification in children. *Science, 244*(4907), 933–938.

Moon, C., Cooper, R. P., & Fifer, W. P. (1993). Two-day-olds prefer their native language. *Infant Behavior and Development, 16*, 495–500.

Moriuchi, J. M., Klin, A., & Jones, W. (2016). Mechanisms of diminished attention to eyes in autism. *American Journal of Psychiatry, 174*, 26–35.

Morrissey, T. W., Hutchison, L., & Winsler, A. (2014). Family income, school attendance, and academic achievement in elementary school. *Developmental Psychology, 50*, 741–753.

Moss-Racusin, C. A., Dovidio, J. F., Brescoll, V. L., Graham, M. J, & Handelsman, J. (2012). Science faculty's subtle gender biases favor male students. *Proceedings from the National Academy of Sciences.*

Murkoff, H., & Mazel, S. (2008). *What to expect when you're expecting.* New York: Workman.

Murray, L. (1992). The impact of postnatal depression on infant development. *Journal of Child Psychology and Psychiatry, 33*, 543–561.

Myers, L. J., LeWitt, R. B., Gallo, R. E., & Maselli, N. M. (2017). Baby FaceTime: Can toddlers learn from online video chat? *Developmental Science, 24*, e12430.

Myruski, S., Gulyayeva, O., Birk, S., Pérez-Edgar, K., Buss, K. A., & Dennis-Tiwary, T. A. (2018). Digital disruption? Maternal mobile device use is related to infant social-emotional functioning. *Developmental Science, 21*(4), e12610.

Nature Editorials. (2012). Nature's sexism. *Nature, 491*, 495. https://www.nature.com/news/nature-s-sexism-1.11850

Narvaez, D., Wang, L., & Cheng, Y. (2016). The evolved developmental niche in childhood: Relation to adult psychopathology and morality. Applied Developmental Science, 20, 294–309.

Negron, R., Martin, A., Almog, M., Balbierz, A., & Howell, E. A. (2013). Social support during the postpartum period: Mothers' views on needs, expectations, and mobilization of support. Maternal and Child Health Journal, 17, 616–623.

Nelson, D. G. K., Hirsh-Pasek, K., Jusczyk, P. W., & Cassidy, K. W. (1989). How the prosodic cues in motherese might assist language learning. Journal of Child Language, 16, 55–68.

Neu, J., & Rushing, J. (2011). Cesarean versus vaginal delivery: Long-term infant outcomes and the hygiene hypothesis. Clinics in Perinatology, 38, 321–331.

Newhouse, R. P., Stanik-Hutt, J., White, K. M., Johantgen, M., Bass, E. B., Zangaro, G., . . . Weiner, J. P. (2011). Advanced practice nurse outcomes 1990–2008: A systematic review. Nursing Economics, 29, 1–22.

NICHD Early Child Care Research Network. (2001). Nonmaternal care and family factors in early development: An overview of the NICHD Study of Early Child Care. Journal of Applied Developmental Psychology, 22, 457–492.

Oakes, L. M. (2015). A biopsychosocial perspective on looking behavior in infancy. In S. Calkins (Ed). Handbook of infant biopsychosocial development. New York: Guilford Press.

O'Connor, T. G., Heron, J., Golding, J., Beveridge, M., & Glover, V. (2002). Maternal antenatal anxiety and children's behavioural/emotional problems at 4 years. The British Journal of Psychiatry, 180, 502–508.

O'hara, M. W., & Swain, A. M. (1996). Rates and risk of postpartum depression—a meta-analysis. International Review of Psychiatry, 8, 37–54.

Olson, K. R., Durwood, L., DeMeules, M., & McLaughlin, K. A. (2016). Mental health of transgender children who are supported in their identities. Pediatrics, 137(3), e20153223.

Olson, K. R., Key, A. C., & Eaton, N. R. (2015). Gender cognition in transgender children. Psychological Science, 26, 467–474.

Pandi-Perumal, S. R., Seils, L. K., Kayumov, L., Ralph, M. R., Lowe, A., Moller, H., & Swaab, D. F. (2002). Senescence, sleep, and circadian rhythms. Ageing Research Reviews, 1, 559–604.

Penela, E. C., Henderson, H. A., Hane, A. A., Ghera, M. M., & Fox, N. A. (2012). Maternal caregiving moderates the relation between temperamental fear and social behavior with peers. Infancy, 17, 715–730.

Pascalis, O., de Haan, M., & Nelson, C. A. (2002). Is face processing species-specific during the first year of life? Science, 296(5571), 1321–1323.

Pérez-Edgar, K., Morales, S., LoBue, V., Taber-Thomas, B. C., Allen, K. M., Brown, K. M., & Buss, K. A. (2017). The impact of negative affect on attention patterns to threat across the first two years of life. Developmental Psychology, 53, 2219–2232.

Peters, S. A., Yang, L., Guo, Y., Chen, Y., Bian, Z., Du, J., . . . Chen, Z. (2017). Breastfeeding and the risk of maternal cardiovascular disease: A prospective study of 300 000 Chinese women. *Journal of the American Heart Association, 6*, e006081.

Piaget, J. (2013). *The construction of reality in the child*. Routledge.

Pierroutsakos, S. L., & Troseth, G. L. (2003). Video verite: Infants' manual investigation of objects on video. *Infant Behavior and Development, 26*, 183–199.

Price, A. M., Wake, M., Ukoumunne, O. C., & Hiscock, H. (2012). Five-year follow-up of harms and benefits of behavioral infant sleep intervention: Randomized trial. *Pediatrics, 130*, 643–651.

Ramírez-Esparza, N., García-Sierra, A., & Kuhl, P. K. (2014). Look who's talking: Speech style and social context in language input to infants are linked to concurrent and future speech development. *Developmental Science, 17*, 880–891.

Rank, O. (1929). *The trauma of birth*. Mineola, NY: Courier Dover Publications.

Rauscher, F.H., Shaw, G. L., & Ky, K. N. (1993). Music and spatial task performance. *Nature, 365*, 611.

Reed, J., Hirsh-Pasek, K., & Golinkoff, R. M. (2017). Learning on hold: Cell phones sidetrack parent-child interactions. *Developmental Psychology, 53*, 1428–1436.

Reid, V. M., Dunn, K., Young, R. J., Amu, J., Donovan, T., & Reissland, N. (2017). The human fetus preferentially engages with face-like visual stimuli. *Current Biology, 27*, 1825–1828.

Renz-Polster, H., David, M. R., Buist, A. S., Vollmer, W. M., O'connor, E. A., Frazier, E. A., & Wall, M. A. (2005). Caesarean section delivery and the risk of allergic disorders in childhood. *Clinical & Experimental Allergy, 35*, 1466–1472.

Richert, R. A., Robb, M. B., Fender, J. G., & Wartella, E. (2010). Word learning from baby videos. *Archives of Pediatrics & Adolescent Medicine, 164*, 432–437.

Robb, M. B., Richert, R. A., & Wartella, E. A. (2009). Just a talking book? Word learning from watching baby videos. *British Journal of Developmental Psychology, 27*, 27–45.

Rosenthal, R., & Jacobson, L. (1968). Pygmalion in the classroom. *The Urban Review, 3*, 16–20.

Rossen, L. M., Osterman, M. J. K., Hamilton, B. E., & Martin, J. A. (2017). Quarterly provisional estimates for selected birth indicators, 2015-Quarter 4, 2016. *National Center for Health Statistics. National Vital Statistics System, Vital Statistics Rapid Release Program.*

Rottman, J. (2014). Evolution, development, and the emergence of disgust. *Evolutionary Psychology, 12*, 417–433.

Roy, A. K., Benson, B. E., Degnan, K. A., Perez-Edgar, K., Pine, D. S., Fox, N. A., & Ernst, M. (2014). Alterations in amygdala functional connectivity reflect early temperament. *Biological Psychology, 103*, 248–254.

Rozin, P., Fallon, A., & Augustoni-Ziskind, M. (1985). The child's conception of food: The development of contamination sensitivity to" disgusting" substances. *Developmental Psychology, 21*, 1075.

Ruble, D. N., Martin, C. L., & Berenbaum, S. A. (2006). Gender development. In: Eisenberg N (Ed.), *Handbook of child development* (pp. 858–932). New York: Wiley.

Saffran, J. R., Aslin, R. N., & Newport, E. L. (1996). Statistical learning by 8-month-old infants. *Science, 274*(5294), 1926–1928.

Satter, E. (2000). *Child of mind: Feeding with love and good sense.* Boulder, CO: Bull Publishing Company.

Scharoun, S. M., & Bryden, P. J. (2014). Hand preference, performance abilities, and hand selection in children. *Frontiers in Psychology, 5.*

Scher, A. (2005). Infant sleep at 10 months of age as a window to cognitive development. *Early Human Development, 81,* 289–292.

Schaal, B., Marlier, L., & Soussignan, R. (2000). Human fetuses learn odours from their pregnant mother's diet. *Chemical Senses, 25,* 729–737.

Schmidt, M. E., Pempek, T. A., Kirkorian, H. L., Lund, A. F., & Anderson, D. R. (2008). The effects of background television on the toy play behavior of very young children. *Child Development, 79,* 1137–1151.

Senghas, A., & Coppola, M. (2001). Children creating language: How Nicaraguan Sign Language acquired a spatial grammar. *Psychological Science, 12,* 323–328.

Shakin, M., Shakin, D., & Sternglanz, S. H. (1985). Infant clothing: Sex labeling for strangers. *Sex Roles, 12,* 955–964.

Shonkoff, J. P., Garner, A. S., Siegel, B. S., Dobbins, M. I., Earls, M. F., McGuinn, L., . . . Committee on Early Childhood, Adoption, and Dependent Care. (2012). The lifelong effects of early childhood adversity and toxic stress. *Pediatrics, 129,* e232–e246.

Siegel, A. C., & Burton, R. V. (1999). Effects of baby walkers on motor and mental development in human infants. *Journal of Developmental & Behavioral Pediatrics, 20,* 355–360.

Siegler, R., DeLoache, J., & Eisenberg, N. (2011). *How children develop, 3rd edition.* New York: Worth.

Skogerbø, A., Kesmodel, U., Wimberley, T., Støvring, H., Bertrand, J., Landrø, N., & Mortensen, E. (2012). The effects of low to moderate alcohol consumption and binge drinking in early pregnancy on executive function in 5-year-old children. *BJOG, 119,* 1201–1210.

Slater, A., Von der Schulenburg, C., Brown, E., Badenoch, M., Butterworth, G., Parsons, S., & Samuels, C. (1998). Newborn infants prefer attractive faces. *Infant Behavior and Development, 21,* 345–354.

Smyke, A. T., Zeanah, C. H., Fox, N. A., Nelson, C. A., & Guthrie, D. (2010). Placement in foster care enhances quality of attachment among institutionalized children. *Child Development, 81,* 212–223.

Snowden, J. M., Tilden, E. L., Snyder, J., Quigley, B., Caughey, A. B., & Cheng, Y. W. (2015). Planned out-of-hospital birth and birth outcomes. *New England Journal of Medicine, 373,* 2642–2653.

Sosa, A. V. (2016). Association of the type of toy used during play with the quantity and quality of parent-infant communication. *JAMA Pediatrics, 170,* 132–137.

Soska, K. C., & Adolph, K. E. (2014). Postural position constrains multimodal object exploration in infants. *Infancy, 19,* 138–161.

Soska, K. C., Adolph, K. E., & Johnson, S. P. (2010). Systems in development: Motor skill acquisition facilitates three-dimensional object completion. *Developmental Psychology, 46,* 129.

Sobel, D. M., & Sommerville, J. A. (2010). The importance of discovery in children's causal learning from interventions. *Frontiers in Psychology, 1,* 176.

Suomi, S. J. (1997). Early determinants of behaviour: Evidence from primate studies. *British Medical Bulletin, 53,* 170–184.

Sweeney, J., & Bradbard, M. R. (1988). Mothers' and fathers' changing perceptions of their male and female infants over the course of pregnancy. *The Journal of genetic psychology, 149,* 393–404.

Taffel, S. M., Placek, P. J., & Liss, T. (1996). Trends in the United States cesarean section rate and reasons for the 1980-85 rise. *American Journal of Public Health, 77,* 955–959.

Taylor, L. E., Swerdfeger, A. L., & Eslick, G. D. (2014). Vaccines are not associated with autism: An evidence-based meta-analysis of case-control and cohort studies. *Vaccine, 32,* 3623–3629.

Teti, D. M., Gelfand, D. M., Messinger, D. S., Isabella, R. (1995). Maternal depression and the quality of early attachment: An examination of infants, preschoolers, and their mothers. *Developmental Psychology, 31,* 364–376.

Teti, D. M., Shimizu, M., Crosby, B., & Kim, B. R. (2016). Sleep arrangements, parent–infant sleep during the first year, and family functioning. *Developmental Psychology, 52,* 1169.

Thackray, H. M., & Tifft, C. (2001). Fetal alcohol syndrome. *Pediatrics in Review, 22,* 47–55.

Thelen, E. (1996). The improvising infant: Learning about learning to move. In MR Merreu & GG Brannigan (Eds.), *The developmental psychologists: Research adventures across the life span.* New York: McGraw-Hill.

Thoman, E. B. (1990). Sleeping and waking states in infants: A functional perspective. *Neuroscience & Biobehavioral Reviews, 14,* 93–107.

Thomas, A., Chess, S., & Birch, H. G. (1970). The origins of personality. *Scientific American, 223,* 102–109.

Thompson, J. M., Waldie, K. E., Wall, C. R., Murphy, R., Mitchell, E. A., & ABC Study Group. (2014). Associations between acetaminophen use during pregnancy and ADHD symptoms measured at ages 7 and 11 years. *PLoS One, 9*(9), e108210.

Tomasetto, C., Mirisola, A., Galdi, S., & Cadinu, M. (2015). Parents' math–gender stereotypes, children's self-perception of ability, and children's appraisal of parents' evaluations in 6-year-olds. *Contemporary Educational Psychology, 42,* 186–198.

Touchette, É., Petit, D., Paquet, J., Boivin, M., Japel, C., Tremblay, R. E., & Montplaisir, J. Y. (2005). Factors associated with fragmented sleep at night across early childhood. *Archives of Pediatrics & Adolescent Medicine, 159,* 242–249.

Traister, R. (2015). Why women can't break free from the parent trap. *The New Republic*, Feb. 2, 2015. https://newrepublic.com/article/120939/maternity-leave-policies-america-hurt-working-moms

Trettien, A. W. (1900). Creeping and walking. *The American Journal of Psychology*, *12*, 1–57.

Tucker-Drob, E. M. (2012). Preschools reduce early academic-achievement gaps: A longitudinal twin approach. *Psychological Science*, *23*, 310–319.

Turkheimer, E., Haley, A., Waldron, M., D'Onofrio, B., & Gottesman, I. I. (2003). Socioeconomic status modifies heritability of IQ in young children. *Psychological Science*, *14*, 623–628.

Underbjerg. M., Kesmodel, U., Landrø, N., Bakketeig, L., Grove, J., Wimberley, T., . . . Mortensen, E. (2012). The effects of low to moderate alcohol consumption and binge drinking in early pregnancy on selective and sustained attention in 5-year-old children. *BJOG*, *119*, 1211–1221.

Vandell, D. (2004). Early child care: The known and the unknown. *Merrill-Palmer Quarterly*, *50*, 387–414.

Van den Bergh, B. R., & Marcoen, A. (2004). High antenatal maternal anxiety is related to ADHD symptoms, externalizing problems, and anxiety in 8- and 9-year-olds. *Child Development*, *75*, 1085–1097.

Van Ijzendoorn, M. H., & Hubbard, F. O. A. (2010). Are infant crying and maternal responsiveness during the first year related to infant-mother attachment at 15 months? *Attachment and Human Development*, *3*, 371–391.

Van Sleuwen, B. E., Engelberts, A. C., Boere-Boonekamp, M. M., Kuis, W., Schulpen, T. W., & L'Hoir, M. P. (2007). Swaddling: A systematic review. *Pediatrics*, *120*, e1097–e1106.

van Wijk, R. M., van Vlimmeren, L. A., Groothuis-Oudshoorn, C. G., Van der Ploeg, C. P., IJzerman, M. J., & Boere-Boonekamp, M. M. (2014). Helmet therapy in infants with positional skull deformation: Randomised controlled trial. *BMJ*, *348*, g2741.

Ventura, A. K., & Worobey, J. (2013). Early influences on the development of food preferences. *Current Biology*, *23*, R401–R408.

Vouloumanos, A., Druhen, M. J., Hauser, M. D., & Huizink, A. T. (2009). Five-month-old infants' identification of the sources of vocalizations. *Proceedings of the National Academy of Sciences*, *106*, 18867–18872.

Vouloumanos, A., Hauser, M. D., Werker, J. F., & Martin, A. (2010). The tuning of human neonates' preference for speech. *Child Development*, *81*, 517–527.

Vouloumanos, A., & Werker, J. F. (2007). Listening to language at birth: Evidence for a bias for speech in neonates. *Developmental Science*, *10*, 159–164.

Vygotsky, L. S. (1980). *Mind in society: The development of higher psychological processes*. Harvard University Press.

Wagner, E. A., Chantry, C. J., Dewey, K. G., & Nommsen-Rivers, L. A. (2013). Breastfeeding concerns at 3 and 7 days postpartum and feeding status at 2 months. *Pediatrics*, *132*, e865–e875.

Wakefield, A. J., Murch, S. H., Anthony, A., Linnell, J., Casson, D. M., Malik, M., . . .
Valentine, A. (1998). Ileal-lymphoid-nodular hyperplasia, non-specific colitis, and pervasive developmental disorder in children. *Lancet, 351*(9103), 637–641.

Walker-Andrews, A. S. (1997). Infants' perception of expressive behaviors: Differentiation of multimodal information. *Psychological Bulletin, 121*, 437–456.

Warneken, F., & Tomasello, M. (2006). Altruistic helping in human infants and young chimpanzees. *Science, 311*, 1301–1303.

Warneken, F., & Tomasello, M. (2007). Helping and cooperation at 14 months of age. *Infancy, 11*, 271–294.

Waters, S. F., West, T. V., Karnilowicz, H. R., & Mendes, W. B. (2017). Affect contagion between mothers and infants: Examining valence and touch. *Journal of Experimental Psychology: General, 146*, 1043–1051.

Weinberg, M. K., & Tronick, E. Z. (1996). Infant affective reactions to the resumption of maternal interaction after the still-face. *Child Development, 67*, 905–914.

Weisberg, D. S., Hirsh-Pasek, K., Golinkoff, R. M., Kittredge, A. K., & Klahr, D. (2016). Guided play: Principles and practices. *Current Directions in Psychological Science, 25*, 177–182.

Weng, X., Odouli, R., & Li, D. K. (2008). Maternal caffeine consumption during pregnancy and the risk of miscarriage: A prospective cohort study. *American Journal of Obstetrics and Gynecology, 198*(3), 279–e1.

Werker, J. F., Gilbert, J. H., Humphrey, K., & Tees, R. C. (1981). Developmental aspects of cross-language speech perception. *Child Development*, 349–355.

Werker, J. F., & Tees, R. C. (1983). Developmental changes across childhood in the perception of non-native speech sounds. *Canadian Journal of Psychology/Revue canadienne de psychologie, 37*, 278.

Widström, A. M., Lilja, G., Aaltomaa-Michalias, P., Dahllöf, A., Lintula, M., & Nissen, E. (2011). Newborn behaviour to locate the breast when skin-to-skin: A possible method for enabling early self-regulation. *Acta Paediatrica, 100*, 79–85.

Williams, W. M., & Ceci, S. (2012). When scientists choose motherhood. *American Scientist, 100*, 138.

Williamson, A. M., & Feyer, A. M. (2000). Moderate sleep deprivation produces impairments in cognitive and motor performance equivalent to legally prescribed levels of alcohol intoxication. *Occupational and Environmental Medicine, 57* 649–655.

Willyard, C. (2011). Men: A growing minority? *APA gradPSYCH Magazine, January*, 40.

Woodward, A. L., Markman, E. M., & Fitzsimmons, C. M. (1994). Rapid word learning in 13-and 18-month-olds. *Developmental Psychology, 30*, 553–566.

Wright, J. C., Huston, A. C., Murphy, K. C., St. Peters, M., Pinon, M., Scantlin, R., Kotler, J. (2001). The relations of early television viewing to school readiness and vocabulary of children from low-income families: The early window project. *Child Development, 72*, 1347–1366. et al., 2001).

Yoon, P. W., Freeman, S. B., Sherman, S. L., Taft, L. F., Yuanchao, G., Pettay, D., . . . Hassold, T. J. (1996). Advanced maternal age and the risk of down syndrome characterized by the meiotic stage of the chromosomal error: A population-based study. *American Journal of Human Genetics, 58,* 628–633.

Zeanah, C. H., Humphreys, K. L., Fox, N. A., & Nelson, C. A. (2017). Alternatives for abandoned children: Insights from the Bucharest Early Intervention Project. *Current Opinion in Psychology, 15,* 182–188.

Zelazo, P. R., Zelazo, N. A., & Kolb, S. (1972). " Walking" in the newborn. *Science, 176*(4032), 314–315.

Zielinski, R., Ackerson, K., & Low, L. K. (2015). Planned home birth: Benefits, risks, and opportunities. *International Journal of Women's Health, 7,* 361–377.

Zimmerman, F. J., Christakis, D. A., & Meltzoff, A. N. (2007). Associations between media viewing and language development in children under age 2 years. *The Journal of Pediatrics, 151,* 364–368.

INDEX

Note: Tables, figures, and boxes are indicated by *t*, *f*, and *b* following the page number. *For the benefit of digital users, indexed terms that span two pages (e.g., 52–53) may, on occasion, appear on only one of those pages.*

examination of, at 36 weeks of pregnancy, 117, 129–30
chemical pregnancy, 25–26
childbirth, 121–22, 123f. *See also* C-section; delivery; labor; vaginal birth
mother's experience of, 120
pushing in, 132–33
childcare
deciding about, 255, 263
high-quality, 261
benefits of, 263
childlessness, as choice, 12
chorion, 27
chromosomal abnormalities. *See also* Down syndrome
maternal age and, 12–13
and miscarriage, 25–26
chromosome(s), human, 58f *See also* X chromosome(s); Y chromosome(s)
circumcision, 127–28
cleft palate, 29–30, 39
clothes, maternity, 65–66, 79
coffee, 36
cognitive development, Piaget's theory of, 215–22
colic, 147–48
colors, gender-stereotyped, 55–56, 57–59, 60f
Common Sense Media, findings on children's exposure to screens/TV, 230
communication
adult–infant, gender differences in, 61
parent–infant, type of toys played with and, 99
screen-time use for, infants' engagement with, 237–39
with toddler, 268–69
by young children, 193–94
conception
problems with, interventions for, 18–19
sex ratios of, 57
time needed for, 21–22
concordance rate, 164–65, 261
concrete thinking, 222
conditioned sucking procedure, 97–98
congenital adrenal hyperplasia (CAH), 51
constipation, in first trimester of pregnancy, 35–36

contractions. *See also* Braxton Hicks contractions
5-1-1 rule for, 131
in labor, 130–31
timing, 131
cooing, 183–84
cord blood banking, 27–29
co-sleeping, 72–74
cow's milk allergy, in newborn, 147–48
crawling
development/achievement of, 172–73, 176–77
and safety considerations, 177
different modes of, 172
crying
carrying and, 155–57
with colic, 147–48
effects on babies
with long-term abuse and neglect, 76
in loving family, 76–77
by newborn, 146–48
inconsolable, 147, 154
reducing, techniques for, 154–57
reduction, skin-to-skin contact for, 157
and shaken baby syndrome, 148
cry it out (CIO) method, of sleep training, 74–75
C-section
benefits of, 124
for breech birth, 127
emergency, 134–35
failure to progress and, 126
infants born via, health consequences in, 121
maternal age and, 12–13
placenta previa and, 67
rates of, 124
culture, and emotion regulation, 208–9

daycare
and health/sickness, 256–58
high-quality, benefits of, 261, 262, 263
pros and cons of, 255–57, 256f
and socialization, 262
deaf children, development of their own sign language, 188–89
deferred imitation, 218–19

interpretation of, cross-cultural differences in, 208–9
negative, heightened bias for, inhibited temperament and, 112–13, 113*f*
newborn and infants' recognition of, 160–61
problems with, 164
falling, during walking, by young children, 175–76
familiarity, soothing effect on newborn, 100–1
Family and Medical Leave Act (FMLA), 253–54
fatigue
in first trimester of pregnancy, 30–31
in third trimester of pregnancy, 103–5
fear(s)
development of, 202, 248
in infants, 201–2
new mother's, 140, 210–11
parents', how to handle, 270
of strangers, 202
feet-down position, fetal, 124, 127
Ferber method, of sleep training, 181–82
fertilization, 19–20, 28*f*
fetal alcohol syndrome (FAS), 39
fetal head, downward position, 80
fetal movement, 103–4, 117–18
feeling, for first time, 66–67
at night, 68–69
in third trimester, 80
fetus. *See also* weight, baby's
breathing movements, 27
in eighth month, 103
in fifth month, 65
in first month, 25
on first ultrasound, 32*f*, 32–33
in fourth month, 49
in ninth month, 117
rapid eye movement (REM) sleep in, 69–72, 73*f*
in second month, 25
sensory experiences of, 70
in seventh month, 91
in sixth month, 79
taste preferences, 92–94, 95–96
in third month, 35
fibroid(s), in uterus, 87–89

fifth month
of life, infant's, 195
of pregnancy, 65
fingers, fetal development of, 45–47
first month
of life, infant's, 139
of pregnancy, 25
flatulence. *See* gas
folic acid
deficiency, and spina bifida, 43–45
supplementation in pregnancy, 43–45
food(s)
contaminated, children's willingness to eat, 203–4, 258
introduction of, to infant, 213–14, 214*f*
precautions with, in first trimester of pregnancy, 36
food preferences, development of, 101, 270–71
forceps delivery, 122
formula, introduction of, to breastfed baby, 195–96, 210–11
foster care, benefits of, 245–47
fourth month
of life, infant's, 181
of pregnancy, 49

gas, in first trimester of pregnancy, 35–36
gender
non-binary, 51
and sex
children's understanding of, 52–53
differentiation of, 51
gender bias, and children's achievements, 59–61
gender differences
in adult–infant communication, 61
expectations and, 59–61
in first year, 57–59
in math, 59–61
gender discrimination
in academia, 4–5
male–female distribution of, 4–5
gender identity, development of, 53–54, 269–70
gender inequality, and gender differences, 59
gender reveal, 105–6

gender stereotyping
    of infants and children, by adults, 55–57
    preschool children's adherence to, 53,
        57–59, 60*f*
    of unborn babies, by their parents, 56–57
gene(s), dominant vs. recessive, 14–18,
        16*f*, 17*f*
genetic disorders
    dominant vs. recessive, 15–18, 17*f*
    sex ratios of, 57
genetic tests
    costs of, 15–18
    preconception, 14–15
    scope of, 15–18
genotype, 51
grasping, by 4-month-old infant, 182–83, 183*f*
grasping reflex, 82
guided play, 223–24
guilt, 204–5
    new mother's, 210–11

hand, fetal, 118*f*
happiness, in infants, 199–200
having it all, 264
head. *See also* head-down position
    infant's, flat, 167–70, 168*f*
headache
    in early pregnancy, 30, 31, 36–37
    in first trimester of pregnancy, 35–36
    at onset of labor, 130
head-down position, 117–18, 127
    soothing effect on newborn, 100–1
healthy behaviors, teaching children
        about, 258–59
hearing, fetal, 70
heart
    embryonic, 29
    fetal development of, 32–33
heartburn, in third trimester, 79
heights, fear of, 177
hiccups, fetal, 29–30, 80, 103–4, 117–18
high-risk pregnancy, maternal age and, 21–
        22, 267–68, 270
Himba women, breastfeeding in, 149–50
holophrases, 194
home births, 124–26
hormone therapy, 18

hospital birth, 127–28
    midwives and, 125
human chorionic gonadotropin
        (hCG), 23, 25
hunger
    in first trimester, 30–31, 35–36
    in third trimester, 79

ibuprofen, risk to fetus, 36–38
imitation, deferred, 218–19
immune system, development of, 256–57
implantation, 26–27, 28*f*
income
    family, and child outcomes, 14
    motherhood and, 14
indiscriminate friendliness, 244–45, 247
infant mortality. *See also* sudden infant death
        syndrome (SIDS)
    bed sharing and, 73–74
    co-sleeping and, 72–74
    sex ratios of, 57
infertility
    female, interventions for, 18–19
    male, interventions for, 18
institutionalized care. *See also* orphanages
    effects on attachment, 245–47
    long-term negative effects of, 247
intelligence, Mozart effect and, 98–99
in vitro fertilization (IVF), 19

jaundice, neonatal, 86
joy, in infants, 199–200
junk food, effects on fetus, 101

kicking, fetal, in third trimester, 80, 117–18
kindergarten, 261

labor
    induction of, 122
    onset of, 130
    preparation for, 118–19
    progress of, 126
    prolongation of
        by anxiety/fear, 118–19
        by epidural, 122–24
        by stress, 122–24
    stages of, 121–22, 123*f*, 126

transition in, 121–22
    unexpected surprises in, 133–35
labor pain, 120–21
    anxiety and, 118–19
    characteristics of, 131–32
language
    development of, 183*f*, 183–85
        reading aloud to infant and, 192–93, 239
        talking to infant and, 192–93, 222–23
        in toddler, 268–69
        watching TV and, 236–37
        word production in, 194
    fetal preference for, 96–97
    second, acquisition
        age and, 189, 190–91
        immersion and, 191–92
        school programs and, 192
language comprehension, by young
        children, 193–94
language delay, 193–94
language learning, by infants
    children's propensity for, 188–89
    motherese and, 187
    mothers' reinforcement of, 187–88, 222–23
    sensitive period for, 189
laughing, by infants, 199–200, 210*f*
learning
    as "baby scientists," 222, 224
    educational TV and, 231, 232
    fetal, 92, 98
    guided play and, 223–24
    in 6-month-old child, 214–15
    of new words, 231–32
    from screen time, 237–39
legs, fetal development of, 45–47
letdown reflex, 153–54
life expectancy, sex differences in, 57
Listeriosis, 36
low back pain, in third trimester of
        pregnancy, 103–5
low birth weight
    maternal age and, 3–4, 12–13
    maternal smoking and, 40
luteinizing hormone (LH), and ovulation, 21

massage, for premature infants, 157
maternal age. *See* age, mother's

maternity leave, 253–54
mental representation(s), 215–18
    multiple, 219–21
midwives
    certification/experience/training of, 124–26
    and home births, 124–26
    and hospital births, 125
mirror, recognition of self in, development of,
        204–5, 206*f*
miscarriage(s)
    caffeine and, 36
    definition of, 25
    in first trimester, 25–26
    maternal age and, 12–13
    rates of, 25–26
    sex ratios of, 57
mobility, development/achievement of, and
        safety considerations, 177
mom shaming, 271–72
Montessori school, 259–61, 267
morning sickness, 31–32
Moro reflex, 82
mother(s)
    face, newborn's preference for, 158, 160–61
    infant's attachment to, 241–44, 247–48
    new
        anxiety in, 140
        brain changes in, 209–10
        emotions of, 209–11
        fears of, 140, 210–11
        guilt in, 210–11
        support system for, 141–42,
            148–49, 150–51
    working, 254, 264 (*See also* return to work)
motherese, 187
motor milestones
    average, 170–72
    chart of, 170–71, 171*f*
    cultural differences and, 172–73
    delay in, 169–70
    differences in, 171–73
    exercise routines and, 172–73, 175
    generational differences and, 172–73
motor skills, development/achievement of,
        171–76, 182–83, 214
    delays in, 178
    and safety considerations, 177

negative consequence of, 178
treatment of, 178–80
play. *See also* toys
  gender stereotypes and, 56
postnatal glow, 7–8, 265
postpartum blues, 140–43, 148
postpartum depression, 140–41
  colicky baby and, 148
  effects on infant, 149
  management of, 148–49
preferences, fetal, 92, 100–1
pregnancy
  high-risk, 21–22, 267–68, 270
  second, 267–68
  unexpected surprises in, 135
pregnancy test, 25
  negative, in pregnancy, 22–23
  positive, 23
premature birth, maternal age and, 12–13
premature infants
  massage for, 157
  skin-to-skin contact for, 157
prenatal care, maternal age and, 12–13
preschool, 261
  benefits of, for low-income/disadvantaged
    children, 261–62
prescription medications, risk to fetus, FDA
    rating of, 36–37
pride, 204–5
programmed cell death, 45–47
psychology, women in, 4
pushing, in childbirth, 132–33

quickening, 66–67

rapid eye movement (REM) sleep
  in fetus and newborn, 69–72, 73*f*
  importance of, 69
  over lifespan, 69, 71*f*
Rauscher, Frances, 98–99
reaching
  by 3-month-old infant, 176–77
  by 4-month-old infant, 182–83
reading aloud, to the baby, benefits of,
    192–93, 231–32
reflex(es)
  in animals, 81

definition of, 81
fetal, 81
functions of, 81, 83–84
in newborns, 81–83
  disappearance in infancy, 83–85
  testing of, 81–82
reflux, in newborn, 147–48
return to work, 254–55, 263–65
rhesus monkeys
  baby, attachment in, 242–43
  temperament in, parenting style
    and, 114–15
rocking, soothing effect on newborn, 100–1
rolling over, development/achievement of,
    176–77, 182–83, 227–28
Romanian orphans, 245–46
rooting reflex, 81–82
  disappearance of, 84
rouge test, 204–5

sadness, in infants, 201
Safe to Sleep campaign, 169
safety, child's, with development/achievement
    of motor skills, 177
Sally-Anne task, 219–21, 220*f*
Salmonella, 257
scaffolding, of supportive behaviors,
    222–23, 224
screen time
  activity replaced by, 239
  children's exposure to, 230
  distracting effect of, 237
  real-world considerations and, 229–30
  recommendations on, 228–29, 230
second month
  of life, infant's, 153
  of pregnancy, 25
self, sense of, 204–5
self-conscious emotion(s), 204–5
self-soothing, infant's learning
    of, 74–75
sensitive period, for language learning, 189
separation anxiety, 241–42, 250–51
Sesame Street
  learning benefits from, 231
  young infant's engagement with,
    238*f*, 239–40

terrible two's, 205–7
testosterone, 51
thalidomide, 42–43, 44*f*
theory of mind, 221, 224–25
third month
  of life, infant's, 167
  of pregnancy, 35
threat, response to, presence of attachment
    figure and, 249–50
thumb sucking, fetal, 81
tobacco use, maternal, fetal effects of, 40
toes, fetal development of, 45–47
tonic neck reflex, 82–84, 83*f*
torticollis, 167–68
  negative consequence of, 178
touch sense, fetal, 70
toys
  gender stereotypes and, 56, 269–70
  "genius," 99–100
  and infants' learning, 99–100
  learning about
    guided play and, 223–24
    in 6-month-old child, 214–15
    and parent–infant communication, 99
transgender individuals, 51, 53–54
  in childhood, 53–55
transition, in labor, 121–22
trisomy 21. *See* Down syndrome
trust, development of, 248
tummy time, 178–80, 179*f*
TV. *See* television
twin studies, 164–65, 261
two-dimensional images, children's
    understanding of, 232
Tylenol, safety in pregnancy, 36–38

ultrasound. *See also* sonogram(s)
  to monitor fibroids, 87–89
  sixteen-week, 50, 62*f*, 62–63, 65
  thirty-six-week, 117–18
  thirty-two-week, 103–4, 104*f*
  three-dimensional, 103–4, 104*f*, 118*f*
  twelve-week, 43–47, 46*f*
  twenty-eight-week, 88*f*, 89
  twenty-one-week, 67–68, 68*f*
umbilical cord, 27
  wrapped around baby's neck, 127, 133

urination, frequent
  in first trimester of pregnancy,
    30–31, 35–36
  in third trimester of pregnancy, 91–92,
    104–5, 117–18

vaccinations
  and autism, 165–66
  dangers of skipping, 165–66
  and daycare, 257–58
  effectiveness of, 165–66
  side effects of, 166
vaginal birth, 127–28, 133
  benefits of, 121
vertigo, in second trimester of
    pregnancy, 49–50
video chat, infants' engagement with, 237–39
vision, in 2-month-old baby, 157–58, 160*f*
visual acuity, infant's, 157–58, 159*f*
visual input, to newborn, and baby's view of
    world, 111–12
visual stimulation
  fetal, 70
  newborn, 70–72, 73*f*
vitamins, supplementation in
    pregnancy, 43–45
vocabulary spurt, 268–69
voice, mother's, fetal recognition of, 96

walker, infant's use of, 227–28
  and motor skills, 175
  and spatial skills, 175
walking
  development/achievement of,
    171–73, 175–77
  and safety considerations, 177
  as fun, for babies, 176
  by young children, falling during, 175–76
water birth, 119–20
weaning, from breastfeeding, 227
weight, baby's. *See also* low birth weight
  in eighth month, 103–4
  in ninth month, 117–18
  in seventh month, 92
  in sixth month, 89
weight gain
  baby's, with breastfeeding, 146–47